Blessing Same-Sex Unions

Blessing Same-Sex Unions

THE PERILS OF
QUEER ROMANCE
AND THE
CONFUSIONS OF
CHRISTIAN MARRIAGE

Mark D. Jordan

THE UNIVERSITY OF CHICAGO PRESS

CHICAGO AND LONDON

Mark D. Jordan is the Asa Griggs Candler Professor of Religion at Emory University. He is the author of several books, including *The Invention of Sodomy in Christian Theology, The Silence of Sodom: Homosexuality in Modern Catholicism, The Ethics of Sex,* and *Telling Truths in Church: Scandal, Flesh, and Christian Speech.*

The University of Chicago Press, Chicago 60637
The University of Chicago Press, Ltd., London
© 2005 by Mark D. Jordan
All rights reserved. Published 2005
Printed in the United States of America

14 13 12 11 10 09 08 07 06 05   1 2 3 4 5

ISBN: 0-226-41033-1 (cloth)

Library of Congress Cataloging-in-Publication Data

Jordan, Mark D.
  Blessing same-sex unions : the perils of queer romance and the confusions of Christian marriage / Mark D. Jordan.
     p. cm.
  Includes bibliographical references and index.
  ISBN 0-226-41033-1 (cloth : alk. paper)
  1. Same-sex marriage—Religious aspects—Christianity.   I. Title.
  BT707.6.J67 2005
  234'.165—dc22

                                                                        2004023660

For my father and my brother

Contents

Acknowledgments

The book that follows was written over many years with abundant help. It began with a course at Chicago Theological Seminary and ended with another at the Graduate Theological Union. In between, my changeable notions, however outrageous, were treated to attentive discussions at Concordia University, Boston University's School of Theology, the Pacific School of Religion, the Episcopal Divinity School, Vanderbilt Divinity School, Rice University, Duke Divinity School, and Bard College. They were also considered, at every stage, by the gifted doctoral students who have been my steady conversation partners. As research assistants and sharp-eyed readers, but most of all as charming intellectual companions, Wesley Barker, John Blevins, Kent Brintnall, David Mellott, Yael Sherman, Ted Smith, Meghan Sweeney, and Stephen Whitaker did their best to improve this book. They could have done more if I had listened better.

During the same period, I was fortunate to be a member of a project led by John Witte and Don Browning at the Center for the Interdisciplinary Study of Religion, with support from The Pew Charitable Trusts through a grant to Emory University. The project sustained the respect and congeniality within which alone fundamental disagreements become productive. Neither the Trusts nor my colleagues should be tarred with my heresies.

Since the mid-1990s, I have talked through these questions with friends: sitting in a sunny café in the Castro or in one of Montréal's darker clubs, strolling through a ravishing Cambridge garden, on break at the GLBT Historical Archives in San Francisco, over sushi in Houston and Nashville or Thai food in Berkeley, in a colonial inn next to the Hudson, while driving to and from airports. Writing about friendship at the end of the pages that follow, I could remember hours with Donald Boisvert, Bob Goss, Laurence Paul Hemming, Ralph Hexter, Mary Hunt, Jay Johnson, Jim Mitulski, Bob Neville, Penny Nixon, Susan Parsons, and Mary Ann Tolbert.

Pentecost AD 2004, in the weeks running up to Pride

Uncivil Ceremonies

∞

"It is a truth universally acknowledged, that a single man in possession of a good fortune, must be in want of a wife. . . ."[1]

(No, that won't do. This is a comedy of manners, but it requires a different beginning.)

In a recent June, month of weddings, a day before the Pride parade, and several years before the issuing of defiant marriage licenses, you could witness a ceremony for "domestic partnerships" on the steps of San Francisco's City Hall.[2] The ceremony was hardly intimate: scores of same-sex couples had come to register their partnerships with the Secretary of State under a 1999 law that granted a very limited list of civil rights, beginning with hospital visitation.[3] But fix on the ceremony—and not just because in America weddings are so much more significant than marriages.

Under a hot sky, framed by the banners of corporate sponsors, the ceremony was conducted by politicians, chief among them Assemblywoman Carole Migden, author of that 1999 bill. Parts of the ceremony certainly sounded like a political rally. Migden was introduced as "Superwoman," and she gave a rousing stump speech promising that the rights "we have" will get "bigger and bigger every year" until we reach "real marriage." Other politician-officiants onstage included Tom Ammiano and Mark Leno, then both city officials. Still, the ceremony was clearly also a wedding. The surprisingly traditional vows were read out by Ammiano and Leno, and then repeated nervously by the couples. They promised "to love and to cherish forever," in sickness and in health, in wealth and poverty, in times good and bad. "Forever": the word was repeated. You would have recognized other signs of a wedding too. Many of the couples came in ceremonial

1

costume—one woman in a tux, her partner in a white-lace wedding gown with veil; pairs of men in matching Hawaiian shirts or leather harnesses. After exchanging vows, the couples kissed. Cameras flashed or whirred, and most everyone was in tears.

The ceremony required one final action: a blessing. A mass registration with the Secretary of State might not seem to require a blessing, but a marriage does. So two novices and one senior member of a religious order were welcomed on-stage. The senior member's religious name was Sr. Kitty Catalyst; her order, the Sisters of Perpetual Indulgence. The Sisters have raised money for charity, done grassroots organizing, and vivified the streets of San Francisco with controversy since the end of the 1970s.[4] The Sisters are men. They often wear black habits of a style most Catholic nuns now disdain, but they were present at the June ceremony in summer outfit. Sister Kitty wore a print dress and wimple: fuchsia, green, yellow, and orange on white. The novices accessorized more modestly with starlet sunglasses.

As for the liturgy of blessing: First the Sisters pulled strips of paper from a purse and read out sayings about love: love is cleaning the toilet, love is ice on the nipples. They read then stanzas from a poem on love, L-O-V-E. E stood for Emotion, which meant that you should be honest and open with your partner. Finally the Sisters blessed the newly vowed couples and the attending crowd.

The Sisters might well be annoyed by my reading too much into their mildly salacious and rather haphazard performance. I will read into it—because their performance shows the necessity and the strangeness of religion in our national debates about same-sex unions. The necessity, because the mixed group of Americans on that plaza, from however many religious traditions, if from any, felt the need for a blessing from sacral figures with a recognized moral genealogy in the community. If the religious action came wrapped in feather boas of parody, it was still recognizably religious—or perhaps more recognizably religious, given the liturgical role of camp for many in the crowd. Only to take offense at the Sisters, only to resent their parody, would miss their strange religious significance—indeed, their specifically Christian significance. The Sisters on that stage made manifest not only the play of civil law and Christian imagery in most American marriages, but also the element of unacknowledged religious parody in many of them. Some marriages celebrated in churches are "Christian" in roughly the same way that the Sisters of Perpetual Indulgence are "Catholic nuns." The costumes and the gestures may be right, but the intention is rather different. Many church weddings have nothing to do with distinctively Christian intentions.[5]

CONTROVERSY, FALLACY, CHATTER, AND REVELATIONS

American Christians now live, in their various churches, a great controversy. At stake in the controversy is whether or not the churches should bless same-sex unions publicly — or, rather, should continue to bless them, since an increasing number of well-established Christian churches already do. My purpose is not to join the contenders. I want instead to think about what the great controversy portends for all those involved. For the Christian churches, blessing same-sex unions might be just the opposite of an assault on Christian marriage. It might be the opportunity to find something Christian in what church-going Americans so blithely call "Christian marriage."[6] The challenge for the churches is not to justify blessing same-sex unions. The challenge is justifying any blessings of unions at all. Here engagement with queer critique could be an enormous help. After centuries of enforced silence, lesbian and gay voices can at last speak back to official Christianity, not only about the churches' slander of same-sex love, but about their practices for other-sex loves.[7] The once-silenced voices get to ask: What have you been doing all these centuries when you were marrying men to women — and what are you doing now? Finding cogent answers to the question will be finding something distinctively or indispensably Christian in church weddings.

For lesbian and gay public discourses, the controversy brings other portents. The movements or speeches we call "lesbian and gay" or "queer" are hardly unified.[8] They carry forward rancorous disagreements, which are particularly bitter around both committed partnerships and religious practice. So Christian lesbians and gays may find themselves asking their "subculture," or political organizations, or circle of friends some embarrassing questions. Do you still count us as fully lesbian or gay if we insist on being Christian? And will you allow a same-sex relationship that looks something like a Christian marriage to count as queer?

Each side gets to ask the other: What comes next? The reciprocal question is the sharpest because blessing same-sex unions cannot be separated either from the future of Christian marriage or from the future of lesbian and gay "identities" (which I prefer to call "characters").[9] Blessing unions will determine the future of Christian marriage because it poses an unavoidable and fundamental challenge to the complacencies of churchly practice. Failure to respond to the challenge will hasten the demise of the church wedding — I mean, will hasten us toward the day when many more church weddings are excruciating parody. Unions are also the future of queer character. Not every queer will want a union, much less a blessed one, but every queer will perform a character modified by the fact that the unions of some queers are blessed by Christian churches. Character is the medium through which a certain eros passes. Character renders the specificity of that eros coherent, but also curiously vulnerable to historical change. The present repertoire of characters may not survive blessed unions. Certainly the repertoire of church weddings will not survive the refusal to bless them.

Debates over blessing same-sex unions are fated to raise queasy anxieties on both sides. For traditional Christian theology, no claim undoes the rationales for marriage quite as quickly as the claim that nonprocreative sexual pleasure might merit or already be a blessing. For many queer characters, nothing is quite so deflating as the prospect that churches might bless their couplings after all. As Stan Persky complains, "Once homo thought: *Desire is nature,* and thus, almost by definition, playful, anarchic, out[side]law, subversive of conventional society; now homo is content to put on its slippers, domesticate desire, join the Rotary Club. If homo ain't interesting, I ain't interested." [10] It sounds as if the whole array of queer life were at stake. On some views of the life, it is.

The anxieties produce endless misconceptions around the encounter of queer and Christian speeches. I have fallen into most of them. Indeed, I now consider them not so much missteps as fallacies that you have to catch yourself committing in order to recognize how tricky it is to talk seriously about blessing unions. For example, I began my writing by insisting that I was interested in *church blessings of same-sex unions* and not in civil recognition of them. Believers and nonbelievers must recognize at least a conceptual distinction between a church wedding and a civil registration. No one should imagine that arguments for or against state-sanctioned domestic relationships are in America simply identical with arguments about church blessings. The more state regulation accords with church practice, whether prohibiting or approving certain unions, the more important it is to say that the two spheres are not one. Yet as soon as you begin to insist on their distinction, you fall into the first fallacy. Christian marriage has long been constructed by church and state together, even when the church in question wanted to assert exclusive jurisdiction over it. In Christendom and the societies descended from it, marriage is a topic uniquely suited to disrupt any distinction between secular and sacred. Marriage remains the great testimony to the inseparability of church and state, to their ancient commingling. So the debates can never be cut cleanly in practice, putting legal issues over here and theological issues over there. The most you can hope for is to be wary about the confusion of legal and religious issues, which will never be unconfused. The secular is a version of the religious—and (now) conversely. [11] Not too many months after the Sisters gave their blessing in front of San Francisco's City Hall, the building was crowded with same-sex couples being (il)legally married with the defiant support of the mayor. The elegant dome became a wedding pantheon. Under it, you could find Jewish *chuppahs* or Anglican stoles, fervent private prayers or invitations to mass liturgies, even as the city's newest deputies read, when requested, formulas of religious blessing.[12]

A second necessary fallacy is to try to divide pro and con in the debate as between *outside the church and inside the church*. For a long time, I had this picture in mind: Everyone opposed to the blessing of unions huddled in a wedding chapel trying to hold the neo-Gothic doors closed; everyone supporting the blessing crowded outside, trying to batter the doors open with a maypole.[13] This image misleads in many ways. It can make it seem that every supporter of blessing stands outside the church, though that is hardly the case. Earnest requests to bless same-sex couples are not an alien menace that attacks churches from the stratosphere. The couples asking for blessing live already inside the churches. They are baptized believers. No pair of gay atheists converts to Rome just for the pleasure of being refused a nuptial Mass. The same is true in Christian theology. Non-Christian queer theorists do not write Christian defenses of same-sex unions. Indeed, many queer theorists consider the dogged persistence of lesbians and gays inside Christian churches pitiable or horrifying. Christian theologies of lesbian or gay unions are written by lesbian and gay believers.

The misleading picture of the barred chapel has become the master dichotomy in our present controversies. It divides all discourse about same-sex unions between a homosexual agenda (always the outside) and a religious right (ever the inside). The dichotomy was not invented by the controversies, but it has shown itself perfectly adapted to them. Some partisans on both sides find it immensely useful to pretend that no one can be both queer and Christian. Self-proclaimed Christian speeches are of course among the most prominent and scorching attacks on same-sex unions. When polls are conducted or platforms announced, most opposition to civil recognition for same-sex unions in America justifies itself on Christian grounds and precisely as if those grounds were settled. Yet Christian history is a long series of quarrels among Christians about an innumerable range of topics, large and small, notably including sex and marriage. The same point needs to be made on the other side of the debate. American lesbian/gay "activists" have disagreed with each other sharply since 1969, the date called out by the myth of Stonewall. The projection of Stonewall as myth enshrines a disagreement, a vehement critique of earlier positions. Before and after Stonewall, religious adherents, including Christian believers of every stripe, have played important roles in same-sex politics. If some activist discourses want to erase the religious, they ought to be reminded of queer diversity—not to say, some history.

The image of the chapel door barred from the inside and battered from the outside misled me in another direction too. In many significant ways, there is *neither inside nor outside* in our quarrels about unions, because both opponents and proponents argue in social spaces where the most powerful images of Christian marriage are beyond the control of the churches. While the opponents try to bar the doors in the name of Christian tradition, there are weddings being celebrated at the altar behind them that are controlled not by theological or sacramental tradition, but by cultural expectations given power through mass advertising or family custom.

Let us be honest: At most church weddings, the chief ritual specialist is not the pastor or priest, but the wedding planner, followed closely by the photographer, the florist, and the caterer.[14] More wedding theology is supplied in fact by *Modern Bride* magazine than by any dozen treatises on holy matrimony. Mechanically reproduced representations of (Christian?) marriage circulate detailed codes of etiquette that prescribe words to be spoken, but also actions to be done, looks to be copied, feelings to be practiced, and unrealizable ends to be craved.[15] The circulating etiquettes quote Christian elements, but transform them in the moment of quotation. Then the mechanical speeches thoroughly infiltrate Christian teaching and worship. On "Christian" call-in radio, in "true Catholic" guide-books for happy homes, we Americans are offered—we are bombarded with—barely edited versions of mass-market marriage. The more elaborate offerings combine sitcoms with pop psychology. The less elaborate are sitcoms with churchy sets.

Americans receive broadcasts on marriage etiquette every hour. They cannot be avoided. They jump out from mandatory public TV screens and from glossy covers in grocery checkout lanes. It is boring even to mention how common they are—and that may be the most telling thing. We are now so dulled that we forget to consider the effect on us of the bombardment of mass images of marriage. Church leaders complain about the effect of negative images on believers: all those stories about adultery and divorce, about easy sex and no children. Sex everywhere! But Christian marriage everywhere too! Only it is not really sex—and not really Christian marriage: just mass-produced talking pictures, in which Christian symbols or rites or words appear as "good visuals" over cycling babble.

My final fallacy was to think it the most important task to *reply point-by-point to the recurring arguments* against same-sex unions, blessed or unblessed. I admire those who have the stomach for this labor. (By comparison, Hercules was at his leisure in the Augean stables.) I appreciate the arguments they have constructed and the clarities they have achieved.[16] I do now wonder about the return on their expenditure of time and self. The exhausting labor does not seem to be rhetorically effective with opponents. It must often remain within limited categories set by controversy. It reinforces the notion that both eros and blessing are adequately captured in words. And so on. Those of us who earn our livings assembling and disassembling arguments can find it hard to resist the impulse to refute, especially when many arguments against blessing unions are so eminently refutable. But I have come to believe that it is more useful to listen in these controversies not for points that debaters can speak against each other, but for figures of speech they are liable to share. Figures cannot be refuted, they can only be disarmed. The safest way to disarm them is to inhabit them, to use them, until you can see when they malfunction. You have to watch yourself relying on them.

These four fallacies are only samples of missteps one has to make in trying to stage an encounter of discourses around same-sex unions. Just the four should show how fallacies combine with each other to reinforce one of the deepest convictions embedded in our chatter. The conviction is that there is a single thing, Christian Marriage, which is now being asked to accommodate this other single thing, Queer Relationship. Neither member of that duo is quite what it seems. Moreover, the duo of terms has got to be at least a trio, since speeches about either or both of them are now driven by representations of mass marketing. The most important fallacy we risk is thinking that we are dealing with speeches when we are in fact dealing with speeches almost drowned out by chatter. The chatter may be easiest to recognize in mass marketing, but it spreads out into every speech about blessing same-sex unions.

In decrying chatter, I risk chattering through needless repetition.[17] The complaint against the quantity of mindless speech around us is so common that it has itself become part of the chatter, in the same way that media satire is a cliché of media. Yet complaining against chatter again — and not as incantation or as irony — may be part of turning down its volume. The first step in resisting habits of chatter is to recognize them as habits. Habits happen in time; they are produced over time by repetition. They are contracted and then cultivated by institutions. One of Kierkegaard's pseudonyms uses "chatter" to name the centuries-old echo in some churches that riddles faith with noise.[18] The naming is inspired, because it reminds us that habits of chattering are produced by particular histories. There is no way to turn down the chatter about "Christian Marriage" and "Queer Relationship" without forcing ourselves to remember how we come to keep talking in those dichotomized terms.

Chatter is not so much content as a habit of use, a mode of presentation. Habit is not the same as tradition. Chatter both "sacred" and "secular" often refers to the library of traditional Christian speeches about marriage. Any reader of marriage theology will know that the library is quite mixed. Right alongside courageous and humane pleas for the beauty of uncoerced and affectionate marriage, there are volumes of forgotten compromises with the procreative or property schemes of vanished states and markets. Yet the difference between quoted plea and quoted compromise is not the same as the difference between theology and chatter. Both plea and compromise can be quoted in reflection *or* in chatter. Beautiful theological visions of erotic union are reduced to chatter in a thoughtless wedding sermon or entertainment news about the latest Hollywood passion. The inheritance of Christian teaching on marriage is not all chatter, but its voices are regularly distorted into chatter—and not simply so far as they contain simple mistakes, proud compromises, or sad failures of nerve. Chatter does not feed on the worst in Christian theology. It consumes by choice the best.

Our chatter about blessing unions is not what was once meant by idle chatter.[19] It is precisely not gossip, whatever the old slurs about "chatty housewives" or "chatty fags" might suggest. Gossip was the kind of human exchange, of conversation face to face, that chatter most drowns out. Gossip gave classes of people denied authoritative speech an alternate network for knowledge.[20] How much richer churchly discussions of marriage would be if they could frankly admit the knowledge of daily gossip, perhaps especially the gossip of "housewives" and "fags," who are, in their different ways, experts on the limits of sanctioned heterosexuality. Chatter is not gossip because gossip can be the living exchange of unpopular wisdom.

The closest cousin to chatter that I can find is neither gossip nor the library of church speeches, but the all too modern category of propaganda. Each morning's newscasts show how comprehensive propaganda can be and how much it resembles the chatter that is advertising. It is hard to know whether propaganda aspires to be good advertising or advertising works best when it is accomplished propaganda. They trade techniques back and forth, as they depend on the same technologies of amplification and circulation. Perhaps chatter is only the more innocent face of propaganda— propaganda without an obviously totalitarian intent behind it. Or perhaps propaganda is the deliberate chatter of the dictator's police. Either way, the resemblances between chatter about Christian marriage, inside churches or outside them, for and against, quickly become frightening.

No serious discussion about blessing same-sex unions in Christian churches can proceed except by acknowledging and then confronting this chatter. No serious discussion about Christianity can fail to admit how much Christian "speech" on many important topics has become identical with chatter. This is one consequence of being after Christendom, of living in societies where one or another Christianity supplies many of the cultural references or images. In the same way that medieval or modern Europeans used Greek or Roman religion as ornamental "mythology," so contemporary American groups use Christian icons as clip-art. To debate Christian topics without confronting that situation is simply to supply a steady stream of Christian words and images for clipping, for quotation in chatter.

Still, you can never know quite when chatter might disrupt itself, when it might carry in its cycling streams a precious disclosure, a revelation. Or divine Revelation: truths "beyond" chatter are given only through chatter. (Christians might translate this as the profession that God took flesh and spoke.) The book listens to chatter page after page, from beginning to end.[21] It examines words and images, counsels on etiquette, that might seem beneath the dignity of theology—if not of queer theory, which is notoriously omnivorous. I believe that theology needs to be less preoccupied with its dignity and more eager to find epiphanies wherever they occur. The artifacts of mass culture supply most marriage theology to believers and unbelievers, including the theology that hardly looks "mass" at all. Chatter about unions cannot be overcome. It has to be resisted with a constant practice of listening otherwise. Any remedy for marriage chatter will begin with what sounds almost imperceptibly through it.

As soon as I try to listen through chatter, I am interrupted by curiously paired arguments that have the effect of stopping words about same-sex unions. The arguments are curiously paired because they are made by declared opponents. The first argument is the "conservative Christian" objection that there is no point talking about blessing same-sex unions because homosexuality is immoral, and Christians don't bless immorality. The second argument is the "queer activist" objection that concern with blessing same-sex unions represents in itself a betrayal of the movement for lesbian and gay liberation. I stress that the arguments are comparable only as producing an effect of silence. They are hardly symmetrical as reasoning or as politics. Because of the institutional powers it commands or abets, the first argument is dangerous in ways the second cannot be—and does not want to be. It is all the odder, then, that they agree in wishing that a certain kind of talk would stop.

BETRAYING THE FAITH

Isn't the most obvious question whether homosexual relations are permissible to Christians? I think not. In fact, this "most obvious question" is actually an obsessive distraction from thinking about same-sex unions. Fear of other issues spied just ahead fuels this "obvious question" as it does so many preemptive condemnations of same-sex desire. For the sake of clarity, let me focus just on a common form of the preemption, often identified as "conservative." It claims that Christians cannot consider blessing unions because of Genesis 19, Leviticus 18:22 or 20:13, Romans 1, 1 Corinthians 6:9, 1 Timothy 1:10, or Jude 7—to mention only the most-cited scriptural passages. There have been others. Bernardino of Siena builds his treatise *On the Horrible Sin against Nature* atop that decisive verse, Psalm 14:1, "They are corrupt, they do abominable deeds; there is no one who does good."[22] The verse refers unmistakably to the rapid spread of affluent sodomites in fifteenth-century Tuscany—according to Bernardino.

For half a century now, there have been philological and theological critiques of the traditional proof-texts against homosexuality. The critiques have managed to dislodge some complacent certainties. It is hard today to find an academic exegete who will argue that the Genesis story of the destruction of Sodom gives a moral law condemning homosexuality— though that story obviously lent its name to the theological category of "sodomy." What was once the most pertinent passage now proves to be impertinent. If controversy continues about the meaning and moral applicability of Leviticus 18 or Romans 1, it is notable that "conservative" scholars now feel compelled to supply labored explanations of what these passages mean. A hundred years ago, Christian exegetes knew exactly what the passages meant and whom they condemned.

Arguments about the "clobber passages" have indeed shifted the terms of debate, but they have not, of course, resolved underlying slips. Reiterations of the old scriptural condemnations typically fail to take any notice of fundamental objections already raised against the categories they assume. For example, when Robert Gagnon claims that "there is clear, strong, and credible evidence that the Bible unequivocally defines same-sex intercourse as sin" and then equates "same-sex intercourse" with "homosexual practice," one has to wonder whether he has heard even the rumors of the theoretical work on same-sex characters published in the last thirty years.[23] Gagnon's (willful?) refusal to engage theoretical critique of sex/gender categories goes hand-in-hand with a refusal to admit exegetical questions that would complicate his lock-step argument.

"Conservative" condemnations can fail to register a whole range of fundamental questions: How does a particular community of debate determine what the biblical texts mean for human life? How do diverse communities broker disagreements over moral interpretation? Why do they decide to use *nonbiblical* categories like "homosexuality" in applying canonical texts? Is "homosexuality" one thing in every time and place, under each set of human circumstances? When is it appropriate to look past the surface of a debate to see what forces of institutional power may be at play in it? Whenever you begin a public debate by asking What moral teaching does the Christian Bible give us about homosexuality? you presume that your public agrees on which biblical texts are relevant and how they are to be read, on how they give coherent and pertinent moral teaching, on the relation of that teaching to scientific discoveries or personal discernments, and on who has authority to decipher and then apply the teaching in the present. What moral teaching does the Christian Bible give us about homosexuality? Asked that way, the question can only show how deeply divided Christians are when they read their Bibles.

The kind of passage they need is not an alleged rule about prohibited acts, but a model for resolving conflicting testimonies to divine guidance within a Christian community. Christian readers would do better not to look to Romans 1, but rather to Acts 10. There, as part of a narrative of the progressive and disconcerting expansion of the Christian community that will culminate in Paul's ministry, the author tells how Peter was led to associate with and then to baptize non-Jews.[24] The story comes as an answer to an internal dispute among Jewish Christians about whether new converts had to observe the fullness of Jewish law, including the law of circumcision. As the author of Acts 10 rehearses the story, Peter has to be pushed by God three times, in different ways, before he will finally consent to baptize gentiles. Peter appears at first as quite the biblical literalist, quoting divine law back to God and refusing to eat what he understands to be prohibited in the Scriptures known to him (Acts 10:14). Peter performs the baptism at the end of the chapter only after he has watched God pour the Holy Spirit out on the uncircumcised. As Peter exclaims, perhaps ruefully: "Can anyone keep back water for baptizing these people who have received the Holy Spirit just as we have?" (Acts 10:47). The present controversy over blessing same-sex unions looks much like the original controversy over universal circumcision and dietary restrictions. The biblical precedents to be invoked for it are not alleged rules about sex, but stories about how Christian communities move forward through divisions.

Unfortunately, church debates typically circle around without remembering Peter or addressing painful divisions. The circles seem to be about homosexuality, but they are in fact about biblical interpretation, method in moral theology, and church authority. In listening to the circling words, I do sometimes despair over our ability to communicate, much less to argue. The various positions are so evidently not talking about the same thing. The first assumptions that conservative Christian exegetes make about homo-

sexuality are the ideological fictions that have been most thoroughly undone by queer theory. The divergence is not a difference between biblical
and secular worldviews, or between traditional and postmodern scholarship (contrasts that are themselves polemical). The difference is about
where language can rest—about how far down Christian debate must
reach. Since I think that Christian theology is obliged to reach as far below
the surface of language as one can get, queer theorists often seem to me
much more exacting theologians than churchly exegetes.

The consequences of not reaching far enough down are plain to the
eye—or, rather, to the ear. One effect of the quarrels over "the Bible and
homosexuality" (and, I suspect, one of their intentions) is precisely to prevent anyone from thinking about unions. To think about blessing same-sex
unions threatens not only a number of established church positions, but a
number of church illusions. For example, asking about unions leads one to
ask what exactly churches have been condemning in persecuting them.
Churches have historically condemned same-sex activity along with a host
of other acts that offer sexual pleasure in excessive amounts or without the
possibility of procreation—such acts as masturbation, fellatio, cunnilin-
gus, artificial contraception, and heterosexual copulation in positions other
than the "missionary."[25] Many or most heterosexual Christians now approve and even practice these "sodomitic" or "unnatural" acts. (Until
June 2003, American Christians often did so in violation of state criminal
laws that drew their authority from once authoritative biblical interpretations.) The present condemnation of same-sex acts appears to be the last
vestige of Christianity's nervous refusal to think sex beyond genital me-
chanics. Refusing to think same-sex couples is another way of doing moral
theology by fantastical anatomy. For a certain theology, penises "can" only
fit into vaginas—not into mouths or anuses, between hands, thighs, and
breasts. They "can" fit into vaginas only to inseminate them. If we dismiss
this (il)logic for heterosexual couples in favor of a more accurate understanding of erotic relationship, why do we resist doing so for same-sex
couples? How can the churches pin on same-sex couples alone moral reasoning that applies much more widely—that the churches themselves applied quite recently to heterosexual coupling? Is that "biblical principle" or
the useful amnesia of a majority?

To take a second example: Actually thinking through the question of
same-sex unions quickly discovers unexpressed tensions in Christian theologies of marriage. If it is true to say that Christian traditions have condemned same-sex unions, it is equally true to say that Christian traditions
have been highly suspicious of heterosexual marriage. The weight of tradition that now stands against blessing same-sex unions once stood, as the

Protestant Reformers well knew, and still stands in part, as any "traditional Catholic" can tell you, against the choice of marriage itself as a Christian vocation. The higher vocation, indeed the only life-choice worthy to be described as a "vocation," or calling, from God, was entry into a life under vows of sexual abstinence. To get Christian marriage between a man and a woman recognized as a spiritual calling equivalent to vowed celibacy or virginity took Christian theologians many centuries. Roman Catholic theologians only reached this point in recent decades. To what extent are current refusals to bless same-sex unions a remainder of that now-forgotten history? And why exactly has it been necessary to forget it? How have our debates permitted the astonishing pretense that Christianity has been a tradition of robust sexual health or (astonishing phrase!) "family values"?

Finally, allowing Christians or their interlocutors to think about same-sex unions would bring them soon enough to confront the churches' ancient misogyny. Much Christian theology about *other*-sex unions has argued that women must be subordinate to men in domestic relationship and in church and that men exercise their maleness precisely by dominating women. The possibility of blessing same-sex unions compels one to wonder how much marriage theology has to be redone for "traditional" marriages in order to undo the old anxieties about gender.

If the possibility of blessing same-sex unions leads us so quickly to consider such disconcerting questions, it is no wonder that quantities of energy are spent to prevent the question from being asked. Jerking the question out of sight in the name of biblical authority is only one rhetorical device. My countersuggestion to all of them is that Christians are now obliged to raise the question and then to think it through while listening to the fullest array of pertinent voices. Let me repeat one obvious but theologically decisive fact. Requests to bless unions are not coming from outside the churches. They are made by Christians of their own leaders. Often they come from individuals or couples who have been active parishioners or congregants and long-time student of the Scriptures. Members of the vestry or the choir, directors of religious education and deacons, not to speak of priests and pastors themselves—these people come forward to ask for a blessing on their serious commitments, very often to an equally generous member of the same church. They come carrying their Bibles.

Much effort has gone into rebutting the allegedly literal readings of Christian Scripture on which church condemnations claim to be based. Much consolation has been gained from the retrieval of biblical same-sex "couples" or other gender deviants.[26] Still, it is better to remember that the disputes in churches are not about the meaning of particular passages. They are about institutional conditions for interpretation. They are, in short, disputes among Christians about who gets to define the faith—which is the same as saying who gets to decide on community membership. The debates are hopelessly and sometimes maliciously confused when they are reported as Christian against gay, as biblical truth against "liberal" political claims for justice. Some denominations or sects do indeed want to redefine "Christian" so that it applies only to those who interpret biblical texts according to predetermined results. They should not be allowed to hijack either Christian Scriptures or Christian faith.[27] Debates over homosexuality within Christian churches are disputes among Christians. They are disputes about how to read the Bible, how to interpret tradition, and how to live faithfully in the present. All parties in the dispute are influenced by larger political or social forces. If those advocating reform or reconstruction of church practices look like political "liberals," those opposing them certainly resemble political "conservatives." Antilesbian or antigay initiatives in the churches are quite often funded by exactly the same donors or mock-foundations that bankroll parallel initiatives in civil contexts. Church debates over Scripture circle endlessly because some are lavishly paid to spin them in circles.

The move to preempt discussion on biblical grounds should be resisted by emphasizing that positivist assumptions of "conservative Christian" exegesis are not the only ways Christians have of reading the Scriptures. There may be much better ways, and they may be discovered precisely after one turns away from current "biblical" debates. A theology does not become biblical by brandishing the words of the Christian Bible. A high percentage of (translated) biblical verses on a page gives no assurance of its fidelity. Quotation and distortion are perfectly compatible—they are old partners. Reflecting clear-mindedly on an urgent question that disconcerts theological categories might be the most biblical practice, precisely so far as it fractures long-dominant readings and allows the scriptural text to speak outside the little boxes prepared for it in polemic.

BETRAYING THE MOVEMENT

The second of the curiously paired attempts to foreclose discussion of unions remains. Usually attributed to "gay activists," it claims that seeking a blessing for same-sex unions represents in itself a betrayal of the movement for queer liberation. Writing out the objection in that way already raises doubts. Has there been only one movement? Must every movement be committed to the model of "liberation"? Is the objection being made against unions or against ritually recognized unions? Would the objection be less vigorous if the ritual community were not a Christian church? The questions will multiply unless limited to one sample. As before, I simplify even that sample to show the form of the argument being deployed.

In *The Trouble with Normal,* Michael Warner includes a chapter entitled "Beyond Gay Marriage."[28] The chapter is a graceful and witty complaint against making same-sex marriage the highest priority for lesbian and gay politics. It goes further: it tries, I think, to foreclose the question about same-sex marriage. Warner's central conceptual argument is that "marriage sanctifies some couples at the expense of others" (82). If you took *sanctifies* technically, you might expect Warner to discuss religious recognition of same-sex unions. In fact, he means the term colloquially; most of his chapter is about political and legal debates. But the misfired expectation can point to something curious in Warner's historical argument—and, then, in the conceptual argument as well.

To make his main historical argument, Warner must actually suppress religious references. "No one was more surprised by the rise of the gay marriage issue than many veterans of earlier forms of gay activism" (84). Why their surprise? "Marriage became the dominant issue in lesbian and gay politics in the 1990s, but not before" (87). The claim may be true if you stress "dominant" enough and restrict the scope of "gay politics." Still the claim seems to me to exclude prominent Christians from the "veterans of earlier forms of gay activism." As Warner himself notes in passing, Christian activists were blessing unions in public at least as long ago as 1970 (87). They did not do it because they were "riding a burst of radical enthusiasm after Stonewall" (87). They did it because they had been thinking about the theology of same-sex unions since before Stonewall. The best-known group now—and the one that Warner cites—is the Universal Fellowship of Metropolitan Community Churches, founded with a Eucharist presided over by Troy Perry in Los Angeles some months before Stonewall.[29] Still Perry's group was only one of a number of Christian or interfaith groups from the 1950s and 1960s, many of which had been trying to incorporate same-sex relationships into religious doctrine and practice.[30] The choice of Stonewall as emblematic origin encourages forgetfulness of many earlier moments of resistance, including the street actions and the other protests carried on in 1965 by a group called the Council on Religion and the Homosexual, which had been founded out of Glide Memorial Church and which counted among its members many Christian clergy.

Gaps in retelling the role of Christian groups in the history of "the movement" will concern us below. For the moment I emphasize that Warner's historical claim conceals the role of religion in recent queer genealogies. If attention to same-sex marriage may have surprised certain activists, it was a venerable topic for others. Marriage seems to appear suddenly in "lesbian and gay politics" only if those politics exclude decades of queer activist work in the Christian churches and other religious bodies. Warner's historical claim keeps some notable religious history out of sight.[31] It also requires him to deny what present events make clear: If there is a grand narrative to be told, it will tell that the tactics of "gay liberation" were used most effectively to accomplish much older ends. Most queer lives in America now suppose not liberationist fantasies of revolutionary transformation, but homophile programs of legal recognition and ethico-religious acceptance. The well-dressed picketers in cardigans have come closest to success. Not a few of the new homophiles are pastors, priests, or rabbis. Many more worship regularly. Their presence today at queer rallies reminds of their presence all along.

The occlusion of religious activism in Warner's main historical claim makes for other trouble in the main conceptual argument, the argument that "marriage sanctifies some couples at the expense of others." I agree with much of what Warner means here, but I notice again that he must push religion to the side. Warner is certainly right that the present legal privileges accorded (heterosexual) marriage cost other relationships a great deal in benefits and support. The injustices are cruel. Anyone who has had to fight with emergency room staff in order to stay with a mortally ill lover knows them. So does anyone thrown out of a lover's apartment or stripped of joint possessions or denied the right to visit children. The list of legal privileges granted married couples is long, and those refused it can count off its items with some bitterness. Still, it is a list of legal privileges, not of the effects of "sanctification" in the religious sense. The exact contents of the list show the centuries-long influence of church law, as its persistence depends in part on the political clout of the churches, but the contents are connected to the performance of Christian marriages *only* historically. There is no need to assume an entailment between Christian marriage and civil privilege. Today Christian rites for blessing same-sex unions do not have to produce civil entitlements.[32]

What, then, if we took Warner's main argument at face value, but separated the question of blessing from the question of civil privileges? The argument might go part way through, but only with qualification. Two Christians can seek to have their relationship blessed within their church in order to strengthen it by praying for God's grace and the community's supporting love, without expecting or intending to gain any legal privileges. Some of those who attend the rite may judge unblessed relationships as incomplete and sex outside of such relationships sinful. They may believe that all queers should be coupled in permanent, monogamous unions under church jurisdiction. Others may resent the prominence given to couples over singles, to ritual or private understanding, to restriction over freedom. The consequences of ritualizing relationships are as complex in queer churches as in heteronormative ones. Still almost all same-sex couples still face an enforced distance between the religious rite of blessing and civil privilege. Their rites rarely bring automatic civil entitlements. It is very important not to let the distance be forgotten because it is a valuable space for resistance—in the name of queer religion.

Warner's critique commits a familiar mistake in debates over blessing same-sex unions: it transfers arguments about unions back and forth from religious to legal contexts as if they were or ought to be interchangeable. This mistake is made on all sides. Advocates for blessing sometimes argue that the rite should be performed in order to have certain legal consequences. This is how Warner tells the story of Perry's first ceremony back in 1970: [33] "Under California law at the time, common-law marriage could be formalized by a church ceremony after a couple had lived together for two years" (87). He makes it seem as if the motive or purpose of the ceremony was to sneak in through a loophole in the state law. Perhaps that was the motive of the two women in 1970, though I am not quite sure how Warner knows it. Perry's own reflections on Metropolitan Community Church (MCC) weddings written in the year following stress rather their "revolutionary" implications for ethics and spirituality. [34] Perry himself has since presided over union ceremonies that were billed as public protests against marriage laws, but they were protests that were also or primarily religious acts. [35] More recent blessings have been used to push at the limits of legal recognition, as when two women and two men used the medieval custom of announcing the banns—still preserved in the law of Ontario— before that province permitted regular marriage. [36] One can agree or disagree with the use of church rites as forms of civil protest. My point is that even when a church blessing is used to exploit existing civil law, it cannot be reduced conceptually, in motive or in effect, to identity with civil law. On the contrary, civil registrations or licenses in American jurisdictions that have allowed them are regularly doubled or completed by religious rituals. Church weddings don't stop when legal recognition begins. I myself believe that many "Christian" marriages shrink Christian aspirations, but I do not believe that those marriages can be exhaustively described in the languages of social status or legal effect. Remember the Sisters: beyond the civil registration, the ceremony required a blessing.

Historically and conceptually, then, Warner's arguments are unpersuasive. The silence they enact around religious issues should be resisted. How far church activism is or is not a part of larger movement politics, how much there ever was or was not a single movement—the important questions remain. Religious groups, and not least Christian churches, have been the sites of intense and thoughtful activism since "before Stonewall." If it is a matter of measuring genealogies, blessing unions will be seen to be just as venerable as any other activist concern. Many same-sex couples are now coming forward in Christian churches to have their unions blessed. It would be condescending, if not something worse, to inform them that their requests are peripheral to the progress of the movement or to hint that they are somehow less lesbian or less gay because of what they ask. If the question of blessing same-sex unions is not silenced by alleged biblical prohibitions, it should also not be elided in calls for political solidarity—and precisely because of queer politics. Unbridled sex is hardly the most transgressive queer act. That is only what queers are scripted by public imagination to do. Praying over queer sex—now that transgresses.

The curiously coupled interruptions to asking about blessing same-sex unions should both be resisted. The question has not been foreclosed. It should be pursued, right through both chatter and silence.

GETTING PARTICULAR

Blessing queer relationships—as if they stood outside the debates, waiting just to be recognized. The old poster art of "gay liberation": a young man and a young woman, gym-formed, break free from their chains, each to find a suitably liberated partner.[37] As if deliciously shaped bodies conformed to articulate desires already stood there, just waiting to be released. As if queer fantasies of relationship were obviously coherent and practicable. As if lesbians and gays knew exactly what they wanted in a partner or a life. Queers have their characters—too many of them, really, and by now glibly marketed. You can sit at home and watch them on TV or find them by flipping through almost any up-market glossy. With a little more effort, you could go to the right video store and rent thousands more, from the shelves up front by the windows or the ones way in the back. The question about blessing unions has gotten too big. Its expansive generality has to be resisted by attention to particulars, to stubborn details and unpredicted differences.

In several ways, what follows is all too particular. The book is particular in its selection and its interpretation, because I am making the selection and I am doing the interpreting. I am what is called a "white gay man" in America who has spent his professional life on the histories of teaching in the more liturgical Christian churches.[38] This position is common to many of those who write or speak in English about blessing same-sex unions. It is a multiply privileged position—and despite the antiprivilege of announced homosexuality. When you speak from a culturally privileged position, you are encouraged by cultural forms to universalize your own experience (beyond ever-tempting vanity). The work of any dominant culture is to make itself appear as universal as nature—and also superbly special. Privilege should write, so long as it struggles to correct its presumption of universality or inevitability.

The book is not theological in any ordinary Christian sense, but it is particular in borrowing some Christian theologians' commitment to use whatever disciplines can be brought to bear on critical questions. The fairest definition of theology may be that it is the discipline of engaging every genre, including genres that claim to be God's own. The reader who likes to tally disciplines will find pages that look like cultural criticism, qualitative sociology, narrative history, literary criticism, and amateur satire. If theology is the ordered juxtaposition of fragments from human knowing in the most comprehensive pedagogy, these pages might seem the beginning of a theology. But they are decidedly not theological in the sense of claiming institutional authority or arguing by approved methods from established formulas. The best evidence for addressing the blessing of unions is neither scriptural proof-texts nor edicts from church officers. Of course, edicts from church officers or Scripture reduced to proof-texts are not the most helpful starting points for any topic in Christian theology.

I do not speak "confessionally" in the sense of proclaiming Christian tenets so as to recommend them. Nor do I give testimony in the first person about my religious beliefs and practices. Testimony is an ancient genre of Christian speech—of queer speech too. The genre can register lives more richly than such professorial genres as the footnote, the essay, or the treatise. The most politically useful speeches on behalf of Christian same-sex unions are testimonies, precisely because they combine liberationist and Christian impulses. But I will not give testimony here, either as a Christian or as a gay man. I comment on Christian traditions as an attentive listener, not as a fervent advocate. Readers who are not Christian may still find the book too much preoccupied with the details of Christian teaching or history. I hope that they might still learn something about lesbian and gay Christians or about analogies with other religious traditions, even if they cannot like any of the Christian beliefs mentioned.

Then there are the other particularities of my main "gay" character. In my usage, "gay man" and "gay male" are redundant phrases because I use "gay" to refer only to men. I emphasize the redundancy here to note two more specifications in my character. The first is the specification as male rather than female. The second is the specification as gay rather than one of the other characters through which male-male eros finds expression.

My performance encounters the dichotomy male/female repeatedly in its doubled or squared version, as the (imagined, inevitable) polarity between gay and lesbian. Since men and women are required to differ, how much more men who love men and women who love women! Most of what follows concerns male desire and male relations. I mark my ignorance of lesbian relationships as explicitly as I can without becoming boring. So I am careful in using *gay* to refer only to men, *lesbian* obviously to women. I use *same-sex* to cover both, as I have already, but with a caution. The theory that gay men and lesbian women are two subspecies of a true species or nature is a theory concocted for the sake of repression. Even in its weaker forms, the theory erases the specific characters performed by men and by women, however interlaced, variable, and contingent these may be. Lesbian women and gay men have been grouped together medically, legally, politically, socially—and before that, after some hesitation, theologically. Still, in thinking about erotic relationships, it is silly to presume that female-female bonds are substantially identical with male-male bonds. So I speak of same-sex unions most often when I consider lesbian and gay relationships as seen from the outside—from the viewpoint of Christian churches that oppose them, for example, or from the viewpoint of abstract arguments that run them together. Even though I concentrate on men, I keep some feminist and lesbian scholarship in view, especially when it resists or outdoes gay reflection. I never attempt to speak as a lesbian or as a woman, but I do sometimes speak as a faggot—which is, in the dominant gender hierarchy, sometimes lower than a woman. I try never to speak as Man, as the presumptively universal essence of one polarized gender.

The second specification of my "gay" performance has to do with the limits of that term. "Gay" is a specific cultural product most fully elaborated by American men who are white-identified, urban-centered, and media-driven. Men from different social locations can of course legitimately claim the label, though many rightly refuse to do so. Still, *gay* refers to a particular role or character; it is not a general term for men who (sometimes, often, always) have sexual relations with other men. Same-sex behavior between men belongs to a number of different characters, including "bisexual," "down low," "macho," "questioning," and "horny." Some of the characters imply gender deviance, and some specifically do not. One or two of them do not even imply *sexual* deviance. In what follows, then, I use *gay* to refer to a particular character or family of characters. When I want to refer to sexual or gender deviance more generally, though never exhaustively, I resort to the term *queer*.[39]

One final particularity remains, the most important: I speak in time. Time runs through debates about blessing unions in every direction. They are urgent debates for our time in this country. They swirl around social constructions of relationship that change in time, and more rapidly still because same-sex desire only recently emerged into anything like public toleration. In their academic forms, the debates get caught up by the accelerated history of certain disciplines—of "queer theory" and "postmodern theology" or their alternatives. Finally, most importantly, the debates are supposed to help desiring love in its transit through the time of individual lives, haphazardly and mutably joined.

The couple is a unit of time. A couple must exist *in* time, since we usually don't speak of a couple until two people have been together for some time. A couple is more importantly a unit for measuring time. Its duration marks time for the partners in it, but also for their families, friends, and communities. A couple projects a happy beginning and a sad end. It fixes anniversaries and sometimes precedes birthdays. It holds memories. The couple is a narrative—and perhaps a cosmogony. It is also the play of time over a series of dichotomies. A couple is supposed to be set against the world—that is one dichotomy. Yet the couple contains within itself a dichotomy of Same and Other. In some theories of the last century, same-sex couples were supposed to consist of unhealthy twins, because queers, unable to cope with adult diversity, could only seek themselves under the impulse of an infantile narcissism. Anyone who knows same-sex couples will suspect otherwise.[40] Gays and lesbians struggle as much as other-sex couples with the dichotomies built into the time of the romantic dyad. So too do those who write about them. The problem for the writer is the voice of the couple. Coupling authorizes or requires the use of a potent "we." The "we" is in fact either a script drafted by committee or else one partner speaking for both. Still it exerts extraordinary rhetorical force—strong enough, in the case of so many "traditional" marriages, to absorb the voice of one (usually the wife) into the voice of the other (usually the husband). Authors of romantic comedies know enough to stop the tale just when the marriage is performed—just when the voice of the couple is fully sanctioned.[41] The comedy stops then not only because disappointments are bound to follow, but because the voice of the narrator is abruptly pushed to one side. Much of this book is written on the way to marriage, but it cannot stop at the altar. It continues to talk on with the confidence that there must be something to say after the dichotomies of couple and world, of groom and groom.

The book is laid out in time according to the most familiar narrative pattern, the tale of the couple. A comedy of manners, it begins as a love story, but notices immediately how many paths lead off from the main plot, how many possible protagonists there are. Indeed, the book shows, chapter after chapter, how gay relationships slip out of the most familiar narrative stages plotted for marriage. It tries to estrange and caricature the familiar narrative, to "queer" it (as the slogan was). Like all romantic comedies, it discloses how accidental and how overdetermined was its point of departure—that crowded platform in San Francisco during the month of weddings.

CHAPTER ONE

Some Boys' Romance

❧

Track 1: Near the beginning of the American television show *Queer as Folk,* there is a Moment. Brian, the cynical advertising executive, has left the reigning dance club to meet his friends for the drive home.[1] He was being fellated in the "back room," but he got bored. Meanwhile, Justin approaches the gay clubs for the first time. He is seventeen and an aspiring (high school) artist. It is his First Night Out. Brian is about to jump into his jeep with his friends when he sees Justin. The young man emerges like a divinity from a cloud of golden steam. The camera makes a snap, swerving zoom into Brian's face. A strobe flashes. A sound effect: low and indistinct, something buried down inside a dance hit. Cut back to Justin. Then to Brian, who is hit by the strobe and the sound effect again. The street is a dance floor. Noticing Brian at last, Justin leans against a lamppost and stares back at him. So *of course* Brian approaches him and *of course* the two roar off in Brian's jeep to his magnificent loft, leaving the friends to find another way home.[2]

The Moment is the assurance of desire, cruising-and-hooking-up combined. It is also the sacrament of true love. In that suspended instant, Mr. Right meets Mr. Right. If the search for Mr. Right has lasted only minutes rather than years, and if his rightness persists for scant hours rather than a lifetime, still the moment of erotic connection remains an episode in the melodrama of true love. Any given trick may turn out to be a soulmate. Any dance tune may become "our song." Brian's friend Mike remarks in a voice-over just before the Moment between Brian and Justin: "Knowing that at any moment you might see him—the most beautiful man who ever lived." The most beautiful man who ever lived is the steam-haloed god meant for you.

Track 2: In the mid-1990s, Sandra Bernhard released a remake of Sylvester's disco hit, "You Make Me Feel (Mighty Real)."[3] Sylvester's original tells the story of a dance-floor encounter that leads back to a home and its erotic possibilities. Hot kisses in the dark, the right background beats: you feel real good—you feel "real." Bernhard rewrites the disco tune as a ballad about coming out in the Castro in the 1970s.[4] Her version opens with stray piano chords. Bernhard hums a dedication to (invocation of?) Sylvester. Then the kick of the bass and drums: time to dance. The lyrics in Bernhard's version fill in narrative details, but the plot of rapture remains.

> It's your first night out, you aren't sure what you're about
> But tonight something's going down. . . .
> You looked across the room and your heart went zoom
> He walked right over, said "I'll treat you right."

This is just the story of Justin and Brian. This is the Moment again. Or again and again, because we are listening to a perennial fairy tale, a persistent reverie. What Bernhard sings to her unnamed "you" (Sylvester himself?) is the story of Cinderella, only the Prince will not have to search tomorrow for his mysterious beauty. The beauty will already be in his bed.

⚭ ⚭ ⚭

In Christian churches and (other) queer cultures, discussions about marriage or mating are controlled not only by enforced institutional silences, by forbidden topics and discarded histories, but also by the endless cycling of mass images of romance. The images appear in many predictable places, from wedding homilies to "date" movies. They also figure where one might not expect them—say, in advertisements for gentrifying condos or TV spots for erectile dysfunction. It is remarkable how regularly the old romantic plots write themselves out in contemporary stories of desire, queer and not. The "romance novels" sold on supermarket racks are echoed by anthologies of erotica on the shelves of gay bookstores. Bodices are ripped here and jockstraps there, but the plots are identical. True desire becomes true love, or true love was true desire. Either redeems.[5] And this redemption is now widely marketed to queer lovers too.

Images for romance come to us in uncountable forms and with impossibly many genealogies. The forms and histories juxtapose or mix Christian and non-Christian elements. Even a short study of the mass images for happy erotic relationship will make clear the impossibility of segregating the religious or specifically Christian from the "secular."[6] Romantic love possesses sacred power: it is supposed to complete us and transform us, to make us happy and secure our place in the world. Language of divine creation and providence is borrowed for the tritest declarations: "We were meant to be together." "We were made for each other." So too are the great motifs of conversion: "I was drifting until I met you. You brought purpose to my life." "Being with you has given me a new life." Soon enough, even the images of redemptive suffering have their place: "He's tearing me apart, but if I can just stick it out, I know that we'll come through on the other side." These motifs are not only Christian, but so far as Christianity is the religious vernacular for many Americans (including non-Christians), the motifs are still standardly figured as Christian.

American etiquettes for romance necessarily transgress on religious territory.[7] Consider some constitutive elements. In true love, you find the one right person and give yourself entirely to him, to her. Don't think of conditions or time limits. Hold on to no secrets, no unforgiven insults, no unhealed wounds. The total gift of yourself to the other completes you, makes you for the first time who you were really meant to be. You give yourself up to find yourself forever. Your gift to each other creates a couple that can stand against the cruel, uncomprehending world of those who oppose your love. If the world doesn't understand, God will understand, because God made your love. You sacrifice yourself for your love. Your love is God. In the cycling codes of romantic etiquette, true love not only relies on religious terms and notions, it ends by arrogating to itself the place of the divine. The heart's secret is idolatry.

Marriage has an ambiguous role in romantic cycles. On the one hand, a romantic comedy is supposed to end at the wedding chapel. On the other hand, the wedding really is an epilogue and not a beginning. True love scorns marriage as it completes it. Loving is supposed to be the motive for marriage, but it often displaces any wedding. The consummation of true love in erotic encounter is its own sacrament of union. No priest but Love. No communion but the mingling of hearts, glances, lips, bodies. A wedding can be added on as a sort of final punctuation, but the action has already taken place. The indissoluble bond of true love will hold through any number of other relationships—through any number of attempts to contract other marriages.[8] Or so the images repeat to us.

There is no need to rehearse one or another story about how Christianity spawned European notions of romance or caused mutations in notions already there. Nor do I have to reiterate what any contact with the American market makes plain: Sex sells, but so does romance. (Or, rather, the coupling of sex and possession in marketing imitates romance as the desire to have and to hold.) The thing to notice is that mass images of romance are by now fully deployed in queer submarkets and queer lives.[9] Indeed, their (religious) power and their (Christian) provenance may be seen perhaps more clearly in gay male marketing, which is newer, smaller, and less familiarly, omnivorously religious than its "straight" counterparts. In efforts to sell gay relationships, latent Christian imagery must appear—and not only by jealous or condemning reference to heterosexual marriage. It must appear because it is still essential to any mass representation of American romance.[10]

Of course, things are not quite so simple as billboards make out. Gay lovers are not just target markets; they are members of a stigmatized minority. Gay couples that profess Christianity can be doubly stigmatized. To them, the mass images of Christian romantic love are interrupted by images of violent church condemnation. Both find resistance in lived experience. "Christian" persecution is projected across the cheery loops of a "Christian" happily ever after. One advantage of the double stigma is that it can disrupt both the romantic etiquettes and the howl of church outrage. Same-sex Christian couples are sometimes accused of being less queer because they are the willing victims of homophobic churches. Their situation could better be seen as providing them with more critical perspective on mass images than nonreligious couples regularly have. Bruce Mau writes of a world in which "less terrain falls outside of the regime of the logo and its image. . . . Attempting to declare the discrete boundary of any practice, where one ends and another begins, has become arbitrary and artificial. On the contrary, the overlap is where the greatest innovation is happening."[11] The hunch about media innovation applies as well to media critique. The safest place for reflecting on mass etiquettes of romantic love is the point where they meet interference from contrary etiquettes. The most hopeful place for reflection on church practice and its theological suppositions is where a self-righteously "orthodox" Christianity encounters the chemically whitened smiles of the perfect couple. The point of interference, of static, is the point at which many queer Christians find themselves.

Observing the interference of competing etiquettes is not escaping them. Watching yourself be instructed simultaneously by solicitations and condemnations, by illusions and delusions, is not the same as having a mind strengthened against sophistry. What one can hope for from the vantage point is a more revealing view of the particular power of their codes of etiquette—and so a more skeptical assessment of programs for radical reform, whether of our "hearts" or the words we use to give them away.

UNDER THE DISCO BALL; OR, FICTIONS OF LOVE

In an aging idealization of gay urban life, the dance club serves as the public square. You go there to display your citizen status, to join factions, and to share in civic ritual. It is also where you go to find love—or to shop for it. Sylvester, Sarah Bernhard, and the writers of *Queer as Folk* understand that perfectly. The constant accompaniment of time spent in this public square is "dance music." Dance music is not a genre so much as a ritual element. It serves its ritual function by keeping an inescapable beat. On top of that beat, various musical styles can be deployed: anthem, bubblegum jingle, rap, techno, and so indefinitely on. Often the most successful dance tracks recur to the original form of "House music": the deep bass line doubled by drum, percussive and rhythmic complications, electronic modulations, then "samples" or snippets of a soaring voice.[12] In the classic "dance diva" mix, the powerful voice belongs to a woman. She may use Gospel riffs or the techniques of ballad, but almost always she sings of love. Indeed, older connoisseurs may already have recognized that the title of this chapter is a pun on a line from that arch-diva of the dance floor, Madonna. In "Material Girl," she (or She) sang, "Some boys romance, some boys slow dance. . . ."[13]

To cite "current" examples would date this discussion much too exactly. Lists of hot "dance music" numbers change weekly, and nothing is so worthy of scorn as last month's Number 1. Regular patrons of a dance club can chart a song's progress by where it falls on the evening's program. A mix appears, tentatively, as a sort of experiment, in the first hour. If it works, if it is "hot," it makes its slow way through the schedule slots to the apex of the evening—to the hour when the floor is sweatily crowded with the hippest patrons. If the floor isn't crowded when the song begins, it fills almost instantly after the first recognizable measures. Then, inevitably, after a week or six, the song disappears from the roster altogether. And woe to the unwary rube who requests it of the presiding DJ. Humiliation is an art required of DJ's as much as of drag queens—or bishops who want to be lords.

The melodrama of a dance hit's rise and fall cannot conceal the great sameness from week to week. Sameness of beat, but sameness in the lyrics too: most diva mixes are love songs with almost interchangeable texts. Their shared song-form is just the form of our discourses about love. To make love-talk, we "sample" romantic discourse as rapidly and as predictably as this week's hit. We pick a phrase here, an image there. We cite and combine etiquettes for the heart. Then, in our discourses as in the dance floor hits, we persuade ourselves that the repetitive mix of quotations is our truest passion. Or the one true passion, because it is always the same. If each track has its "hook," or gimmick, all are torn from the single song book of romance.

The book is not evidently queer. Dance-floor songs are remarkably heterosexual in their presentation. The women who sing them are not pre-

sumed to be lesbians—far from it. Music videos that illustrate the songs almost always feature other-sex couples. The lyrics are inscribed quite explicitly into the main canon of romantic love. So gay men are supposed to
be drawn to them by a sort of gender inversion or emotional drag. After
all, gay men are famous for being adept at putting on the role of the female
romantic lead. The cliché becomes almost irresistible when the dance floor
is filled with a hundred young men mouthing Madonna. Sometimes they
look at each other as they lip-sync the words, with sentiment or ironic
smile. Sometimes they lift their arms and sing to the light-array on the ceil-
ing—I mean, to the stars above. On the video screens, Madonna can be in
drag herself as Marilyn Monroe. She is performing a Hollywood musical
number; she is pretending (?) to be a star pursued by dapper, dancing men.
I'm dancing and singing. I inhabit Madonna, who inhabits me. The lines
prescribed for romance can be taken up by so many voices and such different bodies. Put on the costume and sing the words. Or sing them as your
costume.

Do we locate the queerness of gay romance here, in the camp or drag of
"straight" romance on a "queer" dance floor? Many do so.[14] Madonna's great
ode to the dance floor, "Vogue," borrows the term and the references from
a practice in the drag balls more fully documented by the film *Paris Is Burning*.[15] To vogue at the drag balls was to dress and gesture like a glossy magazine's super-model. Madonna endorses the practice for all genders and
races. Then gay men on the dance floor mimic Madonna singing the song.
Gym boys perform a former leather-lace girl who now sings in glamorously
sultry tones, borrowing words and images from a drag competition that
mimics publicity stills or upscale advertisements. Who's camping what?
Analyses of drag or other camp tend often toward infinite regress, because
their imitation refers not to an original, but to an equally stylized social performance. Recall the category "Real" at the drag balls. A young, poor, African American, gay man is applauded for performing a Wall Street broker.
"Wall Street broker" is in turn a role that cites a series of antecedents that
would prove, on closer examination, to be codified artifacts. Queers performing straight love songs are camping, but then the straight love song is
already camp.

Ample room for queer appropriation is opened by the ambiguous pronouns. "I" sing love to "you." Queer desire can inhabit that relation, as closeted queers can make and market versions of it. Yet the very indefiniteness
of the pronouns also means that queer desire can be elided with ease, as it
is presumptively elided in the dominant use of romantic language. Camping romantic professions may reveal their ambiguities, but they are then liable to be "camped" back into a slightly hipper normative reading. The gen-

der fluidity of dance music remains fluid. Gay dance clubs are (re)colonized by straight couples.

The distinction between "queer" and "straight" evaporates quickly enough in romance. Just where it might seem thickest, it turns to vapor. In love, most of all, the difference between male-female and female-female or male-male might seem fixed—in the way sex or nature is fixed. In fact, the terms and images of standard romance are curiously mobile. At its origin, romance was divorced from procreation and hence from whatever fixity supposedly attaches to reproductive roles or normative gender differences. Romance is not about being man and woman in the world. It is about worshiping love against the world. Romance already floats free from the biological foundations that are supposed to guide the conduct of eros. Diverse erotic loves can inhabit an "I" soliciting a "you" or lamenting a broken heart. Gay men can have key roles in manufacturing mass etiquettes for romance not because of reversed gender position, but because of an intrinsic lack of gender fixity in contemporary romantic positions.

The clichés of consumption and production need reversing. The gay male appetite for romance is one cliché. Gay fandom is reputed to be particularly fierce in its adoration of the icons of romantic love—from opera divas through Hollywood stars and back to dance "divas." Who cries at failed romance? Coeds, housewives, and old queens, according to cliché. Gay production of the images of romance is another cliché. How many Hollywood romances were written, acted, orchestrated, filmed, lighted, or designed from inside a closet? Is this because gay men are really women—as if romance were only the game of women? Or is it rather because our language of romance is curiously indifferent to the genders and sexes that put on the roles it recommends? Roland Barthes's *A Lover's Discourse* is instructive on this point—and not only because Barthes is a gay man writing a catalogue of heteronormative speech. The catalogue itself can be read by anyone as about anyone. There is no way to tell from the love-language whether the lovers are male or female, straight or queer. "So it is a lover who speaks and who says: . . . "[16] Insert your current beloved here.

The pronouns move. So do their genres. Queer men make and consume romantic images in the unlikeliest places. One or another romantic plot underwrites much gay fiction, including fiction designed to titillate. Popular or almost popular novels from before the mid-1960s are notorious for illustrating doomed loves. Gay characters were destined to have love prohibited altogether or taken away immediately once acknowledged. The lovers were required to descend into quick death or sordid insensibility— and preferably both.[17] Still the quest for love often haunts these older novels. Love gains full redemptive potential when it is doomed. Often in these pages true love must be opposed to marriage for all the obvious reasons. In them, men marry to disprove gay rumors or as an antidote to homoerotic feelings. The decision for marriage is often enough the decision against a queer relationship or same-sex friendship.[18] But even in these novels, true love sometimes survives to express itself with the tokens or the language of marriage.[19] Tales of the strangeness of same-sex love turn quickly enough into familiar tales of love's perilous journey.

Blurbs on the covers of queer pulp from the same years promise indescribable deviations, but they speak romance too.[20] "Women lusted after this handsome, virile jazzman; . . . it took him years of agony to realize he wanted a man."[21] The blurb hardly does justice to *Hot Pants Homo,* but it well represents the persistent pulp desire to discover the truth of love. The cover of *So Sweet, So Soft, So Queer* confesses it more clearly: "He burned with a lusty passion as he soared into the ecstacy [*sic*] of love—but this time his partner was a man."[22] "They lived in fear, loved in secret."[23] In the "twilight" world (to use the adjective adored by blurb writers), romantic conventions bind. One of the conventions of romance is that star-crossed love is the more intense because it can never be fulfilled through public marriage. In opposing love to conventional marriage, the queer novels and their garish blurbs rehearse the great tenet of troubadour love poetry: Desires redouble when they are forbidden.[24] The allure of pulp is that its very publication expresses and elicits prohibited desires. To hold the tattered pages passed hand to hand is already to join in romance.

Oddly enough, the removal of actual external prohibitions or repressions has not automatically weakened the allure. Changes in the enforcement and interpretation of American pornography laws led to well-known shifts in queer publishing and other image-making. Gay pulp novels could now become much more explicit, and "above-ground" pornographic photographs or films could be made for gay men and distributed to them with some immunity from prosecution.[25] The increase of sexual explicitness that followed did not stop the circulation of romantic images through queer bodies. On the contrary, a more visible market increased the susceptibility of graphic queer eros to mass romantic images. I can show this from two apparently opposed films: *Pink Narcissus* (1971) and *A Night at Halsted's* (1981).

For a long time, *Pink Narcissus* was officially anonymous, not so much because it was prurient as because its release was the result of a messy fight. In 1971, at the time of the first public screenings, the reviewer for *Variety* reported that the film was made during seven years by a young filmmaker whose nerve failed when it came time to edit a version for release. The "young filmmaker" was in fact James Bidgood. A socialite's costume designer and fashion photographer, Bidgood contributed lush pictorials to physique magazines. For *Pink Narcissus,* his masterpiece, he was the complete queer *auteur:* director, writer, and cinematographer, but also set builder, stage manager, costume designer, hair stylist, makeup assistant, and special effects engineer. The dreamlike beauty of Bidgood's conception of the film is appreciated not so much in the blowup from 8 mm as in his luxurious production stills.[26] At the end, and of course, Bidgood could not bring the project to the perfection he dreamed. The exasperated backer/distributor, Sherpix, hired Martin Jay Sadoff to do the editing and, with Gary Goch, the scoring.[27]

Bidgood fantasized *Pink Narcissus* as an allegory of first innocence, sexual discovery, depravity, and innocence regained. As a young hustler waits in a hotel room for an elderly john, he is both star and witness in a series of dreams or visions. They move from a garden (of Eden?) through history to Hell—and then through a ritual cleansing to self-understanding and erotic transfiguration. The film has enough nudity and sensuous writhing in it to qualify as "erotica." Indeed, *Variety* summarized it as a "homosexual masturbation fantasy, very artistically made. And not hardcore."[28] If masturbation occurs during the film (beware loose sequins), it will be caught up in a story of special romantic salvation. Same-sex desire redeems just as much as (and maybe more than) its other-sex counterpart.

Pink Narcissus collects familiarly "romantic" settings and situations. Bobby Kendall, the star, is a young man discovering his desire in nature. He is also the hooker with the heart of gold, the matador, the beautiful peasant boy, the Roman captive, and the harem slave. He is at every moment—by the very character of the images—the glossy magazine model and the perfect beloved. The production stills are at once a set of publicity shots and portraits in heart-shaped frames. The quality of vision is the quality of first love—of the color-saturated, dramatically lit, glitter-coated gaze of infatuation—for which even the denizens of Times Square and the devils in Hell are perfectly composed. No sordid detail of the beloved's past can stand in the way.

My second example looks on its grainy surface to be just the opposite. *A Night at Halsted's* was filmed in the Los Angeles sex-club of porn star Fred Halsted.[29] The "sets" are dim hallways leading to glory holes, slings, and bunk beds. Think workboots on concrete, mustaches, rough-hewn timbers, stringy hair, and the odd bit of smudged Plexiglas. In the most clichéd manner of pornographic films, the story is a string of sexual situations barely connected by plot and punctuated more by murmured encouragements or groans than by dialogue. Still the sketchy plot portrays a roman-

tic quest for a young man who is tracked through the whole club and all the
night. However many sexual acts might be performed or witnessed by the
hero, only consummation with the "boy" in the boot-blacking stand can
complete the evening. Once he has been had, it is time to go home. In their
different ways, then, *Pink Narcissus* and *A Night at Halsted's* are equally stories of romance, the first as redemptive melodrama, the second as light
comedy. (Indeed, it may be that the standard "all male" pornographic film
simply *is* the most widely distributed gay version of the Hollywood romance—Joey Stefano its Doris Day.) If one film is "artistic" and the other
"hard core," if one prefers chiffon and the other leather, these are trivial differences. Underneath, the same old song.

Other than the genitals involved or imagined, is there anything queer
about these love stories, from camped Madonna through pulp fiction to the
early films? All might be explained as examples of camp or drag. More
clever analysis might want to detect in gay men's avid consumption of the
stories some traces of the old queer "melancholy." Isn't the dance floor, after all, the site of a certain wistfulness over denied or delayed adolescence?
Mightn't Bidgood's obsessive effort to create a surreal allegory show just
how dreary gay reality finally is? And couldn't we read in the compulsions
of gay porn the felt lack of more domestic films—say, home movies of the
happy family? The suggestion is over-subtle. Plots of straight romance are
also about lost youth, Eden, and complete fulfillment. Bidgood's obsessive
attentions are answered in hundreds of straight fashion magazines. He
found them there. The preoccupations of gay porn are often indistinguish-
able from those of pornography for straight men. Of course; and, given the
shifting pronouns of romance, we should ask, How do you tell for whom
pornography is produced? Some straight women love gay erotica and
pornography, and straight men are notoriously fond of lesbian scenes. Who
can control the consumption of image-bodies in their frenzies? And who
believes that their acts or the tokens of their desires say anything about underlying "sexual orientation"? In gay pornography, there are genres and sub-
genres featuring "straight boys." How do you know that they are straight?
They keep pornographic images of women prominently beside them.

If we want to look for what is "queer" in same-sex consumption of the
mass etiquettes of romantic love, we would do better to look at the curious coincidence of the declaration of love with coming out. To declare
yourself, in Victorian novels, is to confess your love, to commit yourself in
momentous words.[30] The words show what kind of person you are. To declare love is to put both your "heart" and your reputation at stake. This is
doubly true for queer loves. When one man declares erotic love for another man, he also declares himself gay. He reveals not only his feelings, but

his being—his "heart" in a double sense. Declaring your love is coming out in a particularly pointed way. The pressure of love, the madness of it, drives you to say who you are.

Saying who you really are is the central act of the liberationist model of coming out. The slogan, "Out of the closet and into the streets!" could, on its face, mean several things. It could mean, for example, that people who have same-sex relations in private should be willing to claim those relations in public as a means of political change. Still the now-orthodox interpretation of the slogan construes "into the streets" as meaning "into the gay identity." You come out of your closet when you step into the public "identity," which is also your true self. Dennis Altman, writing in 1971, quoted the Gay Liberation Front statement from the first issue of New York's *Come Out!*: "WE ARE GOING TO BE WHO WE ARE."[31] Altman explains: "Gay liberation, to a much greater extent than is true of the older homophile groups, is concerned with the assertion and creation of a new sense of identity, one based on pride in being gay."[32] Isn't the same true of romantic love? When I fall in love with the right person, I can be myself for the first time. I am supposed to find myself in the other. Together we should live our true lives in opposition to the world.

However much gay sex might appear to be the antithesis of romance, it is tied to those utopian fantasies by the terms of its own "liberation." What could be more romantic than finding your inmost self by finding out who you really love? A gay liberation movement is a long ballad to the power of love. You can find tricks at its meetings, in its committees and cells, but you are taken by the movement itself, because the movement promises you an unending romance in the character it bestows on you. Romance circulates not only in the marketplace out there, or in the construction and expression of your particular desires, but in the very "identity" that counts you as queer. To be defined by your loves is to be the perfectly romantic being. And mustn't it always have been like this for the select band of the courageous? The romance of present liberation uncovers the centuries-long romance of queer folk.

LOVE IN A QUEER SUBCULTURE

For several decades now, "subculture" has been a leading character in academic controversies over gay history.[33] The controversies have returned more and more irritably to a fixed series of questions: When did something that can be called a gay "subculture" first appear? What are the criteria for calling something a gay "subculture"? What are the entailments, if any, between finding a gay "subculture" and finding a gay "identity" or "subjectivity"? Before they were terms of gay academic controversy, *culture* and *sub-*

culture figured in the speeches of the gay liberation movement. Before gay liberation, the terms were deployed and disputed in various rhetorical patterns of the homophile movement; before that, in earlier groups. These vanished discourses are too various to be surveyed, but they may be sampled in the way a House mix samples earlier tracks. They need to be surveyed because queer subculture is not only a medium through which etiquettes of romance circulate, but is itself an edifice of romance—the object and the product of romantic longings. You can see this if you begin from blander definitions.

In 1951, the Mattachine Society's "Missions and Purposes" commits the new group to fostering "a highly ethical homosexual culture . . . paralleling the emerging culture of our fellow minorities—the Negro, Mexican and Jewish Peoples."[34] The commitment answered the worry in the minds of at least some homophile activists that there was already a homosexual culture, and precisely not a "highly ethical" one. No sooner was the claim made than its reference to culture had to be rendered precise and empirical. In 1961, an early teacher of sociology at the ONE Institute in Los Angeles offered this methodological rule: "Homosexuals can claim to be a distinct cultural minority only as it can be proven that they make a group contribution to the dominant culture which is the specific outcome of the homosexual temperament."[35] The Institute itself set about conducting a survey.

Gay liberation proclaimed itself the rejection of the homophile movement. In fact, its discourses depended on the earlier movement in many ways, not least in regard to gay culture or subculture. A document prepared by Chicago's Gay Liberation Front (GLF) for a conference in September 1970 includes "Culture" as a separate section. It begins with an indictment: "As a group we have been robbed of our culture."[36] The Chicago GLF and Third World Gay Revolution summarize their doctrine in June of 1971: "The personal is the political, the economic, and the cultural."[37] In these documents and the hundreds more like them, terms such as *culture* or *subculture* are supposed to invoke an already elaborated (Marxist, Leninist, Trotskyite, Maoist, Marcusian) theory, so they are frequently and triumphantly exchanged for more technical terms, like *group consciousness,* or *ghetto mentality,* or *class ideology.* Of course, the gay liberationist theory of culture or subculture was not nearly so technical as it pretended to be, and its terminology was anything but scientifically secure.

Revolutionary analyses of culture or subculture had to contend with a growing number of alternate gay notions about them, most of which were tinted some romantic shade. Some of these notions attached to codified sexual practices. For example, *The Queen's Vernacular* (1972) defines "leather crowd" as "the subculture of the leather boys,"[38] while "Greek culture" is an old euphemism in the want ads for anal intercourse. Other notions of culture or subculture gesture toward something like a lifestyle. A clumsy satire published in 1971 by *Gay Sunshine* attacks "the traditional gay subculture": "a fantasy world of poodle dogs and Wedgewood teacups and chandeliers and all the fancy clothes and home furnishings any queen could ever desire."[39] A few years later, writing in the Boston gay press, "A. Nolder Gay" criticizes the thinness of "the gay subculture": "The self-centeredness of the child persists in a number of gay life situations; indeed, in my gloomier moments I am tempted to say that it pervades both the traditional and the allegedly liberated gay subcultures."[40]

Dennis Altman, writing around 1971, speaks most often of a "gay-world," but also of "counterculture" and "pseudo-community."[41] Many "social gayworlds" are characterized for Altman as camp. Camp leads him in turn to speak of a "gay sensibility."[42] Other authors also call "camp" a culture, if not quite a sensibility.[43] Others still make culture and sensibility synonymous — or coeval.[44] In this way, the notion of a gay culture or subculture is brought back around to the cliché that gays are especially "cultured," arbiters of taste, of style, and of every art, both fine and domestic. In a piece drafted in 1975 and recast in 1978, Allen Young notices "two primary definitions of the term 'culture'—first, culture as what is generally called 'the arts,' and, second, culture as anthropologists use the term— that is, the patterns of behavior and institutions belonging to a particular group of people."[45] Young then uses "culture" loosely enough, rhetorically enough, so that the gay subculture becomes something like the flip side of the gay role in culture, simply speaking.

Note in the last few definitions, and particularly in Young's, the multiple links to romance. The art world is, according to the clichés, a world of decadent passions. It loves beautiful artifacts, but also beautiful young men. The acquisition of paintings is accompanied by the acquisition of ephebes. The connoisseur of ballet may also fancy dancers, as the impoverished opera queen may, in the transport of spectatorship from the upper balconies, find more carnal satisfactions. The alignment of gay culture with connoisseurship is not only eroticized, but thoroughly romantic. Queer culture is assigned as the space in which romantic passions are sought and elicited, praised and taught, recorded and adored. Drag is one expression of this, the ticket line of the Metropolitan Opera another.

A different sort of romance can be found even in attempts to reclaim *culture* and *subculture* as terms of queer exhortation or historical description— though the finding will require looking under some absences. Some of the hortatory roles assumed by "subculture" are admirable. At times, for exam-

ple, the notion of gay subculture is defended against the charge that homosexuals can't have real communities. So Stephen Murray rightly replies to
the charge that gay neighborhoods are little more than "lifestyle enclaves"
by showing that they satisfy stated criteria for communities as fully as could
be wanted.[46] At other times, "culture" and "subculture" reassume their
central roles in exhortations to build better gay societies, a role they once
shared with "counterculture."[47] If it has become increasingly hard to sustain the illusion that gay culture is countercultural, rejecting money and
commodities fetishism and the uptown idyll, "our" culture is still contrasted for political purposes both with straight culture and with its own
failings. Gilbert Herdt and Andrew Boxer not only argue for "the existence
of a gay cultural system" in America, they want to assess its "authenticity."[48]
Daniel Harris goes further, pronouncing the demise of "gay culture" just
because it is no longer resists the market economy and the frenzied banal-
ity of mass media.[49]

Given the prominence of "culture" and "subculture" in American gay
discourses, it is not surprising that the terms should also figure in histories
of gay America, especially since many of the historians were themselves
also activists—and therefore romantics. John D'Emilio incorporates the
terms into one of his principal aims: "I have attempted to situate the growth
of a gay politics within the larger setting of the evolution of a gay sexual
identity and an urban subculture of homosexuals and lesbians."[50] Accom-
plishing this aim requires D'Emilio to show, among other things, that "an
urban gay subculture took shape in America during the 1940s."[51] Jonathan
Ned Katz finds evidence of a subculture further back—say, in slang terms
from the 1920s.[52] George Chauncey pushes the origins of "a highly visible,
remarkably complex, and continually changing gay male world" back to
1890: "The men who participated in that world forged a distinctive culture
with its own language and customs, its own traditions and folk histories, its
own heroes and heroines."[53]

Is it clear yet what a subculture is? It cannot be, because the authors are
saying different things. Contrast three attempts at exact definition. For Jeffrey Weeks, "male homosexual sub-culture" in the "modern" sense requires
at least "recognised cruising places and homosexual haunts, ritualised sexual contact and a distinctive argot and 'style.'"[54] For John Boswell, "Individual writers recording their personal feelings in isolation, no matter how
numerous, probably do not constitute a 'subculture' . . . ; but a network
of such persons, conscious of their common difference from the majority
and mutually influencing their own and others' perceptions of the nature of
their distinctiveness" does.[55] For Chauncey, "an organized, multilayered,
and self-conscious gay subculture" has "its own meeting places, language,

folklore, and moral codes."[56] The attempts cannot be combined into a single definition. For Weeks, gay subculture is to be judged by externally observable behaviors, by places, and acts, and modes of speech or dress. For Boswell, gay subculture requires an invisible consciousness shared in such a way as to modify invisible perceptions. For Chauncey, subculture is characterized by competing visual metaphors ("organized, multi-layered, self-conscious") and recognized by a mixture of visible and invisible effects ("meeting places, language, folklore, and moral codes").

The difficulty in defining gay subculture results from the confusing circulation of etiquettes for queer romance. On the one hand, it would seem that the material basis for *queer* culture (or for a queer life) is a sort of rudimentary sexual marketplace. In it, queers can recognize each other and stand on their desires against the heterosexual hegemony and all its pomps. The core of the queer subculture is traffic in queer desires. On the other hand, the elaboration of a culture on top of those desires is a traffic in etiquettes—etiquettes that are, regularly and inevitably, borrowed, camped, appropriated from the hegemony of other-sex romance. Or else stealthily elaborated within that hegemony and then reclaimed from it. Or else produced by the simple inversion of that hegemony. What then is the relation of the romantic etiquettes to the desires and the bodies over which they play?

In many historical accounts, gay subculture has implied or been implied by gay character. Traces of cultural production or exchange motivate inferences about the consciousness required for them or fostered in them. So there are further debates about whether it is possible to sustain a gay cultural script or character outside of a subculture that can reinforce and reproduce it.[57] Debates over "identity" slide into debates over "subjectivity," over the conscious or unconscious appropriation of a gay character. Indeed, in most debates, claims for a gay subculture are interchangeable with claims for a gay identity and a gay subjectivity.[58] For the historians, as for the gay liberationists, having the identity means having or sharing or making the culture. "The evolution of a homosexual identity is necessary to the development of a homosexual culture"—and conversely.[59] The identity is taken as the locus and agent of the subculture, as its interpreter and its expression.

"Identity" is an over-determined notion that has by now worn down. You can still feel in it some of the material out of which it was made. It means something like equality, of course, and so suggests continuity of the same through time. The word evokes more strongly a fixed name or other token (like a number) that has been assigned so that the person can be placed, tracked, or apprehended. This is the identity you give in response to the question, "Where is your ID?" The meaning passes from there to "personal identity" as a sense of self, of being a certain kind of person. To lose your identity, in this sense, is not to lose a driver's license. It is rather to lose your experience of being a self with stable features. The easy shift from the second to the third meaning worries me because I want to open space between the assigned stable identity and the fluidities of the self for bodies and pleasures—just where romance imposes its codes of etiquette with particular force. The assigned erotic character becomes the deepest sense of self. You are how you love, and so you must love in particular ways. Many searches for gay "identities" or subcultures replicate or reinforce romantic codes.

After all, what makes a social role or group "homosexual" or "gay"? If we are hunting for a gay "subculture," what are we hunting for? The distinguishing mark must be something in the desires, sexual acts, affections, and dispositions. It must be the character of a risky and often tragic love for an unattainable object. We are looking for a kind of love that can be expressed only as *sub*-culture, only in code or camp, in ironies and allusions placed against the hegemonic culture. Romance writes scenes for the character of the lover. The history of gay "identity" recovers those scripts. Sexual desires, fantasies, dispositions, and even acts are less amenable to documentation and narration than, say, a shared set of quotations or allusions. The discovery of a subculture is so often the discovery of quotations or allusions, of identity cards traded among its members. The quotations or allusions are distinguished from hegemonic culture precisely because of their Beloved. Being queer is knowing the dress, music, jokes, and myths, but these are distinguished as queer through their reference to a particular and famously trammeled desire. Evidence for queer "identity" is evidence in turn for queer "subculture," which is evidence for a particularly pure form of the romantic myth.

Identities for same-sex desires have been written by many regimes and their agents, including preachers, inquisitors, judges, and physicians. Today they get written increasingly by the purveyors of romance, those charming successors to preachers, inquisitors, judges, and physicians. The purveyors function most like preachers. They are not like medieval preachers thundering condemnations against sodomites, though they do offer something modeled on that Christian sin-identity and do heartily condemn deviations from it. The purveyors of queer romance are wedding preachers who want to preside over every coupling of "identical" genitals. They do so not only by direct prescription, but by reinforcing romance in the imagined space of queer subculture. They speak in and for a subculture that is essentially romantic. It is distinguished, in many contemporary accounts, by a kind of love—by the object of love. Gay subculture is the promised land of love. There love can find itself, express itself, abide with itself. The subculture is an Ithaka to which every young, queer Odysseus travels, through perils, in search of his home, where love waits patiently. String up other suitors and climb into the bed you always knew was yours.

In its better moments, Christian theology (especially "mystical" theology) has traced the limits of languages or images as tokens of the most important desires. It has connected the fracturing of language with the disruption or dissolution of a (false) self and its idols of the beloved. In its radical critique of idolatry's disappointments, Christian mystical theology could provide useful antidotes to the circulation of mass etiquettes for queer romance. Most often, the antidote is neither offered nor received. It is too easily drowned in churchly denunciations of same-sex love. It is endlessly diluted, because the Christian theology of love is now beguiled by the very same romantic etiquettes. Only a long argument could show this with convincing detail, but I can suggest to the skeptical a simple exercise: Spend a few days with "religious education" booklets for Christian adolescents. You will find extraordinary amalgamations of traditional Christian speech and romantic self-help. Critiques of secular romance will be undone, on the same page, by a capitulation to the narrative of romantic love. The capitulation can come in content or in form. Some evangelical tracts adopt the layout of a glossy teenage fashion magazine to give good Christian girls dating tips.[60] In the same way, if less blatantly, Christian counseling for couples borrows the advice and presuppositions of its secular predecessors. Pastoral care leaves little space for critique of the idolatries in heterosexual romance—and less, the more homophobic it becomes. How can it then help to assess the gay models, which it has trouble mentioning?

Faced with the proliferation of mass etiquettes in queer marketing, abandoned by most Christian theology or its civic embodiments, queer love can be tempted to take refuge in the most private spaces—in the secret love-talk of closeted predecessors. Surely in them there must be an escape from the mass images and their Christian complements! But in fact it is within the intimate spaces that the etiquettes dance most energetically.

LOVE LETTERS

Alongside the statements of Christian churches and the policies of "LGBT" organizations, beside the liberationist critiques of bourgeois marriage and the Christian rebuttals to them, lesbian and gay writers have been experimenting with how to write their loves. They have done so publicly in works of literature. They have done so privately (and for a longer time) in correspondence, journals, and gifts of art. I call the private registers "love letters," whether written or not. They show most poignantly the play of romantic etiquettes in the professions of same-sex love.

In approaching old love letters, we need to be careful about assuming a substantially identical queer subculture or fixed repertoire of characters. Such assumptions trouble, for example, Rictor Norton's anthology of "gay love letters" across cultures and centuries.[61] Norton wants to bring together letters or pieces of letters from Greco-Roman antiquity to the American 1960s, with quick expeditions to China and Japan. To sustain the illusion of a recognizable "gay" role across time and place, he must ignore many textual details, including conventions of letter-writing, familiar address, and erudite allusion. For example, his "love letter" from Marcus Cornelius Fronto to Marcus Aurelius is an embellishment on the speeches about seduction in Plato's *Phaedrus*.[62] Again, the letters of Anselm of Canterbury that Norton treats as examples of "the last flowering of homosexual love before fanatical anti-gay prejudice swept across Europe in the thirteenth century" are in fact artful weavings of literary images for friendship, both natural and spiritual.[63] Lust quotes affectionate literature, of course, but not every quotation of it is lustful. What sounds to modern English-speakers like a declaration of ardent erotic passion may be, in an ancient or medieval text, a well-established convention for expressing another sort of attachment. Passion too is a rhetorical convention. Even where older letters do seem to speak about same-sex desire or activity, we cannot infer that the correspondents would have recognized anything like the contemporary "gay" self, character, or role.

Much more would have to be said about these difficulties of interpretation before using ancient, medieval, or early modern examples. I will economize by taking an extended example nearer to the American present. The correspondents are two American men who had a long-term relationship that was, for at least a part of its span, avowedly and deliberately physical. The relationship took place between 1924 and 1945. If the correspondents did not call themselves "gay," they did think of themselves, at least in the beginning, as "inverts," that is, as belonging to a medico-legal category closely related to "homosexual." The men were the literary critic F. O. Matthiessen and the painter Russell Cheney. I want to see in their letters how inevitable are the images of romance, even in the scandalous correspondence of "inverts."

Matthiessen and Cheney met on a ship crossing the Atlantic in September 1924. Matthiessen was in his early twenties, Cheney forty-three. The younger man was pursuing an advanced degree in English literature at Oxford after a brilliant undergraduate career at Yale. The older man was already an established painter who moved around the Mediterranean. After several days of growing shipboard friendship, Matthiessen came out to Cheney late their last night on board—or, rather, confessed that he had been "sexually inverted" in the past. Cheney was eating on a pear that Matthiessen (another Eve) had conveniently offered him. Once he swallowed, Cheney replied, as Matthiessen retold things: "My God, feller, you've turned me upside down. I'm that way too."[64] They parted the next morning having slept together without consummating their new relationship—beyond a single kiss and the plan to meet in Italy at Christmas.

A kiss, a promise, and a rush of letters: Matthiessen and Cheney began to write to each other regularly, feverishly. The first letter from Matthiessen is signed "With all my love" (24). The first from Cheney is more effusive: "Our union is complete. Love is stronger than death, stronger than sin— even than old habits. . . . I sat there convulsed with laughter at the image of myself before my soul was quiet with you . . . I love you and will live as though you were at my side" (24–25). Remember that they had met hardly a week earlier and had spent only one chaste night together. If it is not quite love at first sight, it is close enough: love at first self-disclosure.

Of course, both correspondents felt uneasy in carrying over the standard vocabulary of romance. Matthiessen makes several efforts in the early months to describe what it is they have or are. First he says that they are "living" Walt Whitman, but not the more homoerotic Whitman (26).[65] Barely two days later, he tries again, this time playing off the stronger notion, marriage.

> I saw very clearly that night and called it a marriage. . . . Marriage is a mere term; only as a dynamic vivid thing does it dominate life. That is: you can visualize marriage or you can live it. Now I am living it.
>
> Marriage! What a strange word to be applied to two men! Can't you hear the hell-hounds of society baying full pursuit behind us? But that's just the point. We are beyond society . . .
>
> And so we have a marriage that was never seen on land or sea and surely not in Tennyson's poet's dream! It is a marriage that demands nothing and gives everything. It does not limit the affections of the two parties, it gives their scope greater radiance and depth. Oh it is strange enough. It has no ring and no vows, and no [wedding presents from your friends], and no children. And so of course it has none of the coldness of passion, but merely the serene joy of companionship. It has no three hundred and sixty-five breakfasts opposite each other at the same table; and yet it desires frequent companionship, devotion, and laughter. Its bonds indeed form the service that is perfect freedom. (29–30)[66]

I have quoted the letter at length because it shows so plainly how the effort to distance oneself from heterosexual relations becomes entangled again in the rhetoric of romance. The passage wants to repudiate marriage as it claims a truer marriage. It scorns tedious domesticity in favor of a more thorough companionship. It links its outlaw status to the service of a higher law—because, of course, "the service that is perfect freedom" is one of Augustine's—or the *Book of Common Prayer's*—most famous descriptions of the creature's relation to the divine Creator.

Religious language recurs in these pages, even as the language of marriage is questioned. About a month further into the same fall, Matthiessen responds to a phrase from Cheney: "'The splendid untrammeled freedom of love'—that's the essence of it all, right. Why give it a name that really doesn't belong to it? It isn't a marriage except in a very unusual mystical sense, and so don't adopt the conventional terms to speak of it. Our union has no name, no label; in the world it does not exist. It is simply the unpalpable, inexpressible fullness of our lives" (46). In authoritative Christian writings the "mystical marriage" of Christ and the church or of God and the soul is the archetype of earthly marriage.[67] To say that the two men do not have a marriage *except* in a mystical sense is to say that they have the noblest and best sort of marriage. They are "unlike the majority" and yet capable of "a love more complete and sacred" than any they had dreamed (73).

The mystical marriage, the sacred love, is also fully physical—at Matthiessen's insistence. When Cheney tries to retreat from a sexual relationship into a friendship, Matthiessen insists that celibacy would betray the fullness of their love. He rejects celibacy as something that Christ could practice, but that the follower of Christ should not and cannot embrace. "I want to live according to the dictates of my deepest, purest inner spirit, the spirit of God, the spirit of Love. . . . I worship Christ, but I follow him in the spirit, not in the letter. And in our union, Rat, I feel that I have followed the deepest voice of my nature" (88). Once Cheney has been persuaded, Matthiessen continues to announce the lesson: "I realize that in these last months I am a whole man for the first time: no more dodging or repressing for we gladly accept what we are. And sex now instead of being a nightmare is the most sacred, all-embracing gift we have" (116). Or, rather, the fusion of sex and love between them is the most sacred. When Cheney has sex back in New York with a former lover, Matthiessen sets the act aside as necessarily superficial: "It seems to me that the most significant thing revealed by this situation with Malcolm is the truth of the statement that you can give the supreme expression of your body only to the man you love. That it is such a fundamental all-embracing sacred thing that once you have known it in its full radiance of love, that any other expression seems cheap and unsatisfactory" (127–28).[68]

It can be tempting to explain away the religious overtones by pointing to Matthiessen's own religious beliefs, in which love was indeed the highest expression of the divine: "My whole religion has nothing to do with traditionalism or authority, but finds its beginning and end in ever increasing knowledge of the spirit of love which I find in my own heart" (102). Years later, in the 1940s, he would repeat the same doctrine as the essence of his Christianity.[69] Yet religious language echoes in Cheney too, right alongside skeptical remarks about Christianity. He had recorded, in his very first letter, that their encounter had brought him back to reciting his childhood prayers (25).[70] A month later he is invoking Gospel example: "A little thing like that beautiful legend of Christ and St. John, so close to the ideal we have lived for these last weeks. (You take your choice for part—I don't assume one or the other!! You know what I mean all right, the sacred devotion of love.)" (53–54).[71] When Cheney wants to argue for celibacy in their relationship, he appeals to the humility that Matthiessen has taught him, which is also "the quality that Christ exemplified" (81). A little later, he is reading the New Testament on love in the "simple presence" of his lover's "spirit" (95).

Reliance on religious language does not prove that either correspondent was an especially pious Christian. The soaring romantic tropes familiar to them drew them toward that language. Our romance quotes by habit the most exalted religious imagery alongside tropes of outlawry, transgression, and uniqueness. We fuse religion with transgression to justify our loves. Matthiessen insists upon Christian theological language when arguing with Cheney that they should continue as lovers. He invokes it only a bit more subtly when he insists that the two of them are without guides, without precedents. "That there have been other unions like ours is obvious, but we are unable to draw on their experience. We must create everything for ourselves. And creation is never easy" (71). In love, the creature must take up the solitary labor of the Creator.

Is the important thing here that the two correspondents belong to the same sex? Isn't it much more important that they share a notion of creative, redemptive love? Love talk remains, even in private and oppressed settings, curiously divorced from lived specificities of sex, same or other. What is most striking is that these feverish exchanges occur early on in the relationship—most of those quoted, in fact, between the shipboard meeting and the first reunion in Italy. The language of love, with its circulation of the most clichéd images, flowers in the absence of same-sex copulation.

It fills up the time when they are apart, when they miss each other, but also when they can construct a relationship without each other——indeed, when they imagine an altogether different sort of relationship. Romance is most fluent when the beloved is remote. It spins out "relationships" when the other person is an occasion, not a steady presence. Romance prefers episodic time——the hours of fantasy.

Matthiessen and Cheney are a particularly distinguished couple, and so their correspondence might be considered exceptional. It is all the more striking, then, how inevitably it trades in the most familiar images. The same trade can be found in less distinguished and more private texts, such as the roughly contemporary diary of "Jeb Alexander." This is the pseudonym assigned by his niece and editor to an American civil servant who recorded his relations with other men in Washington, DC, from the 1920s into the 1960s.[72] The published extracts are heavily edited, but they still provide some specimens of his language. It is clear, for example, that "Alexander" described his ideal or idealized erotic relations as "friendship" or "companionship," with the context for both supplied by Whitman.[73] His imaginary lover, his "dream boy, Vincent Eric Orville," is described over many years as friend, companion, or comrade.[74] More vivid notions of permanent romantic fusion appear at moments of intense emotion. Of his brother's wedding, "Alexander" writes: "The use of such phrases as 'forever' and 'till death do us part' affected me more than I had expected to feel."[75] He notes "the anniversary of my first experience of love and its consummation."[76] At the moment when it seems that he may at last have begun an enduring relationship with his true love, "Alexander" writes: "I believe that if I could have him with me I could be happy the rest of my life on a desert isle. Just the two of us alone. I feel that I should like to be father, mother, brother, wife, friend, and lover to him all at the same time."[77] The "wife" is particularly interesting, both as marital imagery and because it is not "husband." Most interesting is the predominance of romance, according to which every possible social and familial relation is realized by a couple in changeless isolation. "Alexander" commits himself to Whitman's notion of "manly comrades," but then he slides into the great ideals of romantic love and even marriage.

Both of these private registers, the correspondence and the journal, predate our aggressive gay market, yet they are caught up in the circulation of etiquettes of romantic love. They exhibit the effects not of targeted ad campaigns but of some older logic. It is the core idolatry of romantic love, which must deny everything, including any other divine, in order to exalt the beloved sufficiently. Radical denial expects (wants!) to be met with social condemnation. True love could not be legally consummated or socially recognized. It is—and insists on being—a passion stigmatized for its intensity. If there were another stigmatized longing, another set of erotic acts branded by society, surely they would be romantic too. Romance is not in the genitals, but in the stigma. Romantic love yearns to have passion outside law. Anything else that looks like passion outside law will also look quintessentially romantic. So is the language of romance straight or queer? It is neither and both. It is the straight diva singer to her straight boyfriend—for a queer audience. It is the male-on-male imagery of Socratic seduction generalized to include women.[78] It is Israelite marriage hymns in the *Song of Songs* reread as the intercourse of male monks and their male God—and then read again at a lesbian union. Romance condenses all loves into a single, saving passion. It offers a single vocabulary for the beatings of every heart.

THE MASTERS' TONGUE

"Gay liberation," like "women's liberation" or "black liberation," was a utopian fantasy. The same utopian fantasy animated all three. The fantasy may have been cast in the terms of vulgar Marxism or politicized psychoanalysis, but it was essentially a romance in which properly directed love— for one's race, one's gender, one's sex—would recreate the world. However many political or social successes were achieved by members of these movements (there have been many), the core fantasy has been endlessly frustrated. The fault lies not in the readings of Marx or Freud, in the perversity of the recruits, or in the machinations of the ruling powers. The fault is in the fantastic character of the imagined future. It is a future unlike any that has ever been—not in its details or its principles, but in its tone or color. It is human life bathed in fantasy light.

As part of the messianic hopes for reforming history, there were projects for the reform of language. Their impulses have succeeded in banning certain derogatory terms for whole groups (except where reappropriated by the group's members) and in rewriting the rules in some linguistic communities (say around *he* or terms for spouses and erotic partners). Still the movements of liberation imagined more complete reform of language— freed speech in which many more distinctions would disappear, including the distinctions supposed by the myths of coupled romance. The failure of complete reform does not make the projects any less interesting. Even if impracticable, fully liberated speech is worth considering as a sort of limit case in thinking about escape from the cycling images of romance.

Could we really talk differently about same-sex loves? The question might be put most melodramatically by conceiving the language of queer love as a ruthlessly repressed minority language, a language whose native

speakers have been forcibly scattered at birth into households of the mas-
ters. What would it be to discover or make the birthright language? The
dramatic question breaks down immediately. There has never been a birthright language, no matter how regularly polemicists invoke one. Queers
have no other "mother tongue." Same-sex love has had to speak itself out of
existing languages that were used most often (if ambiguously) for the purposes of other-sex attraction. Any reform would be of necessity a variation. Speech cannot be created out of nothing, as each effort to make a universal language has shown. Still, if the queer linguistic revolution can never
take place, one can still imagine several different strategies for variation,
especially in the language of romance.

One strategy would *transfer existing languages of romance and marriage* as if
they actually held together. We would speak as if same-sex love actually fit
under the universal vocabulary of romance—until it didn't. Matthiessen
played variations on the notion of marriage, but only briefly. Other writers on male-male love have sustained the transfer of marital imagery. In
Jean Genet's *Our Lady of the Flowers,* Divine dreams or reminisces as "she"
falls asleep beside Darling: "Just then, the *angelus* tolled. Now she is asleep
in the lace, and their married bodies are afloat."[79] Divine and a soldier,
strolling the boulevards, are "united" by Milord the Prince, "his fingers
circled in the form of a ring": "All along the way from Blanche to Pigalle,
others bless them in like manner and consecrate their union" (148). The
young Divine, the boy Culafroy (to give the simplistic biography), is "transported . . . to seventh heaven" by the "nuptial charm" of the hymn *Veni creator* (170). Divine is also "wedded to God," in the highest tradition of the
religious orders (186). Of course, even Divine feels how the marital language falters. S/he knows, with the narrator, the ease of divorce between
men: "Our domestic life and the law of Our Homes do not resemble your
Homes . . . Our homes do not have the sacramental character . . . In the
twinkling of an eye, after six years of union, without considering himself
attached, without thinking that he was causing pain or doing wrong, Darling decided to leave Divine" (110). The charm of this sustained transfer of
images is the fantasy (or ironic implication) that husbands never abandon
wives in "your" homes. Genet's Divine transfers the confusions of romantic marriage with pious credulity. Her queer speech is a faithful mirror in
which the flaws of the original are much too clear.

The limit in the strategy of linguistic transfer is the faithfulness of its
copying. The transferred images can snap back too quickly. Some writers
claim that there is enough shock in applying the language so literally, so
unironically, to two male or two female bodies. The difficulty with the
claim is the universal pretension of romantic images. A literal application

of normative language for love becomes a literal prescription for assimilating queer relationships in a way that erases the sex of queer bodies. For example, in some supportive circles, a tacit compact counts same-sex couples as honorary heterosexuals. They fit right in — so long as no mention is made of what is being fit into what. No mention will be made. The delicious and aching tensions in Genet's transfer of idioms have gone. Nowadays it is only too easy to believe that man and man or woman and woman are meant to be happy in the same way as man and wife — or, rather, that they are to make up for man and wife failing to get on happily. They are called upon to perform heterosexual marriage better than heterosexuals — just as they have been called upon to be paragons of outlaw romance. This is not linguistic resistance. It is linguistic entrapment. The first strategy collapses into a new literal sense.

Another strategy in relation to existing romantic languages takes its cue from *"gay" argot or slang for erotic relationships.* The strategy would twist existing terms by inventive mockery to fit very different relations. Polari (or Palari, Palare), the British slang used by gay men in the 1950s, borrowed the words of straight marriage. "Husband" meant a man's male lover of some elapsed or potential duration, unless one were being ironic. The "wedding night" was the date of first sex — because of course one was being ironic. So "wedding ring" means, in some contemporary slang, a ring worn to indicate that one is in a long-term relationship.[80] (Is that usage ironic or wistful?) The trouble for this strategy is that it is hard to go much further with gay slang, which contains few coinages for love or passion. Invention has been lavished on the lexicon for sex, its practice and procurement.

Could the strategy then turn to sex-words as a significant resistance to the language of romantic love? If what makes my love queer is the genital configuration I crave, then terms for anatomy might be reclassed as terms of affection. Perhaps the exemplary slang is "talking dirty." Unfortunately, much of that talk is often tediously derivative. It sounds like an imitation of mass-market pornography read or seen. (A rule of romance: When in doubt about how to behave, even during copulation, consult novels and films.) Talk during sex can also be astonishingly generic. "Give it to me," "Take it," and "Harder" are not particularly queer. They replicate too exactly certain models of heterosexuality. Terms of address—"Baby" or "Lover," "Boy" or "Daddy," even "Stud"—are repeated or modeled after standard romantic formulas. Looking to queer sexual slang for innovative language risks playing the melody of romance in another key, on different combinations of instruments.

In response, the next strategy for linguistic resistance tries, more boldly, to *rewrite language away from the claims of romance.* It would undertake

radical critique of romantic language, including the binary opposition /
equation between love and marriage or the link of love to true self. Novelists have done best at full imagining of alternate languages, and feminist
novelists perhaps best of all. Consider, for example, the linguistic alternatives proposed in Marge Piercy's *Woman on the Edge of Time*. In a future
America, *she* and *he* have been abolished in favor of *person*. Proper names are
not divided by gender, and they can be changed at will after a certain age.
Parenting is shared within the community, and co-parenting arrangements
are deliberately separated from erotic love, precisely so that children "will
not get caught in love misunderstandings."[81] Eros is not distinguished between same-sex and other-sex. To insist on the distinction would be
"rigid," though "persons" may tend to be "sweet friends" mostly with males
or mostly with females.[82] Multiple partners are presumed over the course
of a life and perhaps even at a single time. An obsessive erotic attachment
to a single other person is a "binding . . . not good for growth."[83]

In Piercy, the language wants to escape the cycling images of romance,
but it can only wriggle free from monogamous heterosexual romance. Romantic impulses, romantic myth-making, the grand romance of a utopian
transformation of the language for sex—these remain. The happy and
splendidly imagined future is constructed in romantic counterpoint to the
wretched present. Every point in the present must be reversed, whether it
is the gender divide, the distinction between love and friendship, or the
quest for a perfect mate. Can we imagine utopia except by reversal? Could
we dream getting from present language to an alternately fluent future except across a revolutionary gap? The gap of linguistic reversal is, in Piercy's
novel, the time difference between present and (science fiction) future.
You can't get there from here—except by a romantic leap through science
fiction.

One last strategy intends to resist romantic language by *exploiting slips
during its ironic performance*. The basic performance could be recognizable
camp, in which the script is always overdone. The resistance is not in alter-
ing the text, but intoning it—as if with the arched eyebrow or pursed lips.
Or the performance could be a less predictable, less studied practice of collage—say, random switches between slang and straight-talk, between masculine and feminine pronouns. The last strategy begins when these ironic
performances slip unexpectedly. It starts in the moment when the heart is
no longer fluent in its dozen learned languages. The strategy has no wish to
appropriate etiquettes of romance by satirical melancholy. It wants to repeat them, vary them, alternate them, recombine them—until it finds itself, surrounded by a surplus of language, not knowing what to say.

The last strategy is evidently my own. I never hope for complete escape, in language or in the forms of relationship. I fashion what I can while assuming that the present disposition will remain for a good while. On that assumption, the blessing of same-sex unions can still look like an interesting and perhaps even "radical" speech act. The most familiar languages of American romance are fragments of older Christian languages. They are remnants of theology. Romance bewitches us by shape-shifting language about God into language about our beloveds. It wants the power of divine presence through words without the disciplines of scriptural exegesis or theological self-negation. One way to resist romance is to carry its language back into the churches—just where it is least expected. Theological remnants were not supposed to come in through that door. When they do, they expose the poverty of church marriage practice and the tyranny of romance—even in church. No one then knows quite what to say. Queer romance, in language and in relationship, might be most resistant and most innovative when it stutters in church.

CHAPTER TWO

A Proper Engagement

∽

BAMBI: ". . . Gay marriage is a joke anyway."

KWAME: "Yeah, Bambi. I thought it was funny too when you asked your boyfriend to marry you . . . four times. And got your gay ass turned down . . . four times."[1]

Jokes, indeed. There are so many of them in that bit of dialogue. Bambi is a gorgeous Londoner, a perfect "twink," who has made those proposals to Robin, a not-so-gorgeous, middle-aged "bear." It usually goes the other way around. When Bambi soon proposes again, he does so by slipping a ring onto sleeping Robin's finger after another night of perfect sex. Robin half awakens, sees the ring on his hand, pulls it off in panic, flings it across the room. He apologizes, of course, and the couple is reconciled and then engaged or, rather, immediately married. For a day or so. Until other trouble comes.

Engagements were not supposed to be like that—at least not in the romantic reruns. After anxious misadventures and not a little surreptitious scheming from his intended, the boy or man finally brought himself to kneel down (or almost), stumble through the words (or most of them), and then offer a ring or at least his heart. The girl or woman had known better and for much longer what the scene would be about, yet she too was swept away. With tears in her eyes, through a diffusion filter that rendered meticulously balanced light magical, she spoke the potent word: "Yes."

The script for the scene of engagement is so trite that Oscar Wilde was already writing London satires on it a century before the invention of Bambi and Kwame. In the first scene of *The Importance of Being Earnest,* as

50

prelude to its real complications, Gwendolen and "Ernest," that is, Jack, have this exchange:

> JACK. Well . . . may I propose to you now?
>
> GWENDOLEN. I think it would be an admirable opportunity. And to spare you any possible disappointment, Mr. Worthing, I think it only fair to tell you quite frankly beforehand that I am fully determined to accept you.
>
> JACK. Gwendolen!
>
> GWENDOLEN. Yes, Mr. Worthing, what have you got to say to me?
>
> JACK. You know what I have got to say to you.
>
> GWENDOLEN. Yes, but you don't say it.
>
> JACK. Gwendolen, will you marry me? (*Goes on his knees.*)
>
> GWENDOLEN. Of course I will, darling. How long you have been about it! I am afraid you have had very little experience in how to propose.
>
> JACK. My own one, I have never loved any one in the world but you.
>
> GWENDOLEN. Yes, but men often propose for practice. I know my brother Gerald does. All my girl-friends tell me so. What wonderfully blue eyes you have, Ernest! They are quite, quite, blue. I hope you will always look at me just like that, especially when there are other people present.
>
> (*Enter LADY BRACKNELL.*)
>
> LADY BRACKNELL. Mr. Worthing! Rise, sir, from this semi-recumbent posture. It is most indecorous.[2]

The "semi-recumbent posture" may be "indecorous," but it is ritually required for a proposal, as Lady Bracknell well knows. I should say, more exactly, that it is required for a "proposal" according to well-distributed romantic ideals that are heavily infused with ethnic and class notions. A formal proposal followed by a proper engagement is a privilege. It presupposes time and at least the illusion of agency in both parties. For the woman to have the freedom to accept or reject a proposal, she must not be chattel, not come from a home that is desperately poor or regularly abusive, not be pregnant in a society that punishes "bastard" births. Even among the wealthy and leisured, an accomplished scene of proposal, indecorous posture and all, is subject to veto for dozens of social and economic circumstances. Jack's proposal is dismissed by Lady Bracknell until she can verify his assets and his lineage. Later acts turn on the mystery of that lineage. If there had been any mystery about the assets, we would have no later acts.

Contemporary Americans of the "middle class" might seem to have better chances to make and receive proper proposals. Many of them pride themselves on equal agency for men and women, as they profess that love ought to triumph over class or money. The mystique of the proposal can grip the imagination of heterosexual couples not otherwise susceptible to mechanically circulated codes of etiquette. Hip friends who have been co-habiting for years find themselves acting peculiarly when it gets down to "popping the question," though they may have been calculating the advan-tages and disadvantages of legal marriage for months. Of course, what ex-actly an "engagement" means for cohabiting couples is not immediately clear. In fact, the modern proposal in high society now seems to be what marriage was for many of the American poor a century ago: a decision to legalize an already existing arrangement because finances are finally in or-der or other circumstances compel. It is curious then that the mystique of the proposal as a romantic beginning remains so strong.

Does the same mystique grip same-sex couples? In one sense, the an-swer is obviously yes, because some lesbian or gay couples reenact the pre-scribed scene down to its last detail: the romantic setting, the bended knee, the ring produced out of nowhere. Strolling musicians then receive their cue. Or friends who have been invited to witness suddenly appear from be-hind potted palms on the verandah of an expensive restaurant or from be-hind real ones at a gay beach. These scenes are likely to increase as some same-sex couples seize upon every last detail of bourgeois wedding ritual as proofs of their having arrived. Yet puzzles about what an engagement might mean are even more baffling for queer couples than for straight.

For as long as American "homosexuals" have been writing in their own voices, they have been trying to contrast patterns in their relationships with those in "heterosexual" relationships. A recurring contrast points to the en-gagement, that is, to the public announcement of the beginning of a durable union—or at least of a social unit that had to be recognized as a union. This and the other contrasts were sharpened and embittered during the first waves of AIDS deaths. "Until death do us part" was then a much more im-mediate prospect for some gay couples than for many straight ones. An en-gagement meant staying with your lover once he was diagnosed or begin-ning a relationship with someone already symptomatic. You knew you had been engaged and then married when you became an "AIDS widow." Unions were sealed in the shadow of the plague, looking forward to a shared future sure to bring severe trials. For others, the sickness of one or both partners became the motive for a religious recognition of a long-standing relationship.[3] If an announcement that you were a couple did not seem substantial enough, the grief after the memorial service certainly did. Some knew they had been engaged because they were left exhausted, bank-rupt, and ceaselessly grieving.

To speak of engagements in plague years might seem inappropriately lighthearted. They can be more easily considered in other circumstances.

Let me then juxtapose two descriptions to show the persistent puzzles about gay engagements, which were there before AIDS began killing so many so quickly and which remain now. The first description comes from the imagined dawn of contemporary gay history in America: it was published in 1951. The second now seems somewhat remote as well, on the other side of the great divide of AIDS. It was published at the beginning of the 1980s. For all the differences in tone and detail, the two efforts show surprisingly similar frustrations over whether gay men can actually get engaged.

BEFORE STONEWALL: RARE STABILITY—
WITHOUT AN ENGAGEMENT

"Donald Webster Cory" was the pseudonym of Edward Sagarin, who would later and in his own name espouse reactionary views of same-sex attraction. In 1951, when he published *The Homosexual in America,* Cory appeared strikingly liberal—if still in need of the pseudonym. In the preface, he justifies its use: "I am convinced that, in the present cultural milieu in the United States, the pseudonymous or anonymous writer can be more outspoken than one who is willing to place a signature on a subjective analysis of homosexuality."[4] The sentence gives much more than the justification. It tells us that the book will be a "subjective analysis," that is, a supplement to the "objective" analyses that frame it. The subjective recital often bows and sometimes cringes before the presumptively objective, positivist sciences of sociology and psychology, of psychiatry and jurisprudence. It requires a preface by "Dr." Albert Ellis, whose words and name place the book in the genealogy of scientific sexology. Only then can Cory present himself as a talking specimen.[5]

The specimen's talk is curious, especially on same-sex relationships. Cory has lived "a quarter of a century of participation in American life as a homosexual" (xiii). The years have not brought happy erotic connections. As Cory tells it, he married a woman at twenty-five after depressing failures to find a stable relationship with a man. "Love with another male . . . was not easy to achieve, and passionate infatuations that seemed permanent were torn asunder after only a short period of time" (xv). Of course, the marriage did not address Cory's desires. He sought the cure of psychoanalysis, but he became convinced that his desires were neither curable nor shameful. "Today, after many years of a successful marriage, with a happy home and with children, and with a firm bond of friendship that has developed with a man who has been an inspiring person in my life, I sit down to relate what it means to be a homosexual" (xvi). Cory relates, rather, what it means to be a homosexual in a heterosexual marriage that has permitted sexual partners and a steady "friend." The threats that compelled so many

American gays and lesbians to marry and then to arrange their sexual lives on the side should not be mocked. Not a few people, especially among church-goers, feel the same compulsion today. Note, even so, that Cory's thumbnail autobiography finds stability for same-sex love only in subordination to other-sex marriage. The same-sex relationship is a side-bar to the real and visible one.

Cory tries to write beyond his own limits in the chapter entitled, perhaps surprisingly, "Love Is a Wonderful Thing." Still the love at issue is immediately understood as "the search for a life-mate of one's own sex" (135). Cory's description of its wonders is, also from the first, rather sex-less: "There is a need to share life with another person; a delight in turning the key and, on opening a door, finding the warmth of another waiting in the home; of having a *friend* with whom to laugh and on whose shoulder to weep; in being a whipping-post for the pent-up angers of the one who is loved, or of having a *beloved* who willingly and happily plays this role" (135; emphasis added). Unless one is to read "whipping-post" as deep code, there is no allusion to sexual desire in the description of fulfillment. "Beloved" is qualified by the previous "friend."

Cory rehearses less personally the themes of impermanence and disappointment—that is, of unhappy promiscuity—for many (most?) homosexuals. "Their love lives consist of a constant change of partners, of infatuations that last for a day or a week" (136). He then rebuts false "rationalizations" that might be drawn from bitter "partner-changing." Some conclude that promiscuity is the better way for gay men, who are meant to copulate but not to "marry" one another. With a slap in passing for Gore Vidal, Cory rebukes any cheapening of love. Real love seeks to form "a permanent and marriage-like union between two men" (136).

In Cory's account, three problems make unions rarer among gay men than in the general population, where they are scarce enough. First, according to Cory, gay men project their own self-hatred onto their partners, without whom they would not have to face daily evidence of their homosexuality. This might now be translated as the projection of "internalized homophobia," though the mechanisms implied in "homophobia" are no clearer than the mechanism that Cory describes: Many men cannot stay in gay relationships because they hate being gay. Cory's second obstacle to male-male unions is pop analysis: "By his psychological nature the invert is frequently not seeking a man, but is utilizing his ability to obtain sensual pleasure with a man as a means of fortifying a flight from some other and more strongly tabooed attraction" (137). Gay men cannot form unions because they are fleeing from an impossible, incestuous beloved—and no one else will do. Inverted desire screens incestuous desire. The third obstacle named by Cory is less elusive: "Inverts" cannot form stable unions because many of them have difficulty "in finding a partner with whom full physical enjoyment can be mutually obtained" (138). There are so few unions because there is so little good sex.

Self-hatred, inauthentic desire, bad sex, or obstacles sociological, psychological, and biological—no wonder men in Cory's world struggle to find a life-mate (138). Yet some do. "Every submerged homosexual circle knows a few examples of such a union, or it may have several in its midst. If the individuals are unmarried, the bond results in their eventually living together; if married, they may make special vows and unusually tenacious agreements with each other" (138). The last sentence must be read carefully. The marriages in question are not marriages of the men to each other. They are heterosexual marriages in which the men find themselves. If they are not (heterosexually) married, then they may move in together after a decent interval (the engagement?). If one or both is already (heterosexually) married, then they may take "special vows" and negotiate "unusually tenacious agreements."

Cory analyzes his best cases, the ones that approach "the heterosexual concept of marriage" (138). He finds that gay almost-marriages can still be distinguished from straight marriages in several ways.[6] Heterosexual marriage selects partners differently, shrinking the importance of sexual attraction and insisting on a "prolonged" courtship, on a trial period that runs through an engagement to the event itself (139). Straight marriages have legal and social inducements to permanence. Unfortunately, gay relationships have neither careful courtship nor the threat of divorce. Partners are hastily chosen and just as hastily dismissed. In the future, society should seek to address "the instability characteristic of many areas of homosexual life" rather than wasting its time in trying to cure or capture homosexuals.

Cory ends the chapter with two stories. They are cast in the "objective" genre of the case-study, however much they might actually be what the new journalism would call composites. In the first story, Claude and John have been together publicly for ten years, since being college sweethearts. They are also business partners. The equality and stability of the business partnership explains the equality and stability of their erotic partnering. "In place of an economic dependence of homemaker on breadwinner, . . . there was a business partnership which created for each an economic need for the other" (142). Common interests, a shared social circle, honesty about their relationship, and the cement of money: Claude and John have it all. Together they are the gay copy of egalitarian marriage.

Herman and Alex, in the second story, must live through the trials of Alex's recurring infidelity. Is this because Herman is "somewhat older" and "the more intellectual" (142–43)? Or is it because "Alex offers youth, beauty, vivacity, charm," while Herman evidently does not (143)? Their relationship is irreparably unequal. The older partner is stoically wise (not to say, pedagogical), and the younger is charmingly unable to stay in the domestic bed. The result? "Each changed his attitude somewhat, and they found a *modus vivendi*" (143). Theirs is not the symmetrical happiness of Claude and John, but Herman and Alex have an enduring almost-marriage, not too different in the end from "unequal" heterosexual marriages in which the more beautiful or desirable partner has permission to stray.

Whatever else one may think of Cory's cases or analyses, it is striking that he assigns prolonged courtship or engagement to heterosexual marriage as a mark that distinguishes it even from the most durable gay relationships. His two case studies have no such probationary beginning. Claude and John are always already married as Cory describes them. The reader hears of no time before they appear in public tightly, symmetrically knit together. The story of Herman and Alex also lacks a narrative of engagement. Their finding a *modus vivendi* is not so much an engagement as marriage therapy, an effort to avoid divorce. In Cory's world, the male-male relationships most like heterosexual marriage are distinguished from it in having no engagement.

AFTER STONEWALL: OPEN RELATIONSHIP—AND AN ENGAGEMENT?

The second text for comparison was published at the beginning of the 1980s by Seymour Kleinberg as an article in *Christopher Street*.[7] Its genre is the in-depth magazine profile of a gay couple, Michael and David, whom Kleinberg met in New York in July of 1979. Michael was then 29 and David about the same, while Kleinberg himself was in his "late forties" (110). The ages matter, because Kleinberg contrasts the concerns of his "generation" with those of Michael and David, who, from the first page, are taken as representatives of "one of those modern open relationships" (109). If Kleinberg cannot be assigned to Cory's generation (he is fifteen or twenty years younger), he is still not the generation that came of sexual age "after Stonewall." Kleinberg's in-between generation was still preoccupied, in his description, with "*promiscuity, infidelity, priority*" (110, original emphasis). Michael and David are not supposed to be.

Kleinberg drew his profile from confidential interviews with the two younger men. They were in couples therapy at the time, but Kleinberg was not their therapist. He approached them as a writer (so he tells it)—or perhaps as a writer and confidant. Kleinberg promised not to disclose what each partner said about the other. He infers that they did not share much

about the interviews outside the sessions. All three men share solidarity
with a certain Manhattan gayness. It appreciates fine food, draws analogies
to classical literature, and presumes Freud.[8] It does not defer to ideals of
positive science (as Cory did), but it expects that everyone will be inter-
minably in therapy and continuously parsing human motives through para-
digms learned there.

David and Michael met at Cornell in 1970, in the year after Stonewall
and with its emblematic significance already appearing (111, 121). Their
relationship changed from a nonerotic friendship, in which David originally
identified as heterosexual, to a sexual bond. During the transition of these
"courting days" (Kleinberg's phrase or theirs?), David was also having sex
with women. After graduation, the two men separated for a year, during
which Michael found another man. Four years after the beginning of their
relationship, David invited Michael to move in with him and began to call
him "lover" (112–13). At the end of their first year, they had a "belated
honeymoon" in Paris (Kleinberg's phrase again?), during which they began
to arrange sex with other men. The profile considers at therapeutic length
the men's difficulties in the last three years, which have concerned sex, its
after-effects, money, and mutual respect. If Cory wanted to speak as a specimen, Kleinberg will write as a psychoanalyst—an analyst in August, on
vacation, free to speak expansively as an arbiter of cultural forms and deci-
phered lives.

It is hard to read through Kleinberg for David and Michael's self-
descriptions. On the assumption that he echoes some of their language or
is paraphrasing their conceptions, there are two candidate periods for engagement. The first is the college courtship, though this was a period without firm commitment either to each other or (on David's part) to a fixed
homoerotic character. It was followed by the separation after graduation
when the two went their separate ways. Whatever understanding they had,
it did not imply a life together after college. The second candidate period
would be David and Michael's first year in New York, which preceded the
"belated honeymoon" (since honeymoons follow weddings), but also the
beginning of (acknowledged?) sexual encounters outside the relationship.
If that year was the engagement, its declaration did not stipulate sexual exclusivity—or, for that matter, any settled notion of permanence. The
therapy in which David and Michael are engaged three years later concerns
their serious deliberation about whether or not to live together.

Neither period offers itself as an engagement according to coherent heterosexual understandings. Of course, it is a mistake to assume that there
are coherent heterosexual understandings. What is a heterosexual engagement after all? For many contemporary Americans, it is certainly not a

binding civil or religious commitment, neither a contract nor a betrothal. "Engagement" now authorizes the couple to cohabit—unless the local priest or pastor fussily requires that they (appear to) live separately for a period before the wedding.[9] The engagement indicates that a man and a woman have become . . . a something, a new unity of some kind.

The profile contains clues that David and Michael have become or are becoming a unity, but they point in rather opposite directions. In one place, Kleinberg notes that the two men are "treated as a couple" when "they attend the weddings or bar mitzvahs of their families" (111). They are accorded the status of a couple at family functions that stress couple-relations, not least when determining family membership. David and Michael are not married, but they get treated as if they were—much as an engaged couple would be. Engagement entitles one to practice being married within family settings. For gay couples, of course, the practice may never end—since there may never be a marriage.

At another point, though, Kleinberg's profile suggests that the real criterion of mature gay love is the opposite of social acceptance as a unit. It is rather the vivid and painful admission that the best sort of unit is always vulnerable and never closed. Kleinberg compares the link between David and Michael with his own connection to "R." R. had been in an eighteen-year-long arrangement with another man when Kleinberg met him, and he kept on living with that man at least half the time (117). Within a few days of meeting, if not on the very day they met, Kleinberg and R. exchanged "deeply felt pledges and romantically optimistic promises of life-long endurance" (116). The pledges and promises were decidedly less important than Kleinberg's desire for R. to be comforted on hearing news of his mother's death—even if that meant being comforted by his long-time lover across town. Kleinberg confuses the autobiographical disclosure by appending familiar reflections on the difficulty of holding together a male-male couple: "Such a relationship, unrecognized in law, unfettered and unsupported by children, rests on material much more volatile than, say, friendship. Not only do they live out the psychic past, sometimes as if in oracularly fated drama, but they are held together exclusively by convenience and desire. Love rests reliably on neither of those pillars" (117). Cory might have written the same. Kleinberg's autobiographical reminiscence suggests that there is another sort of gay love, for which depth is shown not in promises of mutual exclusivity, but in a willingness to let the beloved find deep comfort wherever, inside or outside the relationship. Kleinberg regards it as a sign of maturity that Michael now thinks of his relationship as "two men bound together" rather than "as a marriage" (126).

If an ideal relationship is one that looks beyond pledges and promises, beyond social recognition or sexual exclusivity, I keep wondering what sense it makes to recognize an engagement. In Kleinberg's account, the engagement is always an antiengagement, the moment in which you admit that a verbal declaration gives no assurance of a stable future together. Or it is a nonmoment, stretched out over the length of the relationship: every day together must be the day of your (re)engagement. Kleinberg ends the profile on just this point by giving David the final line: "'I don't predict, but we'll be together a long time. Despite the flux, it will abide'" (129). Disavowing prediction, he makes a prediction. So Kleinberg, disavowing the notion of "careless love" and his feigned surprise at open relationships, concludes with a paean to the love of a couple that has come to understand itself as always in flux.

In both Cory and Kleinberg, gay engagements are either instantaneous or indefinitely prolonged. They happen in the blink of an eye or they can never be concluded. The persistence of the paradox across the three generations represented by the two texts needs emphasizing—and not only for the sake of understanding gay engagements. The easiest contrast to draw between Cory's text and Kleinberg's, or between the generations of Cory and Kleinberg and the generation of David and Michael, is to pronounce one pre- and the other post-Stonewall, or to label one "homophile" and the other "liberationist," or to employ another of the epochal shift-markers around which so much gay history has been told. Kleinberg favors these markers, but his writing resists dramatic contrasts—especially when juxtaposed to Cory's. The drama should be refused. At large scale, it reduces gay history. In these two texts, it conceals recurring questions about queer relationships, including the function of engagement. The questions stand out in a simplified contrast with Christian traditions of betrothal.

Christian churches have had elaborate theories and regulations about betrothals. Differences of detail can distract from agreement about function. In churches, as in the civil societies with which they collaborated, a betrothal was intended to bring some of the ritual effects of a marriage into the time before it could be performed (for one reason or another). The betrothal was sealed by words that made a promise about the future. Announcing betrothal could secure dynastic ambitions or declare that two people were now unavailable, but its main effect was to constitute the couple as a ritual unit, a "family" by anticipation. Betrothed couples would appear together in a future ritual, but they were already combined as ritual agent, able to take assigned roles in family, civil, and even religious performances. That was the model, at least.

How far can members of same-sex couples adopt it? Same-sex partners can of course announce that they want to be regarded as a couple in the strongest sense the term can have absent full social, legal, and religious recognition. They can intend to invoke a new ritual agency as couple. They can mark off a new time for themselves that is anchored in the future. The future is supposed to be an intended ceremony of some kind—but it is also too often and too implicitly that (messianic) day on which "full" marriage will no longer be denied. Many of the same-sex couples that stand in line to get marriage licenses the moment they become available seem to have lived in that sort of messianic hope. Veteran swimmers under ice, they held their breath for years in aching lungs. As soon as the ice breaks—no matter how small or jagged the hole—they race toward it and arc into the air, panting, tears in their eyes. Who can mock those tears? But no one should be confused by them. Getting married has typically been in "Christian" societies a confusion of family, civic, and religious (or quasi-religious) meanings. Same-sex couples cannot now have unambiguous engagements because they cannot participate easily in the full range of those confused meanings.

Same-sex couples are now supposed to be excluded from (the confusions of) Christian marriage in many areas, beginning with the engagement. The engagement becomes the first point at which larger fights over relationships can grab hold. If they exclude us, why try to count ourselves in by other means? Why perform the overture to an opera that we can't enjoy? At the same time, I suggest, disagreements over queer engagements reveal tensions (to use no stronger word) that run through queer thinking about relationship. Same-sex lovers in America are not immune from the confusions of Christian marriage even when they repudiate it. Nor are all their confusions attributable just to Christian marriage. Engagement rituals have been controversial within queer communities for many reasons, but not least because they raise a fundamental question: Should queers aspire to raise their erotic relations to ritual unity, social or familial, religious or not? This is a question about social recognition, but it is also a question about ritual and about eros in time.

Those abstract questions may be more tractable when put historically. Fights among queers over same-sex engagements repeat unresolved debates in recent queer history. The debates erupted between Cory and Kleinberg, who hints at them without retelling them. Issues in the debates remain unresolved in part because they treat real human confusions, but also in part because those confusions have been multiplied by repressed polemic. In their recent past, American queer communities reverberated with unyielding critiques of any effort to contain eros within time. While some of the critiques condemned religion as hopelessly oppressive, others were voiced by active Christians. Either kind could be absolute in doubting the couple. Without pretending to do anything like a comprehensive history (as if any history could be comprehensive), I want to tell a few easily forgotten episodes from anti-Christian and Christian critiques of coupling. The episodes will show not only that the newly "theoretical" critique became, however improbably, a sort of vernacular, but that the debaters, even in their pure theory, could not escape confusions about eros and time. Eros was supposed to belong to the Movement. No sexual future was to be annexed by private rite. Yet desire still wanted to make its promises—just as Cory and Kleinberg confessed.

LIBERATION FROM BOURGEOIS MARRIAGE

For Michael and David, for their confidant and participant-analyst Kleinberg, "Stonewall" was already not an event so much as an emblem. It was an emblem of public visibility, of coming out "gay and proud" (Michael, 121). "Stonewall" means the demand to take on or put on garish visibility—precisely not the visibility of sunset-lit cocktail parties with classical allusions and therapeutic chatter. It is the imperative to be in the streets. Does the emblem also demand that couples be in the streets as couples? Isn't "gay and proud" visibility demanded for an individual who cannot be engaged to or by any other individual except transiently—and through an organ?

Questions about the force of "Stonewall" as a demand, as an imperative of visibility, lead quickly enough to others. After all, why was this particular emblem chosen? What was it meant to accomplish and what exclude? I find no elegant answers and perhaps no convincing ones. "Stonewall" condensed as an emblem out of an extraordinary play of contradictory principles and contending actors. It was a product and a movement. It was publicized and already earnestly sought. Any effort to explain the emergence of the emblem by appeal to some simple set of causes or some generalizing theory would be both foolish and disrespectful.[10] Still I can notice some of the limits and the optical illusions of the emblem. One of the limits of Stonewall as an emblem is that it excludes religion.[11] The emblem presents a deliberately secular mythology, in which the only sacred space is the caucus room and the only liturgy, the uprising of the oppressed. It makes religion invisible in gay life as *gay* life. Stonewall is hardly unique in being a secular emblem for social progress, but the effect may be particularly important here, especially with regard to questions of marriage. The homophile movement was an uneasy coalition of religious and antireligious groups, comprising antireligious Marxists or Communists, religiously indifferent socialists or libertarians, and religiously motivated activists. With the triumph of the emblem of Stonewall, antireligious or nonreligious groups gained greater control over the telling of lesbian and gay history. By contrast, the emblematic prominence of Martin Luther King privileged a decidedly religious narrative of the struggle for racial equality.

Once you see this limit in the emblem "Stonewall," you need not overturn it in order to proceed with a religious account of gay thinking about couples. You should push the dominant emblem far enough aside so that religious energies can be glimpsed—and precisely around the couple, where the distinction between sacred and secular makes so little sense. We need to enrich the available narratives, as we need to trouble the notion that "Stonewall" refers to some new theory or discourse, to a distinctive view of gay life and its potentialities for coupling. What strikes me is just the transmigration of certain critiques of marriage across "epochs" and "movements" from the early 1960s well into the 1970s.[12] The critiques are traded back and forth across the emblematic divisions between "homophile" and "New Left" or "liberationist," between avowedly anti-Christian and professedly Christian. The critiques condemn vowed or negotiated monogamy, but they also attack couples as "chattel" relationships, units of capitalist production, examples of submissive citizenship, and poison to desire. The critiques can then give way to utopian reverie, fantastical wishes for originality in social relations—or, indeed, new versions of Christian community and its rites. The critiques should be recalled not only to show the religion behind them and in them, but to counteract the silencing of radical opposition in some contemporary queer self-representations. Part of tidying up queer politics for an effective marriage campaign is disciplining queer disagreement.[13] "Tidying up" means pushing out of sight—or memory.

The critiques did not begin with liberationist speeches in the late 1960s. On the contrary, they were being debated in early publications of the homophile movement. For example, the first volume of *ONE* magazine contains an article by E. B. Saunders entitled "Reformer's Choice: Marriage License or Just License?"[14] The issue's cover reduces the title to a simpler question: "Homosexual Marriage?" The main complaint of the piece is that both the Mattachine Society and the magazine have skipped over marriage without considering how important it might be for incorporating "deviates" or "homosexuals" into mainstream society. The author imagines the world of 2053 "in which homosexuality [is] accepted to the point of being of no importance" (10). Would homosexuals then be bound by the same sort of sexual regulation that bound heterosexuals in 1953? Would there be homosexual marriage, adoption or assigned child-rearing, and the threat of adultery? Would the "rebels" of the homophile movement endorse monogamy and other restraints in exchange for acceptance? "Actually we have a greater freedom now (sub rosa as it may be) than do heterosexuals, and any change will be to lose some of it in return for respectability. Are we willing to make the trade? From the silence of the Society, perhaps not" (12). For the author, "legalized marriage" would be "a logical and convincing means of assuring society" that homosexuals are "sincere in wanting respect and dignity" (11). It is a necessary element in any successful movement. Yet the Mattachine Society and *ONE* magazine acknowledge it only in passing, as "all-right-for-those-who-want-it" (11). Long before liberation, the movement will tolerate couples, but it prefers individuals — or, rather, unattached adherents.

Saunders's arch and fussy piece is prescient. It foreshadows many of the motifs that reappear during the next five decades of debate about queer marriage. Saunders points to a struggle for civil marriage as a likely tool for gaining acceptance, but emphasizes that it will place under tighter social control the outlaw sexuality on which queers pride themselves. Acceptance means conformity. Saunders frames the issue as a choice: advocates of same-sex recognition can either adapt queer sex to straight marriage or encourage further changes in straight marriage. He or she then rejects the second possibility: No homosexual reform should "attack" heterosexual marriage or "make [it] even shallower" (11). A movement for homosexual recognition cannot then refuse to think about its consequences for both marriage and homosexuality.

If the essay by Saunders was effectively anonymous, it did not emerge from institutional silence or fall into it. Later issues of *ONE* carry a string of replies in the form of articles and letters to the editors. An anonymous correspondent from Berkeley writes, "What is marriage? It is a heterosexual concept buttressed and blessed by the Church and the State since man emerged out of the miasma of pre-history. It is based on protection of the young and the mate; it is based on the necessities of property inheritance; and it is bounded in a mass of taboo which no one fully understands" (11).[15] In the same issue, R. H. Karcher adds, "And part of the abnormality (or is this abnormal?) for most homosexuals is their seeking many companions. They would fight enforced monogamy tooth and nail; if not in the open against the proposed legislation, then simply by ignoring it (breaking the law) after it was passed. . . . The laws [or marriage] are a hand-me-down from ancient religious rites" (14). A woman writing from New York, and relying on the authority of her "wise" mother, is no more optimistic: "There isn't, never has been, and can't be a long 'marriage' between two men in which they remain faithful" (19). Another writer, probably also a woman, certainly from Los Angeles, disagrees: "We have generally the same concepts of decency and fidelity to our 'spouses' as the heterosexuals. (After all, they raised us.)" (22). The questions register in organizational records as well. In the spring of 1953, the Mattachine Society in Los Angeles was discussing the question, "Why do homosexual marriages fail?"[16] One of the issues raised was whether it is "possible to have mental fidelity without physical fidelity."

The piece by Saunders notably lacks any "theoretical" structure of its own. Its position is that of "stuffy and hide-bound" reflection, and its tone is just the sort to be mocked by liberationists. Yet mockery or imported (and undigested) "theory" do not advance liberationist writing much beyond the Mattachine Society's uneasiness with respect to couples and their place in familial systems. Liberationists espouse a collective view of human life, as they rely on off-the-shelf analyses of socioeconomic class and historical evolution. Still, liberationist rhetoric appeals directly to the individual as chief agent of sexual liberation. The individual as sexual pilgrim persists from homophile arguments to liberationist proclamations. In both, the erotic self is often the enemy of the committed couple.

From the hundreds of speeches, resolutions, placards, posters, pamphlets, leaflets, newsletters; from the lists of non-negotiable demands and the caucus working papers, the protocols for consciousness-raising and the open letters of denunciation, I can select only the smallest sample of liberationist writings. Let me begin with some passages in the piece by Carl Wittman known as the "Gay Manifesto."[17] Wittman came out as a homosexual in print during 1968.[18] By 1969 he was involved with the west coast's Committee on Homosexual Freedom.[19] He participated in the group's unsuccessful picketing of States Steamship Line for its dismissal of a gay employee.[20] Wittman wrote his "Gay Manifesto" in May and June of 1969, that is, in the weeks just before the Stonewall street events. The piece was first published at the end of 1969 and then widely reprinted in the underground press and distributed by a number of groups, including Christian groups in the Bay Area.[21]

Wittman treats marriage in his section headed "On Roles."[22] He has just finished denouncing "mimicry of straight society" with an imperative: "Stop mimicking straights, stop censoring ourselves." Marriage then obviously appears as "a rotten, oppressive institution" from straight culture that ought not to be mimicked. For gays to enter into marriagelike relationships is bad "burlesque" and "an expression of self-hatred." Couples ought instead to find alternatives to marriage, a phrase that heads Wittman's next subsection.[23] Gays are free to define "for [them]selves a new pluralistic, role-free social structure." It may be pluralistic, but Wittman sets three limits on permissible erotic relationships. They should not be sexually exclusive, make promises about the future, or dictate inflexible roles. When Wittman goes on to speak of "couples," the term has to be understood under those three conditions. Gay social structure "must contain both the physical space and spiritual freedom for people to live alone, live together for a while, live together for a long time, either as couples or in larger numbers; and the ability to flow easily from one of these states to another as our needs change." The enemies are exclusivity, permanence, and rote performance.[24]

Every one of Wittman's claims could be multiplied by twenty or thirty parallels in other authors, often more radical.[25] Following Engels, the bourgeois family—nuclear, authoritarian, patriarchal, monogamous—is identified as a principal agent of repression.[26] The ideologies built into it are the cause of innumerable ills, including fascism, racism, and all forms of bigotry. So the goal of the gay liberation movement cannot be "better bars, recognized marriage, entry into the military or even jobs."[27] "'Gay Marriage'" is "the bastard child of Straight Respectability": "Get away from marriage. Get away from family tightness."[28] "We want the abolition of the institution of the bourgeois nuclear family."[29] "In the battle against Amerika, all gay organizations (whether they want to be or not) are revolutionary because they challenge the family—mainspring for religion and the state ('God, Family, and Country')."[30] And so on.

The critique of bourgeois family sometimes prescribed sexual practice. A few liberation fronts advocated a complete withdrawal from gay bars, bath houses, and cruising spots in order not to be trapped in heterosexist and misogynist systems. For others, more piquantly, the critique of monogamous family issued in an ethic of obligatory promiscuity.[31] Beginning in June 1971, Charles Shively published an emblematic series in *Fag Rag* under the slogan (and series title) "Cocksucking as an Act of Revolution."[32] The essays repudiate not only monogamy, but the couple. Shively is a lyricist of body parts, a lesser Whitman, and so refutes by a combination of shock and vivid evocation.[33] Consider one opening gambit: "The model of man and wife pervades everything and shapes our thoughts about how we should make love. Between heterosexual pairs this might seem 'natural' (or at least fitting), but why should faggots ape straight ways? Why should we follow the British Parliament which legalizes sodomy between two but not *three* consenting adults? Each faggot has a mouth, anus, and penis which can all be used at once."[34] Shively follows with a list of allegorical examples drawn from among his friends, each of whom is given a Greek name. The literary conceit recalls the rejected, "homophile" codes of double language, but the names chosen are those of military (if not quite militant) heroes. Shively's ex-lover, dubbed "Aristogeiton," is deputized to argue that "pair-bonding trains us to be good little consumers," to reduce our erotic relations to property titles. A few paragraphs later, Shively asks whether we might replace couples with larger sexual groups. "Unfortunately, group sexual experiences are even less recognized than homosexual couples. Groups may exist physically once in awhile [*sic*], but they have not become part of our consciousness. The rule in almost all group encounters is ONCE ONLY!"[35] Whether or not sustainable erotic groups become possible, couples should not be sustained. "Two people having sex is usually very exclusionary. It may be very ecstatic, free and pleasurable for the two people, but the very ecstasy of the two only heightens the being-left-out-feeling of those not included."[36]

A year later, Shively produced a more fantastically prescriptive essay. It begins with standard doctrine: "The nuclear family is the foundation stone of all that is established. Because we are so radically opposed to the breeding family unit with reproduction as its ultimate aim, our sexuality makes us revolutionary."[37] Unfortunately, Shively complains, the revolutionary potentiality of gay sex is constrained whenever gay practices imitate the capitalist system of commodity selection. The antidote is "indiscriminate promiscuity." "We need to copulate with anyone who requests our company; set aside all the false contraptions of being hard to get, unavailable — that is costly, on the capitalist market."[38] By implication, if a gay man wants to stay in a couple, he opposes the revolution and underwrites not only the bourgeois family, but the entire system of commodity capitalism.

In these pages, Shively's critique of capitalism passes occasionally into a critique of Christianity. The Gospel stands alongside the Market as the enforcer of an exclusive and unequal distribution of bodies. In the essay on indiscriminate promiscuity, the only scriptural citation is Matthew 25:29, which is quoted to the letter: "'For the man who has will be given more, till he has enough and to spare; and the man who has not will forfeit even what he has'" (4). The verse is part of "the conventional wisdom of centuries against which we now speak" (4). For Shively here, familiar Christian condemnations of promiscuity need not be considered, because their logic is just the logic of anticommunist ownership. Elsewhere, his attack on Christianity would be more dramatic.

In June 1977, under the provocation of Anita Bryant, Shively's contingent at Boston's Gay Pride parade marched under a banner that read "Christianity Is The Enemy!"[39] Once on the speakers' platform, he burned in succession his Harvard doctoral diploma, a dollar bill, an insurance policy, a letter refusing his request to teach gay studies, and the sodomy statute of Massachusetts. At the climax of the speech, Shively read out Leviticus 20:13 and its death penalty for those Israelites guilty of male-male intercourse. He then dropped the Bible into the flames. The crowd erupted. A man jumped on stage to pull the book from the flames. Shively was compelled to yield the microphone to Brian McNaught, one of the best-known gay Catholic activists. And so on. The ensuing melodrama is less significant than the sequence of Shively's burning: diploma, financial instruments, (biblically based) statute, and Bible. Christianity had been "the enemy" for Shively long before Anita Bryant's crusade because it formed an integral part of the power ideology that regulated queer sex—by death, if need be, but also by subjecting it everywhere to the economy of the monogamous couple.

Pure liberationist theory leaves little room for the couple except as a transient arrangement. Two erotic seekers may bond for a while, but they remain first and foremost members of a collective movement, which is loudly skeptical of any entitlements for couples as such. The collective does not want special legal recognition for couples, much less to accord them ritual agency in family, law, or religious rite. The decision to become a couple even for a while is dubious enough. How much worse would be an announcement that two men or two women want new social or ritual status because they intend to be coupled forever. Their engagement could only betray a treacherous nostalgia for the perquisites of the straight suburbs.

REVOLUTIONIZING THE CHRISTIAN COUPLE

You might predict that radical critiques of the family, which so quickly identify oppressive Family with oppressive Church/Market, would have been resisted by lesbian and gay Christians caught up in the movements for rights or for liberation. The prediction is and is not accurate. While contemporary Christian writers were perhaps not so radically suspicious of possibilities for stable coupling, they were ready to go quite far in appropriating the radical critiques of bourgeois marriage. But the range of attitudes is large, and I can only illustrate a few of them. I do so from one cluster of Christian discourses around the Bay Area between about 1965 and 1975. From them I select only the examples likely to illustrate both how the critique registered in Christian discourses and how coupling continued even so.

Five years "before Stonewall," there was a remarkable weekend gathering of fifteen members of San Francisco "homophile organizations" and fifteen Protestant clergy. The meeting grew out of collaboration between members of an urban ministry at Glide Foundation and homophile leaders, organized at least in part by Phyllis Lyon and Del Martin.[40] The weekend "consultation" was bold for an early effort: it included a Friday tour of bars and participation Saturday in a secret picnic of the homophile League for Civil Education. There followed, within a few days, the founding of the Council on Religion and the Homosexual (CRH), a group that survived in

San Francisco into the early 1980s and that had for a time affiliates in several cities around the country. Parallel stories could be told about other church groups and, indeed, about the active involvement of many Christian organizations in homophile and liberationist activities.[41] I choose the CRH as one among many for its antiemblematic value. It sponsored an event that might easily have become a national emblem for queer emancipation and yet did not: the New Year's Mardi Gras dance of January 1, 1965.[42]

Preparations for the first consultation included several different documents. For example, using the Mattachine mailing list, Don Lucas distributed a questionnaire to 150 "homosexuals," 40 of whom replied. He summarized the results for the consultation. His only mention of same-sex unions is this: "One individual recommends a change in dogma to provide for homosexual marriage performed and sanctioned by the Church."[43] The language suggests that the respondent is Roman Catholic, but no further exploration or clarification is recorded. The "Outline to Guide (Not Limit) Our Discussion" prepared for the consultation contains no mention of the rites or ethics of same-sex unions.[44] Neither did the long theological presentation by Kim Myers, at least so far as it appears "quasi-verbatim" in the report of the consultation.[45]

There are traces of questions about relationships early in the council's history. Within two months of its founding, members of San Francisco's Daughters of Bilitis who had attended the original weekend prepared notes for a public discussion called "Homophile Religious Experience and Expression."[46] Listed as reference for the session was *Christ and the Homosexual* by the Congregationalist minister, Robert Wood.[47]

> Rev. Wood believes many homosexual "marriages" break up because they have no bond holding them together. He feels that if society and church recognized the love relationship of the homosexual and authorized a marriage ceremony between two people of the same sex, many homosexuals would then live out their lives together, feeling their union blessed by both God and society, and would be more useful members of church and society.
>
> Do you think he is right? Do you think his idea at all practical or feasible? Do you think it is "unholy"? Would you like it to be in force? Would you make use of it if it were? Would you feel more stable if such were the case?[48]

Because of its dependence on Wood's book, the list of questions does not consider reconfiguring same-sex relationships as other than "stable" and presumably monogamous dyads. Nor does the planning document record the participants' responses.

Traces of the marriage question appear in official documents of the

CRH, but so do traces of its critique. Earlier in the summer of 1964, a committee had been formed, chaired by Phyllis Lyon, to draft a set of "Goals and Purposes" for the new council.[49] The final document, approved in 1965, contains no explicit mention of same-sex unions and certainly no demand for their churchly blessing. There are two suggestive entries, however:

> 4. To systematically study the deeper dynamics of authentic human relationships from biblical, theological, and social science perspectives.
> 5. To engage in research activity toward further understanding of homosexuality within the larger framework of the present sexual revolution.[50]

A few months later, in the wake of the blustering police raid on the New Year's dance, the CRH published its *Brief of Injustices*.[51] The *Brief* is mainly concerned with the excesses of the police and related governmental agencies (such as Alcoholic Beverage Control). It ends by alluding to the effects of legal and social persecution on homosexual relationships. "We believe that the only sensible criteria for judging human relationships is [the] maturity, necessity, and justice inherent in each relationship. Social and legal justice is essential" (4). Until the laws recognize that criterion, "the homosexual is forced to perpetrate the last great injustice on himself, that of failing to realize the best in himself and his part in cultivating the best in society" (4). Failure in relationship is failure in social role: social reasoning here displaces religious claims, perhaps because of the quasi-legal genre. This is a brief for the street, because no court will take it.

During the same summer of 1965, at least three members of CRH were invited by Nelson Pike, then Episcopal bishop of the Diocese of California, to join a "Joint Committee on Homosexuality." The committee met from 1965 through 1967. Minutes of its meetings show that same-sex relationships were discussed and that pieces of the antimarriage critique were both voiced and qualified. At one point in 1966, for example, members of the committee were asked to speak about "morality as it relates to the homosexual."[52] Don Lucas is paraphrased in part as follows: "Problem for the homosexual in marriage relationship—patterns after the heterosexual and gets bogged down trying to emulate. Homosexual relationship can be patterned on situational ethic. Where relationship has meaning and fulfills purpose, give and take, this is ethical, good and right for the individuals involved. Promiscuous nature represents flight, search for identity in someone else."[53]

By 1969, at its second "Symposium on Life Styles of the Homosexual," the CRH was hearing a paper by Robert W. Anderson on "Gay Marriage

between two Males." At about the same time, in the council's first volume
of *Essays on Religion and the Homosexual,* Gale Thorne published "A Sexual
Bill of Rights," which included these two clauses:

> 1. The right for any persons, acting in good faith, to live in a love rela-
> tionship, no matter who they are, what marital status they have, or what sex
> they are.
> 2. The right to try for a responsible life with any other or others with-
> out castigation, harassment, intimidation, or possible internment.[54]

Note in the first clause the emphasis on "love relationship," as distinguished
from "marital status." Note, again, in the second clause, the ideal of "a responsible life," but also the allowance for multipartner relationships: "other
or others." The clauses are particularly interesting because they seem to
echo the "right to marry" asserted by the 1948 *Universal Declaration of Human Rights* without falling either into the dyadic, heterosexual language of
that *Declaration* or its privatized notion of the individual rights-bearer.

Religious issues, including the possibility of religious rites, recede in
these last documents. In the contemporary records of related groups in the
Bay Area, there are more radical Christian voices and more provocative
Christian practices. In 1970, as we have heard, Troy Perry performed the
first same-sex "marriages" within the Universal Fellowship of Metropolitan
Community Churches. This was not the first time a Christian minister had
united two men or two women. Traces and rumors of same-sex "marriages"
stretch back for centuries in Christian churches.[55] Nor was Perry's voice the
first to advocate Christian marriage between two members of the same sex.
Still Perry's incorporation of the ritual as a public and regular act of worship for his group brought a new visibility to the question of same-sex coupling, within and outside Christian groups.[56] So the incidental or implicit
considerations in the CRH's first consultations and publications were now
replaced by a much more explicit discourse.[57] But it is worth stressing that
some Christian liberationists around the Bay were eager to claim continu-
ities with earlier Christian thinking. Sally Gearhart and William R. Johnson's *Loving Women/Loving Men: Gay Liberation and the Church,* published in
1974, contains fierce revolutionary rhetoric. Yet the volume starts with
two pieces from the files of the CRH: an abridged summary by Donald
Kuhn of the 1964 consultation and comments on homosexuality in the
Christian Bible first presented by Robert Treese in 1966. Gearhart and
Johnson's narration of "the gay movement in the church" includes the CRH,
the MCC, and several events that were already afoot before the police arrived at the Stonewall Bar that night.[58] Gearhart herself served as co-chair
of CRH.

Revolutionary or radical possibilities did sound more frequently as new groups were established. An anonymous writer for *Agape and Action* in 1970 lays out the possibilities with remarkable generosity.

> It may be that the tendency of many homosexuals to be promiscuous is simply a symptom of their despair: an easy way to feel real, visible, and touchable, sex as a deadening escape from pain instead of a constant and growing revelation. Or the opposite may be true; that homosexuals who seek endlessly for that faithful marriage are just trying to play bourgeois heterosexual. Or it may be that homosexual love is bound to be, as it was in more open times, a band of men, a brotherhood, and that the commune and a 'group marriage' scene is the sane and 'normal' way for homosexuals.[59]

This is a Christian writing for an ecumenical queer audience well connected with Protestant churches and seminaries.

My illustrations of queer Christian discourse from around the Bay show several things. "Homophile" and "liberationist" religious groups did consider a wide range of views about same-sex relationships from the mid-1960s on. They knew radical critiques of sexual exclusivity, permanence, and state religion. They also recognized that some lesbian and gay people wanted social recognition of the relationships they had already entered— relationships that often resembled monogamous marriages. Still, the illustrations show that same-sex relationships were treated as established facts or utopian possibilities. The right to have them may be defended, but criteria for choosing or evaluating them are not set forth. The relationships do not appear as ritual episodes or unfolding discernments in the present. So if these early Christian documents talk about getting relationships recognized by society or the churches, they never mention engagements on the way to recognition. Engagements become a (paradoxical) topic only after there is a regular ritual of blessing. You can see this in my final illustration, from a publication of the San Francisco MCC congregation. In it, the confusions over engagement—of eros in time—return after radical critique.

Douglas Dean, editor of the congregation's short-lived glossy, *Cross Currents,* published in its inaugural issue an article entitled "Gay Marriage."[60] The article begins with the fact that same-sex marriages are performed in various MCC congregations—indeed, that as many as four have been celebrated on a given day at the church in San Francisco. The question for Dean is not whether the rites should continue, but what norms should govern the unions. "How, then, can principles be established which will allow an individual freedom of choice and yet maintain the sanctity and holiness of the wedding ritual?" (6). He understands current MCC policy to require that a couple must have "been together" for at least six months.[61] Yet "being together" is not the same as being sexually exclusive. "Some pastors have counseled a couple contemplating marriage to the effect that they must not consider such a step unless they are prepared to be completely true to one another in a physical sense. Other pastors do not put so much stress on this issue, perhaps believing (privately) that other kinds of fidelity are more important" (6). The engagement has happened already; it is curiously elided or displaced. Presumably there is a gap between the approach to the pastor and the actual wedding date, though the existing policy does not specify how long it should be. The declaration of an engagement does have to be preceded by at least six months of "being together." If the terms and limits of the marriage are debatable, so certainly are the events of that half year. It need only to have been a time when the couple was a couple, however that is construed. The practice of union projects a ritual time for the couple backward at least six months.

Dean conceives the real and recurring temptation in engagement or marriage as lust after outsiders. He admits that it is probably more of a problem for men than women. His conception is nicely illustrated by a photograph of three unclad men in which the central figure, facing away from the adoring partner he embraces, glances over at a bearded stranger—who stares off into an abstract distance, oblivious of the roving eye. The antidote to roving seems to Dean to be a revised conception of marriage that privileges "spiritual fidelity" without insisting on sexual exclusivity. "There is no reason, after all, while we endeavor to form some standards of ethical conduct among ourselves in our gay communities, that we must copy the standards of heterosexuals. We all know that heterosexuals do not abide by their own declared standards, anyway" (15). The notion of heterosexual hypocrisy is combined with the imperative not to emulate heterosexuals in order to motivate a new conception of Christian fidelity for same-sex couples. Of course, there is still a conception of fidelity—and it still attaches primarily to couples. The marriage ceremony presumably increases or intensifies their being a couple, though only in terms of some inexpressible "spiritual" fidelity, no matter how the arrangements for cohabitation or copulation are worked out.

Just here we seem to slip into other paradoxes about gay engagement—other versions of the time-paradoxes noticed in Cory and Kleinberg. In Dean's article, gay engagements do not mark an estate or accomplishment so much as the beginning of a risky and variable series of negotiations over a *modus vivendi* that will continue to be risky and variable. They are directly related to a further ceremony, to a marriage, not by intention, but in retrospect. If two men or two women have "been together" for six months, their union may be blessed. They are not required to intend the six-month period as preparation for the union. They may have gone through the six months resolving every other day to pack up and leave. They can accomplish an engagement without ever intending to be engaged.

The curiously retrospective engagement is a feature of many gay relationships—and not only those between Christians. Gay "engagement" seems always already the marriage. The engagement is projected backward from a later relationship, half seriously. "What anniversary do you celebrate?" gay couples ask each other. They mean: Do you count from your first acquaintance, your first date, your first sex, your first overnight, your first moving in together . . . ?[62] The anniversary is marked off retrospectively in a continuum of possibilities. The choice of an anniversary, the choice to have an anniversary, performs an engagement after the fact.[63] In the middle of a haircut, my barber corrected himself in the flow of a story: "His husband—only I really shouldn't call him his 'husband,' because they've only been together for three years and so they're still boyfriends. You cannot be husband and husband until you've been together for four years." Ah, but when do you start counting? The answer seems to be that you count backward—not forward to a marriage celebration, but backward from a marriage accomplished, before or after Liberation, whether you are Christian or not.

ENGAGEMENTS WITH AND WITHOUT WEDDINGS

The confusion of engagement and marriage is hardly confined to gay relationships. It afflicts many contemporary Christian ones as well.[64] But the confusion thickens in the case of male-male or female-female relationships because of the original separation between relationship and legal or ritual recognition. Queer relationships are imagined as beginning outside the law, outside religion, and outside families. They used to result in quite real criminal prosecutions, expulsions from church, and exiles from family. Sometimes they still do. As the consequences for queer coupling become less brutal in some places, imaginary or conceptual puzzles surge forward. If a single copulation can imply that two men have placed themselves outside society, rejected the prescribed rites, and constituted themselves as an antifamily, what possible function remains for an engagement? The engagement can only appear in an ironic backward glance. "That's the night when we got engaged." "That was our engagement—before we moved in together." "We were only engaged then. He didn't show me all his faults." The ironies will amuse only so long as there are other engagements, defined on quite other terms, against which to play.

Playing with us/them dichotomies can be fun for a while, but it is no reliable substitute for addressing confusions—confusions that have recurred in so many of the texts this chapter has sampled, from Cory forward. Of course same-sex relationships suffer from religious and civil persecution, from the lack of customary rites and familial acceptance. They suffer as well from the petulant refusal to elaborate rites or establish new families once persecution begins to lift. Couples and the groups built around them are deeply embedded in oppressive economic and social systems. So, now, are "sexual outlaws" and their circuit parties. Replaying the old dichotomies postpones essential self-examination. Queer advocates of engagement need to ask themselves what exactly they are in such a rush to join. Queer critics of engagement need to wonder whether the claim that two men shouldn't be a couple isn't just a version of the claim that they can't. So many of the fights over same-sex coupling sound to me like evasions of deeper issues, including whether queer desire hasn't been defined as something that cannot last—because it is queer or desire or both. That definition must not be accepted as self-evident.

A rejection of hegemonic marriage in favor of its alleged opposite satisfies intellectually only so long as one assumes that erotic relations are exhaustively divided by that dichotomy. To my mind unions, let alone relationships, belong to a capacious genus. The varieties of marriage practiced in America are only some of its species. There are many others, actual and potential. Why assume that the species of same-sex union worth blessing should be derived by negating one or another model of Christian marriage? Why restrict thinking about preparation for blessing just to some historical simplification of engagement or its direct opposite? Especially in churches, self-examination requires a vigorous projection of unexpected alternatives.

Queer engagements will only make sense when new senses can be given to queer coupling. My interim proposal is that queer couples should not be defined only in terms of sexual sharing or sexual exclusivity, financial compacts or joined households, care-taking or child-rearing—not to mention coordinated outfits or matching rings. A definition I find implicit in many accounts, however confusedly, sees a couple when there is joined ritual agency. Two men become a couple: they are not "being together," they are doing together. What they do together is not specified according to the traditional terms of civil or Christian marriage. It does not require that they restrict sex, pool money, share a domicile, or raise children (though each of these will figure in some queer relationships). To be a couple, they must seek to be recognized as *ritually* joined. Staging a ritual to announce, mark, or celebrate the union is one way to seek this recognition, but it is not of course the only way. The recognition may come in what others presume when they share confidences, withhold criticism, offer counsel, or issue in-

vitations. Invitations are particularly significant. On the great holidays and
at events like weddings, a guest list is a decisive ritual instrument. It registers ritual bonds. It records effective kinship. Two men who want to become a couple have to seek invitations and other tokens of ritual recognition by declaring their ritual agency together.

Does shared ritual agency make an engagement or a marriage? It makes
an engagement, I propose, only if it establishes a time of preparation in
view of a further rite, an upcoming ritual action that will be even more deliberate. Here enters the uncertainty. An engagement waits on a future that
may never arrive—and not just because of the malice of a civil or churchly
majority.

An engagement is broken when it is called off by one or both parties. In
traditional protocols, rings and love letters are returned, assurances of mutual discretion made, and the hunt begun for a more suitable match—or at
least a quick one. For an engagement to be broken is for it to fail. Almost
as embarrassing, and certainly riskier, is an engagement that goes on beyond its time, past the appointed moment for the marriage. In Texas in the
1950s, an engagement might be announced, formally or informally, in the
junior or senior year of high school. The young woman would begin building her "hope chest." As the linens accumulated, as the trousseau mounted,
hope stretched thin. After seven or eight years of an engagement entirely
amiable on the surface, there came the rupture. The woman, now not so
young, would have run off with her hope chest to marry someone else in
Oklahoma, because it had finally dawned on everyone that her intended
was never going to marry . . . a woman. This, I confess, is a discreetly al-
tered story from my childhood, but stories like it pass down through many
other families.

Queer engagements are not liable to quite the same perils, but there is
a danger that the "engagement," however marked or remembered, will
prevent a wedding. Many gay engagements render the marriage rite redundant. Once the engagement is recognized, there may or may not be a
marriage. I am particularly interested when this happens to gay Christians,
because the cycle of Christian rites ought to encourage them to subordinate
betrothal to blessing on the union. But for many queer Christians, too, engagement becomes marriage and so rules out a wedding. As one lesbian
Christian tells it: "We never made vows to each other in public. We kind of
negotiated an ongoing commitment."[65]

In 1993, Andrew Yip conducted a study in the United Kingdom of sixty-
eight gay couples who had been together more than a year.[66] The couples
were recruited for the study through national organizations of lesbian and
gay Christians (142). Obviously Yip's sample was skewed toward those

who took the intersection of Christianity and sexuality seriously enough to move them to join up. It was further determined by the fact that one of the recruiting organizations was the Anglican Clergy Consultation, a network for the Church of England's gay priests and their partners. Self-identified Anglicans and Roman Catholics together make up 86 percent of Yip's sample (144). You might expect that the results would be very churchy indeed. It is all the more surprising, then, that *none* of the couples had celebrated a blessing ceremony, even though the mean length of partnership was almost ten years (20, 145).[67] One couple had performed a private ceremony of their own, and another was considering a blessing ceremony as the marker of their tenth anniversary (20, 23–24). A few other couples expressed their support for some sort of event, though often precisely not a church blessing. The rest of Yip's couples pronounced strong opposition to a religious ceremony—because it aped heterosexual marriage, because it colluded with civil and churchly refusal to grant full status to same-sex unions, or because it simply added nothing (24–26).[68] Yip presents Christian couples, then, who regard any further ritual as optional or offensive.

What kind of engagements do they have? They have, I think, marriages without engagement or wedding. The loss of both is the loss of two important ritual markers and of an important period of preparation between them. Recall, now within the context of Christian liturgy, the usefulness of the engagement that follows on the opening joke in *Metrosexuality*. Bambi, the perfect "twink" who keeps proposing to his ring-phobic "bear," learns soon enough that Robin cannot be faithful. Despite his friends' best efforts to distract him, Bambi sees Robin kissing another man on the street. The infidelity makes Bambi realize that Robin cannot make the exclusive commitment for which Bambi is ready. Their stuttering engagement, which fills only the time between the giving and discarding of a ring, is a time to get bad news. It is a time to discover a partner's unreadiness for sexual exclusivity. In the same way, engagement between those seeking a Christian blessing makes sense to me only as preparatory time before a second rite. The engagement becomes a betrothal, and a betrothal, in many of its Christian versions, should be a probation, that is, testing and discernment.[69]

Along with other Christian churches that bless unions, MCC congregations now recommend or require counseling sessions with the pastor or some other specialist before a wedding. Counseling is a medicalized successor to spiritual direction. Time for counseling can be translated into older language as a period of spiritual investigation. The months or years of Christian betrothal have often been squandered on satisfying legal or financial requirements, when they have not been used to bring children to marriageable age. A betrothal serves unions better, whether queer or straight, when it is understood as serious inquiry into the advisability of completing the union. The right spirit of inquiry can be heard in the queries suggested to members of the Putney Friends Meeting who are considering marriage, same-sex or other-sex, under the Meeting's care.[70] The last query, and in many ways the most pointed, is this: "Are you aware that the marriage relationship needs constant care and nurture to insure good growth? Are you willing to recommit yourself, day by day, year by year, to try again in spite of difficulties, to recognize, accept, love and delight in each other's individuality?" For some Christian congregations, betrothal might well begin with a liturgical declaration, a rite of betrothal or at least a ritual declaration to the congregation (like the ancient "banns," but with a different purpose). The rite of betrothal would frame any particular modality of self-examination, such as counseling, in ritual space. It would endow the two people with a provisional ritual unity, though their future union would not so much be taken for granted as offered for scrutiny.

A rite of betrothal and an ensuing period of investigation might be particularly important for male-male couples (though, of course, not only for them). Not a few queer men tend to bring forward characters into blessing that are unsuited for any union. I may be a gay Christian who wants ardently to celebrate a union with my lover—and still my performance of "gayness" may contain characters that were codified precisely to exclude durable union. A liturgical betrothal would offer the chance to recast or rewrite those characters under ritual impulse and in the presence of alternate characters. Certainly no Christian congregation could ask a gay couple to enter into betrothal unless it were ready to assist them by invoking a whole choir of queer saints as "patrons," advocates and models, of characters that do flourish in union.

The months between betrothal and marriage might also encourage both the partners and the congregation to think more clearly about the character of the bond to be blessed. (This may actually be more important for straight couples than for queer ones, insofar as they may tend to think that the nature of the marriage bond has been clearly established for them.) A blessing may be sought to mark a transition in the sexual or economic lives of the partners. They may move in together or they may adopt new rules about sexual exclusivity. For many couples, though, the blessing will not mark a dramatic change in the rules for sex, the sharing of resources, or the home address. For them, as for their congregations, the change signaled by the blessing must be conceived more provocatively. Preparing for the blessing may mean reconceiving the moral or spiritual obligation to each other that the partners assume. It may help to build stronger support for shared parenting or caretaking. The period of betrothal will certainly demand more public clarity about how the relationship figures in community life. Most important, a probationary period should lead the couple and those around them to meditate on the transit of eros through time. A time of preparation between erotic intention and public blessing recalls the liturgical logic of life stages, but also the persistence through variation of an erotic bond.

Concerted reflection, by those about to be joined and by those who support them, is the worthiest of traditionally authorized functions for a Christian betrothal. It makes sense only in relation to an ensuing rite or final celebration at some definite time in the future. If the relationship has already reached whatever fullness it can, if serious consideration about its wisdom is belated or pointless, then it is better not to talk of an engagement. Nor should a Christian engagement serve as a sort of antechamber to civil recognition. Those who need rituals while waiting on the state to offer "full" marriage should look elsewhere. Again, if there will be no future rite to mark a more serious or binding commitment, then why "get engaged"? To make engagement only the period between inviting people to a party and throwing it is to make engagement just what the wedding industry desires: a frantic season of wedding planning. Might as well stop now.

CHAPTER THREE

Your (?) Special Day

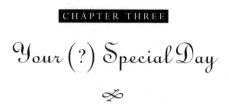

In its December 2002 issue, *XY* magazine features a wedding of sorts on its cover: two young men in Edwardian "morning" clothes exchange vows before another young man dressed as a high-church bishop. An uncropped version of the photograph fills two pages inside the magazine. It reveals that the wedding was attended by a young man in military dress uniform and an alien in ecclesiastical vestments. Another snapshot shows the young couple leaving the chapel under a cascade of rice.

The title of the portfolio is "Normal Heights." It mocks the domestic myths of the 1950s by filling them with queers—I mean, recognizable queers—I mean, queers who publicly affirm their nonheterosexual character. A related spread performs the same substitution for covers of well-known glossy magazines.[1] Among these, there is a satirical cover for *Teen Bride*. On it, a shirtless adolescent wears a white bridal veil. He holds a football, and his game-face has been painted with eye-black. The tattoo of a scorpion peeks out over the band of his briefs, which are (inevitably) an inch or two above his belt. The only other tease on the satirical cover promises an article on "Bachelorette Party Ideas for You and Your Boy." The cover differs from the others in the spread by having little text. Is this because the writers could not think of any other joke articles? Or because the wedding industry is already such a parody of itself? Or because there is, even in satire, some trouble in substituting a queer teenage boy for the adolescent bride of mass marketing?

The curiously spare magazine satire points to the sprawl of the wedding industry across America. How to get any sense of it? The usual attempt seeks out statistics. For example, by 2002 the average cost of a wedding was reported in one survey at just over $22,000.[2] The same group of respondents said that they had overspent their wedding budgets on average by 43 percent. Debts incurred to stage a wedding sometimes outlast the marriage. In many more cases, they put a severe financial pressure on the newlyweds and may contribute to an early bankruptcy.[3] A leader in wedding advertising claims that total spending on the events comes to $50 billion annually.[4] And so on. The numbers can be frightening or outrageous, but they remain abstract. A more vivid overview of the industry comes when you sit down with a recent copy of a glossy magazine for brides-to-be. No one should be permitted to write about Christian marriage before performing this ascetic exercise.

My exemplary issue is Condé Nast's *Modern Bride* for February/ March 2003.[5] I have spent many hours with its "706 pages of inspiration." The issue makes no mention of same-sex unions so far as I can discover. Indeed, I can find no explicit reference to same-sex desire. Some bridal magazines are reported to be considering the inclusion of unions in the future. My guess is that any queer ceremonies that do appear will be unions between women. The overwhelming fact of gender in these magazines is not presumptive heterosexuality, but the address from women to women. The "bridal service industry" offers itself as a smiling shopkeeper to brides, not grooms. One might be authorized to imagine either of two lesbian brides reading it, but neither of two gay grooms.[6]

The address to women is explicit. *Modern Bride*'s editor writes of her own tribulations in finding the right wedding gown as she makes the crucial connection between shopping and coupling. "You have to do a lot of searching and experimenting before you find your one true love. (Kind of like dating, right?)" (26).[7] Dozens of pages later, "real brides" give advice in response to the anguished question, "My fiancé doesn't seem to care that much about wedding details. Any ideas on getting him more involved?" (104). The "real brides" offer some perky suggestions, but these are engulfed by the address of the rest of the magazine. The address is not mainly through words, in any case. The magazine is mostly advertising, of course, and the advertising is mostly pictures, not words. The pictures are for and about female shoppers. They show (white) women's bodies almost exclusively.[8] They display women posing coquettishly for other women—or, rather, and officially, women showing other women how to be coquettes in the eyes of men. The coquettes do not give much thought to any sex after posing. If the female readers of this issue of *Modern Bride* have a great deal to buy, little or nothing of it is related to copulation or reproduction. One advertisement offers contraception, while another touts a remedy for menstrual cramps (63–64, 73). The urgent purchases are (in order of advertising prominence) a dress, a honeymoon package, a ring, and duly registered household products. Forget about genitals. Bridal bodies must be concealed, transported, tagged, and equipped for domestic service.

The bride has to select so many products and services that she should start on it at least twelve months in advance.[9] Obvious tasks include interviewing wedding planners, but she should not overlook cosmetic surgery. Laser treatment for spider veins in the legs should begin three to six months before the wedding, while teeth whitening must commence four weeks out (59, 66). In the end, twelve months are hardly enough. Responses to the 2002 Condé Nast survey suggested that the average length of planning is now nearer sixteen months. It takes more than a year of "the wedding countdown" to "that all-eyes-on-you moment" (90). Planning fills in the time that might have gone to the deliberations of betrothal. It is supposed to be the chief preoccupation of "the engaged life stage" and perhaps its chief passion as well.[10] Is this because so many "engaged couples" are already cohabiting—slightly more than half among respondents to the same survey? Romance has been confirmed by practice and probably consummated as well. The new task is to express it in a properly outfitted ceremony.

Still the work of the planning is not couple's work. It is "woman's work"—or rather the work of the woman and a whole crew of wedding professionals. Queers and especially gay men play their traditional role among the servants in the comedy of straight marriage. The indispensable "beauty pros" stereotypically include a flaming hair designer. Limp-wristed men are assigned to do the catering, arrange the flowers, or play the organ. In some church traditions, they are tacitly allowed to receive the vows and give the blessing. More recently, queers have been featured in supporting nuptial roles as the friend, confidant, or colleague whose counsel, wit, or money saves the day for heterosexuality.[11] Commenting on a handful of recent films, Estelle Freeman writes of the "gay participant whose presence in the ceremony and exclusion from its results seems to guarantee heterosexual marriage."[12] More numerous than gay participants are the stereotypically gay technicians hired by the bride to prepare her body, the site, the service, and the reception. Gay men may even be required to ready a groom for proffering an acceptable proposal—or so several episodes of *Queer Eye for the Straight Guy* emphasize.[13] Without queer expertise, a straight guy is always the groomsman, never the groom.

For bridal magazines, expertise in wedding planning is gendered female. It is something for women and men-who-are-like-women. Real men—the sorts of men who make solid husbands—do not figure much in wedding advertising. They do appear in the editorial photographs, especially in the "candid" shots of "real" people or weddings.[14] If editorial matter is excluded, however, the national advertising in the sample issue shows relatively few men and then in secondary roles. Mostly they are seen outside the wedding chapel, either before the wedding or after it. They can also be useful for carrying television sets in the background of the new home (40). Most importantly, they appear just with you—you the bride—in luminous romantic isolation. A man can propose to you on the beach in a light rain, or run with you there under a kite of tulle, or drink from a coconut, or just pose with you seaside, in daylight or at sunset.[15] (Why are grooms so fond of sand?) His presence requires that pearls be worn while naked, that strawberries get served on silver, and that a suitable registry be found for a suite of accessories.[16] He is the perfect companion for a seven-foot whirlpool bath in the shape of a champagne glass (648). When men finally get dressed for the wedding, they remain figures of solitary reverie. Just the bride and groom: they kiss in a leafy bower or in diffusely lit dream or while floating above an exotic resort; they ride a bike along a country lane, walk (rush?) to a hotel room, "relax" in a field of white, or dance in abstract cutout.[17]

Among these images and their implied etiquettes, one exception is a remarkably androgynous young man who appears four times in a multipage spread (94–101). In all the photographs of this series, he stares away from the camera, left or right or down. In the first two, his dress shirts are halfway unbuttoned. In the last two, his pink shirt with the ruffled front has no sleeves.[18] Any of the outfits would serve him well on the gayest of dance floors. He is so outrageously queer in his look that one has to wonder whether he represents a color-coordinated groomsman, a decorative accessory, or the gay best friend. His queerness directs now-suspicious attention back to the androgyny of a few of the romantic leads—to the man making the beach proposal (2) or the curly-headed groom who squeezes into the binding so that towels may be displayed to full advantage (227). And is the man (?) with the black beret the intended spouse or the dress designer (464)?

The queerness of the male bodies in the magazine is significant for two reasons. It first reminds us that gay men do have traditionally assigned roles as assistants to heterosexual weddings. It then raises questions about the fundamental equation in the magazines between bride and ritual beauty.[19] The bride, much more than the groom, is the incarnation of beauty at a wedding. The event's beauty is female. All eyes are on her. What happens, then, when the gay assistant steps forward to take the place of the bride? Or when two of them present themselves as . . . two brides? Two grooms? Who is the beautiful one? And who prepares that beauty? No longer the stylist and confidant, now, suddenly . . . the bride? Not really—not even in allegedly queer wedding planning.

QUEERING THE WEDDING PLAN?

In September 2002, the Bravo television network first aired an eight-part series entitled *Gay Weddings*.[20] The series is framed as a "reality" show. It follows four same-sex couples as they plan, prepare, and perform union ceremonies. Even without the "revelations" of entertainment reporting, any viewer more than half awake can tell that the show is rather more stagecraft than "reality." Certainly the couples are hardly typical, despite the obvious gestures toward "diversity." Just as certainly their "actions" are orchestrated and arranged with a keen appetite for melodrama. The viewer is asked to believe, for example, that Scott would confide to some friends and the hovering camera his therapist's negative judgment on his partner, Harley—and then lie about it sixty seconds later when Harley walks back from his turn at bowling (ep. 2). The series is not a documentary of wedding planning by four same-sex couples. It is a sitcom illustrating how the wedding industry's fantasies flicker when they are imposed onto same-sex unions.[21]

Let me introduce our couples properly. Sonja, 39, an ER supervisor, is with Lupe, 32, who works in marketing. Sonja and Lupe are the only people of color among the eight. They are also the least affluent and the most subject to public discrimination. Sonja has a teenage son by marriage; he gives her away. The series makes no other mention of offspring, past or future. The two other women in it are Dale, 32, an entertainment lawyer, and Eve, 30, a graduate film student. They have to negotiate endlessly with family in order to get enough money for the wedding, but they are represented as otherwise less vulnerable to financial or social pressures. Now the boys. Harley, 28, in sales, has spent the last two years with Scott, 32, a consultant. They live in Palm Springs, where Scott sings in the gay men's chorus, and where Harley's mother, Michelle, visits frequently. Harley and Scott will be married in Puerto Vallarta, since, as Scott says, "That's where we made a connection" (ep. 2). Finally, we have Dan, 37, a vice president for global marketing at a "Hollywood studio," and his partner of two years, Gregg, 35, vice president at Atlantis, the gay travel company. Dan and Gregg will be married in Los Angeles, though they seem rarely to be there. They are energetic travelers. Dan surprises Gregg by boarding a cruise he is running in Hawaii. Dan brings back a sentimental gift after days in Europe. Snapshots show us that they met on an African safari. "Thank God for e-mail and thank God for cell phones," as Gregg says (ep. 5). Amen.

A few themes in the show link all the couples. Dale says, speaking for many, "How did weddings evolve into this big ordeal" (ep. 1). It is an ordeal in the old sense, a trial to determine the couples' worthiness. As with any ordeal, there are unexpected perils and moments in which defeat looms. If nothing else, dramatic tension requires them. Scott confides to his video diary at the end of episode 1, "Truthfully Harley and I have been talking about whether or not to get married or even stay together." Tune in for the next episode to see whether they make it. Throughout the series, viewers see tears of frustration over family rejection and other unexpected *contre-temps.* Even the golden boys, Dan and Gregg, suffer last-minute anxieties (ep. 7). A white-on-black title tells us, "Four hours before their wedding . . . Dan and Gregg write their vows." They struggle to do it with every sign of stress, from fingers slipping off the keys of a laptop to writer's block. Four hours later, just as they are to process into the service, Dan thinks that he will vomit. Phil, the "wedding officiator," says, "This is what you guys have been planning for how many months? You've got to enjoy it." Only as the two end their recessional after the service can Dan say, "Ah, we did it." It is not clear whether he means that they have performed their union or survived the planning.

As an ordeal, planning for a same-sex union might seem to require confronting homophobia in churches, other public institutions, and families. The series tries feebly to remind its viewers of those political or spiritual struggles, even for the privileged male couples. Dan and Gregg's friend Bob takes the opportunity of a boat excursion to insist that since the church does not bless them and the state does not recognize them, "it's about your family and friends and what it means to them" (ep. 2). A little later Gregg says to an inquiring waitress, "There's nothing legal about what we're doing . . . [we're] doing it for our family and our friends." Yet the family too figures as a source of oppression. Dan's family contingent at the ceremony consists of just three cousins, since his mother will not come. As Phil reminds us, "We know that there are people who for one reason or another have chosen not to be here." In Palm Springs, too, family condemnations must be resisted—though not from the party-loving Michelle, Harley's comic and generous mother. Scott's parents fly in from somewhere in New England to watch him sing an oratorio of gay life, Robert Seeley and Phillip Littell's "Naked Man." The mother is brought to tears, but the laconic father stands by his conviction that men marrying men cannot be normal. At the ceremony, of course, even the father will be converted. The wave of sentiment capsizes scruples.

Religious conflicts are played out in the same way, as transitory quarrels amenable to the therapy of feeling. Scott tells early on that he was once a Catholic seminarian and that he "lived in Catholic churches for several years" (ep. 1). He prefers Catholic-sounding liturgy and would have a Catholic priest present (under what auspices?) if only Harley would allow it. In the end, the ceremony is performed by two friends (one each): Tracey, an

"ordained minister," and Trent, a seminarian. Their denominations or ecclesiastical constraints are not mentioned. As Tracey insists, the main (religious?) point is to do what the two guys want or, rather, can agree on. We
know even less of Phil, who presides over the union of Dan and Gregg. He
appears late in the process and without introduction. The closest he comes
to invoking religious tradition is the explanatory announcement, "We also
bring together tonight the Jewish tradition and the Christian tradition in
this wedding ceremony. And the Jewish tradition is to conclude a wedding
with the breaking of a glass" (ep. 7). Religious "tradition" means innocuous
ornament. Tradition can be another strain on the male-male couple, but
not because the available ministers are particularly zealous about either orthodoxy or liturgy. Conflict comes from the clash of ritual tastes or expectations within the couple itself.

Despite the dramatic emphasis on family judgments and the gestures toward churchly injustices, *Gay Weddings* cannot quite turn the ordeal of planning into an antihomophobic crusade. The ordeal remains plainly the wedding planning itself. A recurring subtext of the series is that queer couples
are stressed in the same ways as straight couples by the innumerable shopping choices to be made. The most passionate controversies are played out
not over civic or religious homophobia, but over product selection. Harley
and Scott bicker endlessly: how many guests housed in what buildings;
platinum or white gold for the rings; the date for mailing invitations; their
exact position on the beach during the ceremony. Wedding planning confronts a relationship with occasions for serious moral disagreement: the exercise of personal expression as authorized by the wedding industry. To
survive the ordeal, you must prove yourself an accomplished consumer.
You can run the gauntlet of boutiques and emerge with a coherent event.
You can have your perfect day look plausibly . . . perfect. You will do it.

Not alone, of course. You do not have to endure the trial alone. Scott
and Harley confer with one wedding planner in Puerto Vallarta by phone,
then walk the beach with another. When she suspects that they might want
something grander (gayer?), she refers them to Michael, whose poised
presence and refined tastes recommend him for casting in that other Bravo
classic, *Queer Eye*—although Michael must here contend with the competing tastes of two gay guys rather than the squeamish docility of rumpled
straight men (straight-men?). The climax is reached when the two guys and
the two planners must agree, around the table, on center pieces and place
settings. "You're a pushy little bitch," Harley snaps at Michael. Later he explains to the camera: "Michael wanted to tell me how my wedding would
be." Of course he did, as emissary of the wedding industry. If the ceremony
is to be your perfect day, it cannot possibly be yours. It never has been. If

Harley had succeeded in chasing off Michael and his over-elaborate table arrangements, he would still have had to contend with the quite specific commodity-expectations he carries within himself.

The constraints of the wedding industry are felt even by Dan and Gregg, who have much ampler means. They are felt by them perhaps more strongly. Theirs is a Hollywood wedding in multiple senses. Dan retains Carleen from Merv Griffin Productions to plan the event, having met her at the Golden Globe Awards dinner. Carleen brings "all her secret weapons to the table" in planning (Dan, ep. 4). The "weapons" vanquish many foes to make the most improbable combinations work. The ballroom of the Park Plaza Hotel is transformed for the reception by carefully lit palms, glowing tables, bustling waiters, and an African American disco group. There are two bag-pipers and a drummer. There is a gospel choir. In the ceremony itself, the ring is rushed forward by . . . the men's dog. As soon as the happy couple kisses, white confetti is blown over them and clapping resounds. Why not give them a standing ovation? It was, as the grooms say, "show time" all day long (ep. 6). Alas, even the near-omnipotence of Merv Griffin Productions cannot shield you entirely from the ordeal. For example, Dan and Gregg have to make their own table assignments on a large chart and then distribute them into the appropriate invitations. Yet a world-class wedding planner evidently spares you much, including the risk of transgressing the gender logic of the wedding industry. Carleen is a woman who can act on behalf of two men in the traditionally female role of wedding shopper. What she chooses for them will insist that they are grooms, not brides. She stresses, for example, that the reception room has masculine colors. She presents the sample table settings as accomplished facts, to be approved but not adjusted, except toward masculine simplicity.

Gender assignments persist when the wedding industry turns its attention to couples of the same sex. In same-sex unions too, the fetish of the white wedding dress can only be indulged by women. Dale and Eve spend much of their screen time shopping for dresses. The men have no corresponding ritual attire. They are thus deprived of the primary purchase fetishized in *Modern Bride*. A title brings us to Harley and Scott as they "shop for their wedding clothes" at a national retailer, but they are looking for cruise wear, not the ritual garments of the white wedding (ep. 1). Since their wedding is also a vacation in Puerto Vallarta with family and friends, they might as well be shopping for a tropical honeymoon. Men are allowed to do that. Men can also buy rings, and so we see Gregg and Scott at the jeweler's. Beyond that, industrialized gender constrains. Dan and Gregg appear at the ceremony in matching black suits and tan tartan ties, but not in morning clothes or other grooms' wear. The only moment of cross-wedding-dressing comes at a "bridal shower" for Dan and Gregg. At this mainly male event, the two men are required to put on white veils before opening their presents. The scene plays like amateur drag night at a gay stand-and-model bar, if it is not just the cross-dressing antics still allowed at a straight bachelor's party. The gifts are safely masculine: weekend escapes, framed romantic portraits.

Is there a punch line to the Bravo series? Its producers might claim that the episodes show that same-sex couples want to commit to each other just as formally and publicly as other-sex couples. "We're just like you: we have stresses and family quarrels and last-minute nerves, too." I would reverse the suggestion: what the series shows is how uniform is the logic of planning for a white wedding. The ordeal remains the same, because it is certifying a standard social accomplishment. The choices to be made are determined more by socioeconomic group than by sexual orientation. So too the relation to religion: for the men on Bravo, as in so many affluent weddings, religious rites are brought forward as another range of options on the master menu. References to queer oppression are likened to other sorts of family misunderstandings. Or else they function as ethnic badges, in the same way that one mentions a proud Scottish heritage by way of the Cape Breton Islands (Dan's family, ep. 6). "I'm a Scotsman—here's the tartan." "I'm queer—here's . . . " What social signifier fills the blank? The only token of queerness at Dan and Gregg's wedding is the concealed sex of their bodies.

Perhaps the most striking thing is how the Bravo series confirms the gender of wedding planning even while it tries to invert it. Arranging the wedding is woman's work. So we were assured by the wedding magazines— and so some queer wedding planners also concede: "Cross our hearts, this is not a sexist remark: this whole thing may come easier to you if you're a lesbian couple than if you're two men."[22] Why? "Gay men . . . have suffered wedding deprivation on two levels: (1) as homosexuals, perhaps never contemplating the notion for themselves; and (2) as grooms, traditionally treated as little more than accessories at their own weddings." For the Bravo series, the most elaborate planning was done by the two male couples. The queer wedding planners would rush to agree: "We know for a fact that men have planned weddings that are every bit as magical as those of their female counterparts. (Sometimes they border on spectacular.)"[23] Queer men plan a spectacular wedding. Is that because (according to gender stereotypes) they are *queer* men or because they are *men* and so better able to afford the right kind of help? The queer wedding plan begins to look less queer all the time. When gay men step out of the roles as assistants to the bride, they become, not more queer, but less—at least on reality TV.

CAMPING AS RESISTANCE AND AS SELF-DELUSION

Queer communities have long camped straight weddings. For example, one of the most famous skits by the 1960s San Francisco troupe, The Cockettes, replayed Tricia Nixon's wedding. It was a satire of White House politics as much as of American society weddings, but it surely satirized those. More commonly, but no less fabulously, the white wedding gown has played a significant role in any number of drag routines. By contrast, it is surprising how un-campy, how earnest, how eagerly serious queer wedding guides can be—and perhaps never more so than when they are trying to be funny.

Bravo's *Gay Weddings* provides an emblem again. Its title sequence begins with a simple, almost jerky version of Mendelssohn's "Wedding March" over extreme close-ups of pink decorations applied to a white cake. Cut to the top of the cake, with a ceramic bride and groom in formal wedding wear. The figure of the bride wobbles and then topples as the music segues into a jazzy, free-form vocal, which serves as the comic zinger. She is replaced by a groom. The substitution—as the music has informed us—is supposed to be funny, and perhaps especially funny in showing us two men rather than two women. (At the end of the title sequence, after each of the couples has been pictured and named, we do see a cake with two grooms and two brides.) The mere sight of two grooms is supposed to disconcert and so to provoke carnival laughter, the liberating laughter of society turned upside down. At the same time, the Bravo series wants to mark political progress. Gay weddings are a step toward the full acceptance of lesbian and gay couples. The breezy comedy of the title sequence sits uneasily alongside the earnest conviction of social reform. No matter how often we camp, our weddings are not jokes. Our weddings are real. They mark epochs. Stop laughing.

Lesbian and gay marketing events perform the uneasy juxtaposition on a grander scale. The "first annual Gay and Lesbian Wedding Expo" was held in West Hollywood in February 2003. In fact, the event was one of many. The "world's only Gay and Lesbian Wedding Fair" had been held in Chicago eight years earlier.[24] Any wedding fair will do as an example—or any planning website.[25] A newspaper account of the West Hollywood event repeats the lessons for all. Its main hook is that "a wedding is a wedding even where there are two brides or two grooms."[26] Note "wedding" rather than marriage, and note that a wedding is presumed to be an important and serious thing. One prospective groom tells the reporter that such a ceremony answers to the universal human need for an "'other half.'" A nondenominational minister who works with a wedding officiator service explains that lesbian and gay weddings "'do a lot to heal some of [the] spiritual wound-

ing'" caused by social rejection. Two women reason that increasing acceptance of lesbian and gay weddings is a sign "that times are changing." This is
such an awkward and sober burden for a sales event to carry.

The "victories" of the progressive incorporation of queer into the wedding industry are equally ambiguous or ironic. Crate and Barrel has adjusted the language of its computerized registry to include every sort of
couple.[27] This is a good thing, the argument goes, because the presumption
of heterosexism is being chipped away — or because queer couples are now
being counted (by such an authority as Crate and Barrel, no less) as equiv-
alently married. Isn't it rather the case that queers too are being invited to
squeeze into coupled consumption? The controversial inclusion of same-
sex wedding announcements by the *New York Times* should be greeted with
equivalent caution. The *Times* retains some cultural authority (though perhaps most with those least likely to be opposed to same-sex unions), so inclusion by it might rightly be considered a social "victory," a sign of
progress. Still the grounds for getting an announcement into the *Times,* of
all places, might give pause to those who want to separate ritual recognition of relationships from the totting up of social accomplishments. The
actual announcements in the *Times,* like applications to elite colleges, are
ingenious combinations of improbably varied accomplishments. The inaugural item on September 1, 2002, described the civil union of a Yale-
Fulbright international financier with a Brandeis-Harvard-Columbia public
affairs consultant.[28] A nice couple, to be sure, but is the announcement lib-
eratory politics?

The uneasy earnestness of the queer wedding industry needs to be analyzed not only for its conflict of motives, but for their issue. Queer politics
in America has often been marked by the rapid alternation of biting humor
and angry piety. Already in the late 1960s, speakers at public meetings
could be faulted both for not being campy and for not being serious, with
the second the more durable charge. The double nature of camp invites both laughter and shouting, both mockery and tears. "It was camp,
it was a joke, it was a sly perversion of life-imitating-Hollywood-schlock-
imitating-real-life, but it was authentic."[29] The bitter irony of camp juxtaposes the ludicrous and the earnest. It is the genius of camp to balance the
two, to resist the dreary triumph of earnestness. So it is unsurprising that
the queer wedding industry should mix shock with sentiment, as it is unsurprising that it should favor sentiment in order to make sales. I am surprised by how rapidly earnest sentiment manipulated by commodities
fetishism trumps the critical purchase of camp, with all that it offers for religious and political thinking.

Compelling evidence comes from *The Essential Guide to Lesbian and Gay*

Weddings. The first edition was published by Harper San Francisco in 1994; a second, somewhat revised edition appeared in 1999 from Alyson, one of the leading publishers of queer books, including erotica. The handbook was written by Tess Ayers, "a former television producer," and Paul Brown, who "has worked in theater and television and has coordinated numerous weddings and special events."[30] Television and theatrical production supply the best models for wedding planning and, indeed, for its inaugural act of imagination: "Pretend you're in a wedding movie, starring yourself" (40). Experience in television production or event planning (Brown's other qualification) may really be the best preparation for compiling a book that guides its readers in selecting script elements from a large, but carefully limited set of formulas. Pretend that you have picked up a studio compendium of elements for assembling a B-grade romance.

The book is a how-to manual, with cartoon-like illustrations, lots of lists and sidebars, a breezy style, and hundreds of shopping tips. It would be unfair to push it further than it means to go. The fact that it whizzes through gross historical mistakes is not significant. Its gestures toward social or political reform are. The gestures emplot queer culture within both mainstream markets and social reform. (Religion will not figure often in the book, and when it does appear it is a minor instance of the social or the theatrical—but more on this later.) In order for queer relations to be put within these larger plots, three things are necessary: confidence in progressive acceptance, ingenuity for creative adaptation, and a conviction of reality. You can catch the three at work already in the book's introduction.

The first step is to put the edgy, queer past into a narrative of social acceptance—particularly by the media, but also by major corporations and marketers. "When we started researching the book back in 1992, the idea of a same-sex wedding planner was borderline nervy, maybe even radical. The good news is that now, six years later, more and more people have had, been to, or at least heard of a gay commitment ceremony" (xiii). The good news is the gospel of acceptance, by which the "radical" becomes the familiar. The second step is to assert that queer people can negotiate the adaptations needed for acceptance by reimagining the rituals of straight society. "This book was written because it was difficult to maneuver your way through straight wedding planners to try to make them work for gay ceremonies. . . . So we set out to write a how-to book that would not only give you information concerning same-sex weddings but that also helps free you from the bounds of what you may think a traditional wedding is supposed to be" (xiii–xiv). Negotiating acceptance becomes itself a sort of liberation, a substitute for the "radical" past. Instead of marching in the street, the same-sex couple can now free itself from the shackles of its notions of the ordinary wedding—while marching down the aisle. The next step, the third, is to uncover the conviction that has propelled it thus far: "When we say wedding we mean wedding. . . . Since this is a wedding book, equivalent to the books that your straight friends might read, we have included everything that, in a different world, a better world, a more equal world, would be part of a gay wedding" (xiv). Your weddings are real weddings. You must think of them, in the light of future equality, as fully equivalent to straight weddings, at least so far as planning goes. Participating fully in wedding planning is living for the future of full equality. Attaining the revolutionary future used to require revolutionary combat. Now it requires only smart purchases.

The first section of the book, "Waxing Philosophical," carries on these preliminary engagements between queer love and social convention. Before turning to the actual business of planning, the same-sex couple has to be bolstered in its resolution to get married and reassured about its essential queerness. At the same time, its anxieties about convention have to be elicited and assuaged. So the book hops from grand themes to advice about conformity. A number of the grand themes are by now thoroughly familiar. The motive for marriage is love. The supremacy of love implies the right to a wedding. A queer couple expresses the motive and exercises the right through the activities described by the book. "By planning a wedding ceremony, you are participating in an age-old rite that honors the purest and most basic union between two people" (6). Again, the *Essential Guide to Lesbian and Gay Weddings* not only figures same-sex unions as a form of political activity (5, 29), but inscribes them in a monumental history (Nietzsche's phrase) of "your lesbian and gay ancestors" (13). The members of the couple are "pioneers" who perform with unequaled boldness the liberationist sacrament of coming out (29, 34). By having a same-sex union, they are "Coming Out and Out and Out and Out" (29).

At the same time, as if in counterpoint, the readers of the *Essential Guide* must confront repeatedly the dictates of "custom" and "the etiquette gurus" (24). They have been urged to redeem the institution of (straight) marriage by selecting the best from it and rejecting the rest (4), but they have also to be reassured that getting cold feet is "absolutely normal. It happens to straight people all the time" (25). Same-sex couples are "ambassadors" who get to "shatter right-wing stereotypes," but they need "a game plan to figure out—in advance—whom [they] are and aren't going to tell" (32). In getting married, queer people are "taking what's theirs" (11), but they are also trying to make the relationship "more like the real world" (23). "We think anything's okay, as long as it's what you want to do" (31)—but "we" mediators of straight wedding rules must give "you," the anxious reader, both our approval and our formulas.

Here is the fundamental rhetorical paradox of the *Essential Guide:* It must mediate between what are alleged to be deeply queer desires and the wedding conventions of various (homophobic) societies. The paradox is visible in many places. It often gives structure to single sentences. Consider this early piece of advice: "The proposal is your own private opening ceremony, before the rest of the planet becomes involved in your union, so why not make it a Hallmark occasion?" The proposal, "the true beginning of the wedding" (18), is the "private opening ceremony" on the way to a public (closing?) ceremony. The proposal is the private beginning of the union ceremony rather than of the relationship, since union ceremonies often happen many years into relationships (9–10). The union ceremony cannot be regarded as uniting anything, as joining what has been apart. It must understood rather as "a whole new arena of honesty" (22), as a "a crossroads of acceptance" (23)—that is, as general publication in established forms (not only to family and friends, but to caterers and florists—or the *New York Times*). So it is fitting that the "private opening ceremony" of a festival of publication should itself be conceived in terms of a printed greeting card: "a Hallmark occasion," indeed.

The contemporary wedding planning book, queer or straight, is at least two different books. The first is a consumer's map, a series of tips for cunning shoppers as they negotiate their way through the wedding bazaar. The second book is a manual of etiquette. No matter how often its authors mock the complexities of the traditional wedding, they must also bow before them. No matter how often a planning book urges the couple to make its own choices, it must instruct them in appropriate choosing. Some of this advice is practical and even tender. Do not write long vows, counsels the *Essential Guide,* because you are liable to be saying them with dry mouths. Yet much of the advice is addressed to the anxiety that one will not be doing things right. Anxiety, rather more than the quest for a good deal, motivates purchase of a book on wedding planning. You buy it because you understand that planning your ceremony is an ordeal fraught with risks of enduring disgrace.

It might seem odd that same-sex couples should be driven by the anxiety to appear socially accomplished. Having broken with fundamental familial principles, why strain at the correct order for elements in a wedding invitation? More pointedly, having engaged in criminal sexual activity (at least until *Lawrence v. Texas*), why worry that celebrating a union will run afoul of admittedly arcane social lore? To which the obvious and frequent answer is: How not? An exact attention to social arcana has often served in gay life as displacement for social acceptance not available elsewhere. Older gay men who suffered routine police harassment could be notoriously severe about place settings. One night in jail, the next night chewing someone out for a mis-positioned dessert spoon. A similar mechanism can explain attention to wedding decorum in some queer couples. The explanation confirms the darkest suspicions of those activists who oppose same-sex marriage as the ultimate mainstreaming.

A wedding planning book, no matter how "imaginative" or "liberating," is a book that addresses anxiety by providing options within an agreed frame. A couple can fly a wedding flag outside the chapel or send out invitations on the B-side of a rock-and-roll 45, but they choose to do so within the frame that posits a chapel and invitations. Beneath the zany possibilities and the breezy jokes, a planning book reinforces anxious earnestness about getting the ceremony right. Getting it right means playing variations on straight weddings—even when this is conceived as redeeming straight weddings by choosing the best elements from them. Such earnestness forfeits radical possibilities for cultural critique. To revert to an earlier complaint, it surrenders camp. By "camp" I mean both that indefinable performance with enormous political possibilities and the particular cultural heritage of the best-studied gay cultures. Its loss not only removes a tool for political critique, it erases cultural specificity.

A telling moment comes when the *Essential Guide* considers whether a same-sex union should make any reference to the lesbian or gay character of the couple. "One of the first things you need to think about is whether you want the ceremony to deal directly with your being gay" (122). This must seem odd in a book that has praised its readers so often as political pioneers. The very chapter on the wedding ceremony begins by repeating the lesson: "You are on the cutting edge here, kids" (109). Yet it remains an option not even to advert to the fact that the wedding happens to involve a same-sex couple. A sidebar warns of the dangers: the Reverend Rosalind Russell complains of an overly political and "angry" lesbian celebration: "I felt like saying, 'Get over it! Look at the beauty of your love!'" (122). To exclude anger is to exclude camp.

The *Essential Guide* makes clear that silence is an option, not a requirement. It permits wedding ceremonies in which there are lesbian and gay references. By raising the possibility of a complete silence, however, the book tips its hand. In order to be able to include these entirely unqueer ceremonies within its menu of choices, it must deny the stronger forms of political critique for which the loss of specific reference would be the loss of agency altogether. The equable tolerance of wedding planning rules out the intolerance of radical queer criticism. The book gives no suggestions about

incorporating strong elements of camp into its services, as it gives no examples of what might be called strongly political ceremonies. The coun-
terexample to Russell's critique of the "angry" lesbian service is only the
claim by a rabbi that "it is important to say the words *gay* and *lesbian* from
the pulpit during a ceremony" (122). If that is the other end of the spectrum of wedding planning, there is no room in it for camp or for strong
politics.

The planned wedding remains curiously bound by the gendering of its
origin as bride's work. It is bound as well by its reliance on the model of informed consumer choice from a list of options. The informed consumer
knows the pros and cons within the options, but cannot be allowed to ask
where the options come from or why a decision about such things should
be made at all. The two constraints may be only one. Shopping too has its
gender, and gender brings its expectations. Camp is, in one of its costumes,
the art of mocking gender expectations by ironic shopping. So I try to
imagine what it would be to camp the planned wedding: teased-up drag
queens in Chanel suits scribble on clip boards as the husky groom in leather
puzzles over dainty place settings. But the picture looks to me like broad
satire, not camp. It cannot inhabit what is to be twisted in the way that
camp must. Here, as with the football boy on the cover of *Teen Bride,* the
winking excess of the original leaves no room for subtle inversion. Bridal
magazines already camp the roles they pretend to exalt. Planned weddings
already offer fairly bitter satire of erotic bonds.

With the loss of the possibility for camp, and not coincidentally, there is
the loss of the wedding as a site of creative religious agency. Whatever the
religious components of a planned wedding might be, they cannot be its
central components. Freeman suggests that trace elements of religious
symbolism might permit the forces of managed marriage to be overcome.
"The history of control over marriage suggests that the residual customary
and religious elements in the ceremony might provide imaginary ways out
beyond the state's promotion of monogamous, enduring couplehood."[31] I
only add—what Freeman would not deny—that models of wedding planning, queer and straight, do their best to remove any residue of religious
imagination.

THE DEATH OF GOD—IN WEDDING PLANNING

In America, the wedding remains, along with the funeral, a ready occasion
for circulating apparently Christian symbolism into the general culture.
The most familiar words of Christian liturgy may be, "Dearly beloved, we
are gathered here today to celebrate the union of this man and this woman."
Public display is a function of the old (and perhaps now antiquated) cultural

privilege of specific kinds of Christianity, but it is also intrinsic to Christian rites. In modern practice, at least, a wedding is a form of sacramental theater. Its performance displays Christian prayer to the public as much as the pope's blessing "to the City and the world." Christian weddings should not be a vernacular for expressing wealth, family status, and social fluency, but some (other) display is essential to a wedding as a public act. What does it mean for a wedding to be one of the most acceptable occasions for the circulation to the public of Christian iconography?

To begin with, it implies a persistent confusion about what is Christian iconography and what not. Most of the elements of the "traditional Christian wedding" are only accidentally Christian. At best, they are the ethnic forms of people who were once mainly or normatively Christian. At worst, they are recent inventions tacked on to Christian weddings by social convention or clever marketing. That is why the iconography of the white wedding, like the Christmas tree, can spread so far beyond the borders of Christendom. Both wedding gowns and Christmas trees sell in Japan, where Christianity remains a minority religion. Neither those who sell them nor those who buy them regard their use as a profession of Christian faith. They are right.

The planning of a "traditional" wedding or indeed of any standard American wedding is not essentially a Christian activity. Those who regard Christianity as a dangerous or bankrupt ideology will of course tend not to distinguish carefully between it and the uses made of it. So Ingraham treats religious weddings as part of the wedding industry.[32] In this, she inadvertently follows the lead of wedding planning, which regards religion as one option within the approved range. Wedding is the master category, the master rite, within which religious wedding is a subtype and Christian wedding the local variant. You are going to have a wedding, that is the important thing. Now you get to choose its details, among which there may or may not be religious references. Because little money can be made off of the specifically religious aspects of a wedding, and because that money is to be made by other institutions, the wedding industry has little to say about religion in weddings—and less to say about God.

The *Essential Guide* repeats the reduction of religion to an optional accessory. Its motive is not so simple as greed. The handling of religious options is dictated partly by vernacular tolerance or openness and partly by a sense of the ancient quarrel between queer people and organized religion. Religious buyers of the book may come from any point on the dizzying spectrum of American religious consumerism. Nonreligious buyers may find religious references tedious or offensive, either because of personal suffering or because of some religious groups' notorious opposition to lesbian and gay life. Faced with a diverse readership, the *Essential Guide* goes lightly through available religious options. It does so by relying on the notion that there is an event—the planned wedding—that exists before and apart from any religious site, organization, officiant, or ritual.

The *Essential Guide*'s longest discussions of religion have to do with selecting the site and drafting the ceremony. Religious sites are discussed on four pages of the fourteen in the chapter about location. The book offers its usual practical advice, only a part of which is concerned with religion. Of the fifteen questions the couple should ask about using the church, for example, one only concerns permissible liturgies: "Are there any rules about what our ceremony and vows can be like?" (89). The same is true for the manual's discussion of religious motivation. Couples who choose "to have their weddings sanctified by the blessings of clergy" may do so "because it's a time-honored fashion . . . or because they want to be close to somebody who they feel is closer to God than they are" (87). Allowing for the clumsy humor of its alternatives, the passage yields nothing to the notion that the religious site might be sacred. The holy cannot be allowed to appear as an alternative to the planned wedding.

Religion must be especially shrunk or silenced when it threatens to appear as a real alternative. Step back to the *Guide*'s first sentence in the section on religious sites: "We don't care who you are or what your sexual orientation is; when you get right down to it, there are basically only two choices of ceremony: civil and religious" (87). What can the alternative mean? The book has stressed repeatedly that the weddings it plans have in themselves no legal effect. "Civil" has no content here except as nonreligious. The religious, in its turn, is given the content either of an extralegal formality or of a primitive, antidemocratic notion about approaching God through an intermediary. "Religious" means not civil, and "civil" means . . . not religious.

The circular alternative, "civil and religious," is more than mimicry of straight marriages. It helps conceal an unacknowledged third: the planned wedding itself is an event neither civil nor religious, an event that stands before both civil and religious. The planned wedding has taken over as the master category that reduces both the civil and the religious to mere options. There is a complex story here, which is much like the story of the American funeral. In the last 150 years, "funeral directors" have constituted themselves as the primary ritual experts who superintend the site, the technical services, and the liturgical craft of the funeral.[33] They offer the expertise within which the older ritual form—say, of Christian burial—now figures as a style package. A new kind of rite has been created, the rite of the "funeral" that is, in its essence, neither Jewish nor Christian, neither civil nor religious. It is the generic funeral with its list of optional services, including your Christian minister (if you have one) and the loved one's favorite hymns (on tape). The rise of the funeral director as ritual expert establishes a new category of ritual that claims for itself a position above the religious rites its displaces. The funeral director displaces the rabbi, priest, or minister as officiant in the mysteries of death. The agents of the older gods capitulate in the face of another priesthood, whose creed is cosmetics and closure.

Something analogous has happened with planned weddings. The wedding planner, like the funeral director, appears as the purveyor of a comprehensive event, the wedding, within which older religious rites can figure only as traces of vanquished powers. In performing the reversal of position, wedding planners have been luckier or more cunning than funeral directors. They have not had to learn any messy techniques (like embalming) or to acquire real estate (like the funeral home). With existing facilities and other people's skills, they have marked out a new ritual sphere, the planned wedding, that consumes other buildings, skills, rites, and ritual experts while pretending to coordinate them.

What to call the space or sphere of the new rite? It is tempting to call it "civic" and to think of it, loosely, as part of a shared American civil religion. By analogy, the funeral industry has functioned with great visibility not only in the public imagination, but in relation to the mysterious world of laws about dead bodies. The funeral director knows how to get death certificates and how to dispose legally of the remains. Here the analogy may not hold. The wedding planner is not in so clear a civic position, especially for same-sex weddings. There are no certificates or laws, except perhaps laws to be avoided. So the ritual of the planned same-sex wedding floats in a space that is neither civic nor religious. It would be tempting to call it the space of Victorious Love, since that is the name of the deity most often invoked. It would be more precise, if less elegant, to call it the space of the Plastic Symbol, since it invites the couple to shape new meaning by the exercise of consumer choice. According to Condé Nast, "85% [of Americans] marry in a religious ceremony."[34] Is that a comment on their intention or their taste in décor?

Unfortunately for planners, wedding ceremonies still permit the old rites and the old gods to intrude. So the chapter on the ceremony is the other section in the *Essential Guide* that offers an extended discussion of existing religions. The book provides a "rundown on where some religions stand concerning gay marriages" (113, referring to 113–117). The list highlights Judaism, the MCC, the Quakers, and the Unitarian Universalists. It then lumps together, under "Other Religions," Methodists, Episcopalians, Presbyterians, Buddhists, and two "'renegade'" groups, Dignity (for Roman Catholics) and Restoration Church of Jesus Christ (for Mormons). The list is, of course, neither proportionate nor comprehensive. It is an awkward gesture toward the old religions—though, to its credit, more visible than most in bridal magazines. Even the *Guide*'s gesture becomes ambiguous when it is put in context. The summary of religions is followed not only by a pitch for "alternative clergy" (acting illicitly or with ordination from unusual groups), but by a list of "variations" that includes handfasting, jumping the broom, and rituals with water, fire, and food. The pages sound entirely too much like the episode of *Absolutely Fabulous* in which Whoopi Goldberg plays a counselor who offers same-sex unions under a waterside trellis with foot washing and handfasting. "I have speaking in tongues just as a sideline."[35] The satire is astute, because the new priesthood of counselors is a model for the lesser order of marriage planners.

In the *Guide,* there is no satire, no camp, only pious earnestness. For it, the moment of maximum choice in the same-sex planned wedding is the construction of the ceremony. "You get to create your own symbols that are new and appropriate—symbols that reflect your own personal realities, as well as the reality of you as a couple" (109). The planner can help best by offering suggestions detached willy-nilly from older religious or ethnic customs. Making new symbols means in reality choosing sentimentally among deracinated existing symbols. "It's your wedding ceremony and anytime you choose to draw on established traditions, you will be doing so with an acute awareness of why you're doing it" (109). The moment of maximum freedom at the center of the wedding ceremony, the moment at which you lay hands on the Plastic Symbols in order to mold them, is a moment informed mostly by "an acute awareness" of your own motive. Your motive is . . . nostalgia? Hubris? Love Victorious?

The gauze of sentimental freedom covers conjuring tricks. The wedding planner is offering not only a menu but a sequence in which the menu items will appear. So the *Essential Guide* presents a plan for the wedding ceremony that is, of course, like Protestant and Reformed Jewish weddings and unlike Catholic, Orthodox, Muslim, or Hindu weddings. The *Guide* employs the language of a mainstream mix. It supposes that a couple will want vows, of course, since vows are the "heart and soul of the wedding ceremony" (123). The two partners should also decide on an introduction, perhaps with "an invocation (calling on God's presence)," then some "prayers" or a "consecration," and finally, a "benediction (blessing of your union)" (120–21). The familiar liturgical words are there, with parenthetical explanation. Of course, the couple will craft vows of its own (122). So too with the rest of the ceremony. "Writing your own ceremony or choosing it from existing ones can be the most rewarding process you go through in getting married" (120). In most cases, writing it means choosing it—piecing it together "personally" from bits and pieces of extant liturgies, social conventions, family stereotypes, or any odd piece of popular culture. "Quote your favorite songwriter or use lines from *Casablanca*. Borrow a saying from a Hallmark card if it speaks to you" (122). Liturgical creation is *bricolage* in aisles of greeting cards.

The wedding liturgy is not a binding rite to which one submits. To admit that much would be to undo the premise of wedding planning—the very assertion of independence from the old religions. There can be no hint that some religious practices might be of an entirely different order than civil unions or sentimental assemblies of tag-lines from greeting cards. Religion must remain an accessory. It is a storeroom of inert words, images, and customs from which you cull whatever bits fit into your self-styling. Your "self"-styling is, in turn, the profession of the wedding planner. Religion as a radical alternative to civic life, religion as a potent source of political revolution, religion as a rebuke to sentiment—the possibilities are excluded *a priori* by the planner's high office.

The wedding planner has displaced the old religions, but not social anxieties. Fear of the wedding as a critical moment of social accomplishment, as an event that constitutes and continues families, that shows the essence of couples for good or ill—that need remains. The genre of the wedding guide depends on it. The office of the wedding planner responds to it. One escapes from the old religions into the cult of social graces.

⁕ ⁕ ⁕

In conclusion, I offer the briefest guide, in easy-to-follow, question-and-answer form.

Q: How can we queer a wedding plan?

A: That is not an option on the list.

Q: What will happen if we hire a professional to plan our Christian rite?

A: You will usher in other gods and their imperious priest.

Q: So what should we do?

A: Use the time for a betrothal, then explain to your friends that you are inviting them to a blessing, not a lifestyle mart. After putting on dish-washing gloves, set aside any bridal magazines and planning guides as cautionary tales for theologians.

CHAPTER FOUR

Finding Some Marriage Theology — Before the Ceremony

❦

A collective illusion, suffered by some queer activists and by Focus on the Family among others, declares that there is or has been a single theory of Christian marriage. To sustain the illusion you have to discard most church history and to strap on big blinders for the present. Otherwise you will notice that there is no coherent Christian tradition to claim, much less a Judeo-Christian one. There is no unanimous model to combat. What you will find in the history of theology (itself a narrative construct) is a long series of disagreements, some violent enough to split churches. Earlier still there is the awkward struggle to steady Christian ideals of sexual asceticism atop the evolving notions of marriage in Israel. No single marriage theology has held sway in all Christian churches, not least because of Christianity's deep ambivalences about sex and about Israel—which were, in the theological imagination, often enough combined.

Christian and Jewish traditions disagree about a number of fundamental issues, including the value of celibacy, the permissibility of polygyny or concubinage, and the grounds for a divorce that permits remarriage. To a remote observer, indeed, marriage is a good point at which to show how oddly yoked the two religions appear to be. In earlier Israelite marriage especially, a reproductive imperative determines many particular arrangements, including multiple wives or concubines and the requirement that a brother procreate with his widowed, childless sister-in-law.[1] The arrangements are "patriarchal" in numerous technical senses: a husband may have many wives according to his means, but a wife no more than one husband at a time; the husband may divorce his wife, but the wife only rarely decide to leave her husband; and so on.[2]

Contrast the views recorded in various pieces of the canonical New Testament, where the "good news" is often a call to a new life beyond biological family and sexual desire. In the Gospels, Jesus says dark things about families, while he praises eunuchs and angels. In 1 Corinthians 7, Paul does, of course, permit marriage—but only as a concession to irresistible lust. The better way is to remain unmarried. If Christians could read the New Testament afresh, they might be struck by the absence of positive portrayals of marriage in it. Who is the example for the married Christian? Not Paul, who extols his singleness. Not the Apostles, who, whatever their marital state, follow Jesus as if they were unmarried men. Not Mary, whose virgin motherhood is narrated by Luke and whose perpetual virginity preoccupied later traditions. Not Jesus, who is the very figure of solitary purity. "What would Jesus do?" Not marry.

It cannot be surprising, then, that Christian marriage theology was slow to develop or that its development was liable to contradiction. If there are authoritative theological passages that can be used to encourage or console married Christians, there are other passages, always ready, that can be used to undercut any pretensions of marriage to be a notably Christian calling. So of course there is no single "Christian tradition" of marriage. Christians have disagreed with Christians about the value of celibacy and the grounds or procedures for divorce. They have disputed the role of civic authority in marriage and the spiritual value of married life. Disagreements about the nature of marriage were at the heart of Protestant and Anglican reformations, as they are now at the heart of increasingly disruptive quarrels between "liberals" and "conservatives."

Any honest discussion about blessing same-sex unions within Christian communities must admit these old tensions, to give them no sharper name. It is not honest to claim that there is a unanimous "Judaeo-Christian tradition" of marriage that is now being assailed, for the first time, from the outside. Even slight effort to study marriage in Christian Scriptures or church history will discover that the opposite is true. Claims for a unified tradition, hyphenated or simply Christian, are in fact claims about something else. They may be claims for a certain definition of Christianity that excludes a host of alternate scriptural interpretations and most of the Christian communities known in history. They may be claims on behalf of a church structure or agency deputed to rehomogenize tradition from day to day. Often enough, and most confusingly, "Christian tradition" is the name given to an amalgamation of whichever political platforms, social prejudices, and journalistic scraps are now being preached in the church of one's choosing.

To locate the theology of marriage in relation to same-sex unions requires considerably more honesty about what Christians have actually said and done. In what follows, I begin from some of their actual confusions, not to homogenize them, but to show how hard it is to stage an encounter with any coherent set of speeches called "Christian marriage theology." I pay the respect of attention to some of the main types of marriage theologies, as I retrieve deeper cautions for theology that a critical history raises. Still my main point is that the search for a theology of marriage does not end where many expect. Only then, in an unexpected setting, do I raise the question: How might Christian theology describe what a nuptial blessing does?

THE CONFUSIONS OF CHRISTIAN MARRIAGE

Historically Christians have asked themselves and one another a host of questions about marriage, from the most fundamental to the most technical. Is marriage permitted to Christians? Is it desirable for them? If it is permissible and desirable, what is it for? Who performs it? When exactly has it been fully performed? Between whom can it be performed? Is its performance a central Christian rite like baptism and Eucharist or is it less important and perhaps only partly Christian? Can the performance be repeated (in case of bereavement)? Can it be dissolved (without death)?

Over centuries, the questions became topics for entire subfields in theology. Consider, for example, elaborations of the criteria for who can enter into marriage. Criteria of eligibility have specified age, form of consent (both individual and familial), physiological capability, sexual inexperience, degree of church membership, spiritual condition, and freedom from earlier obligations. Long analyses have divided the correct sequence of the marriage event, from promise ("betrothal," "engagement"), through public ritual, to private consummation and (even) the birth of the first child. Christian churches have promulgated elaborate prohibitions against incestuous marriage, which have excluded not only quite remote biological relations, but a host of spiritual "kin."

A survey of the history of Christian marriage and its theologies is not needed when hunting for the place of marriage theology.[3] One does need a map both of the main points of controversy and of the sorts of principles that have been invoked or invented to deal with them. Controversial points and responsive principles will have to be gathered from the smallest selection of examples, since anything more would quickly become much more. So let me distinguish only four pertinent topics of controversy and then comment briefly on each. The four topics are: marriage as a Christian path or calling; its subjection to church regulation; its indissolubility; and the importance of procreation in it. The topics will recall the terms of certain famous theological quarrels, but they should also bring to mind key passages from Scripture and their persistent images. I reiterate that this overview is a theological analysis or thought experiment, not a survey or narration of the many episodes in Christian theology's treatment of marriage.

Perhaps the deepest controversy surrounds the *status of marriage as a Christian path or calling*. Only a few Christians have argued that the Gospel prohibits marriage. Many more have held that marriage is an inferior Christian status. The higher way is the way of virginity or, at least, chaste singleness after the death of a spouse. The conviction is powered both by a suspicion of sexual pleasure and a conviction that marriage, with its property and preoccupations, belongs to "the World" rather than to "the Kingdom." Marriage is the mainstay of perishing "flesh." When it is permitted to Christians, it is granted as a concession to the present order. "'For in the resurrection they neither marry nor are married, but are like angels in heaven'" (Matt. 22 : 30).

In parallel accounts, marriage has appeared as a natural institution purified or elevated by Christian demands. Most Christians have believed that there was marriage outside the church and, indeed, outside of Israel. Marriage originated with the created order and belongs to the "law of nature" (to use one Christian idiom). So the early churches could accept Christians who had been married either in Jewish or pagan ceremonies. At the same time, the churches could view marriage as something that happened outside the church — or at the church door, on the boundary between church and civil regime. Marriages were not restricted to the Christian revelation and so were not contained within it.

Even the New Testament's most Christocentric passage on marriage recognizes an outside. Ephesians 5 : 22–33 constructs a famous analogy: as Christ is to the church, so is a husband to his wife. The analogy has force because marriage is presumed to be familiar already to the readers and hearers as not specifically Christian in its essence. Christ's relation to the church can be illuminated by marriage only if marriage is not already conceived in Christocentric terms. Once the analogy is established, it can be reversed so that Christ's love for the church adds a further ideal to the relation of husband and wife. Still the marriage must already exist before the analogy can begin. Marriage is not created out of Christ, however much it can be raised up through his example.

The analogy crosses into the next topic for perennial controversy: whether or how far *Christian churches should regulate marriage*. Despite the notion that marriage was a part of nature, Christian churches began to claim jurisdiction over marriages between Christians and, in some cases, over marriage simply. The oldest and simplest form of the claim asserts that Christians are held to a higher standard of conduct in married life than are other people. Christians may bring a pagan marriage into the church, but once they do so, they should behave as married pagans no longer. When the churches began to develop marriage laws, rites, and (finally) theories or theologies, they began to exert increasing jurisdiction over how marriages were begun, conducted, and ended. In western Europe, the jurisdiction was exercised through a swelling network of church courts. It was also exercised by writing Christian notions about marriage into the "civil" law of Christendom. If the existing form of Roman church jurisdiction over marriage was challenged by the Continental and English Reformations, regulatory power took other forms, often more comprehensive, in the reformed churches and their states. Abolishing church courts may only transfer control to civic magistrates who are Christians of the right sort. Civil law was pressed to become more explicit about marriage precisely to do work that once had been done by church law.

At present, neither the ascendancy of church courts nor the tranquil sharing of marriage between church and states seems a political possibility in many industrialized nations, but that hardly means that the churches have given up regulating Christian marriage. As civil law grows more neutral toward marriage in multireligious societies, the churches themselves are encouraged to codify their own internal regulations. If Americans are unraveling the compact of Constantinian Christendom, we are not returning to the situation of marriage in the earliest centuries of the church. The state may well step back from churchly disputes over marriage, but many churches will continue to dispute and to claim ever more robust jurisdiction.

The changes become clear around the next topic of perennial controversy, the *indissolubility of marriage*. To say that a marriage is indissoluble is to say that the couple cannot be uncoupled. "What God has joined together, let no one separate" (Matt. 19:6; cf. Mark 10:9). Only rarely have Christians understood the claim absolutely, as allowing only a single marriage for all eternity and without any possibility of separation. There are traces of this understanding in 1 Timothy 3:2, where the requirements for an overseer (later read as "bishop") include that he have been married only once. Why only once? Partly because it is a proof of temperance, but partly because some held that Christians in general should be given only one chance at marriage. Many more Christians have allowed remarriage in the case of the death of the spouse and separation (if not remarriage) where the spouse interfered with either the believer's faith or ministry (1 Cor. 7:12–16). Christians have disputed for centuries whether adultery in a spouse gives adequate grounds for separation or divorce and remarriage. The canonical Gospels record Jesus saying different things about the case (Mark 10:11–12 and Luke 16:18 against Matt. 5:32 and 19:9).[4] More recently, many churches have followed civil law in recognizing a much wider range of reasons for divorce, including little reason at all. This is the flip side of collaborating with states on Christian marriage: when states change, churches can be led to change too—and rather abruptly.

Running through the Christian controversies about dissolution, remarriage, and adultery is the controlling image of joined flesh from Genesis 2:24: "Therefore a man leaves his father and his mother and clings to his wife, and they become one flesh."[5] The image dissolves the longer you look at it. Coming as it does in the account of the creation of Eve, it tends to stress the isolation of the couple and not just their separation from the (husband's?) family of origin. Because Adam and Eve are the first couple, they have no human parents, much less an extended family or a network of kin. Their union as couple occurs in perfect solitude, without any other human witness (at least within the confines of the story). If Adam and Eve are the paradigm Christian couple (and not "Adam and Steve," as we are daily reminded), then Christian coupling must be the opposite of the large family gathered around the Thanksgiving table in a neighborhood of friends and relatives. Adam and Eve: the couple perfectly alone.

Another odd feature of the story is that Adam and Eve are depicted as having neither sex nor children while in the Garden. Their being one flesh is a reference more to Eve's coming from Adam than her being joined to him genitally. For Christians, certainly, the image has often been qualified so that it referred to marriage (or at most sex in marriage) rather than to sexual union simply. If Paul uses it to scare the Corinthians away from prostitutes (1 Cor. 6:16), few Christians have held that illicit copulations, like fornication or adultery, create one flesh. Much less do incestuous or "sodomitic" acts. Marriage makes one body out of two—or, rather, three out of two, because the joined flesh of husband and wife becomes the new flesh of the child. Alas, it does so only through sex.

The *role of procreation* is the last topic I selected from the ceaseless debates among Christians over marriage. Many Christians have spoken or speak now as if Christian tradition offers procreation as the sole purpose of marriage. They confuse several grounds of controversy. There are New Testament passages that justify marriage without reference to procreation. For Paul in 1 Corinthians 7, marriage is conceded as a remedy for lust, not for the sake of begetting children. Even writers who invoked procreation in the defense of marriage could not rely on it by itself. Procreation must always be subordinated to other principles, or else it slides into the reproductive logic that many Christians reproved in ancient Israelite practice. If procreation is the sole end, then sterile marriages should be dissolved, and multiple partners or concubines encouraged. Finally, procreation has always been tempered within marriage by appeal to higher aspirations, such as Christian friendship or spiritual advancement. For Augustine, in a highly influential marriage treatise, procreation is allowed as an end early in marriage, but once the couple's ardor cools, they should move on to better things.[6]

The clearer way to conceive this last topic of debate is to say that Christians have appealed to procreation in order to justify not marriage but sex in marriage. At the same time, they have cited procreation to limit the quantity and variety of marital sex as much as possible. If marriage is the only space in which Christians are permitted to have sex, the space it offers is cramped and under constant surveillance. The principle of procreation has worked in tandem with its opposite: the persistent suspicion of erotic pleasure. If God has graciously given humans a remedy for lust, they should certainly not abuse it or take it for granted. The remedy is all too limited in its allowances for partners, acts, desires, intentions, and effects. The principle of procreation, far from making Christian marriage a humid haven for eros, becomes another way to banish it, by policing the only place where Christians can have sex.[7]

The space for sex in Christian marriage has also been constrained by quite particular assumptions about Gospel figures. For example, many Christians assume that a marriage happens only when there has been consummation. In fact, important theological traditions hold that consummation cannot be required for a valid marriage because Mary, the mother of Jesus, was a perpetual virgin. Her marriage to Joseph was never consummated, and yet it would be impious to say that Mary and Joseph were not really married. Better to adjust marriage theology so that a valid marriage requires, not physical consummation, but free consent expressed under specified circumstances.[8]

These four topics are only a few out of many that have preoccupied Christians contemplating marriage. They should clarify recurring theological quarrels. They can also help in translating more technical controversies about marriage into plainer speech. For example, churches have contended over whether or not marriage was a "sacrament." You can translate the controversy differently depending on the sense you give "sacrament." The controversy can be about whether Jesus performed marriages or ordered his Apostles to perform them (since sacraments are instituted or commanded by Jesus). Again, the quarrel can be construed to emphasize issues about the minister or effects of a wedding. But I think that it is more illuminating to read debates about the sacrament of marriage as a controversy partly over its naturalness (topic 1) and partly over the appropriate extent of church regulation (topic 2).

No list of theological topics, no matter how artfully combined, can illuminate Christian marriage debates without the help of an acute historical sensibility. The historical sensibility must keep in view the array of institutions that make up what gets called, so reductively, "the church." Competing church agencies or organizations interpret marriage differently in a single time and place. For example, medieval theologians and church courts within what was supposed to be one and the same church often disagreed over the meaning of the "marriage debt," the sexual obligation owed by spouses to each other. Changing church motives have to be sought as well whenever you tell the story of a single church's teaching during a century or two. A more difficult challenge is to keep an eye on all the ways in which "Christian" marriage has been cross-hatched by local societies— by their politics, laws, and customs. The most basic terms in marriage take different meanings within opposed social arrangements. "You shall not commit adultery" means something different in a society that permits polygyny or concubinage than it does in a society that prohibits them. Again, "indissolubility" means one thing when the average duration of a marriage is 15 or 20 years; it means something else when the average duration is 30 or 35. Finally, the prohibition on incestuous unions does not remain constant when the definition of "incest" fluctuates wildly over so many degrees of biological and spiritual affiliation.

Efforts to find a core teaching about marriage that never changes must ignore the connections that theological words have to each other and to the practices they authorize. Cutting a few formulas from one theologian in order to equate them with formulas from others, quite distant, is like trying to prove the unity of all painting by cutting out little patches of the "same" blue from Michelangelo's frescos and Matisse's canvasses. A string of (translated) words on marriage in Augustine is not equal to the string of the "same" words in John Paul II—unless one already accepts what the comparison is trying to prove, namely, that there are invariant core meanings. Theological traditions have often been built by collage, but the most influential collages have acknowledged their newness. A medieval disputed question collects earlier statements around newly controversial topics, but it does so in candid awareness that it is advancing the topic.

The meaning of marriage in particular is liable to be missed—or grossly misunderstood—unless it is read against the other arrangements that surround it. A push to construct a tidy history of Christian marriage or to recover its coherent theory must leave out many things, not least the parallel

institutions that it has assumed or tolerated at various times. Stirring stories of the development of Christian marriage can be overturned by recalling the relationships or statuses that they neglect to mention. It is a commonplace (at least among those with historical sensibility) that Christian
marriage did not always imply the suburban, nuclear family. It encompassed
various forms of extended or blended families, with their provisions for unmarried adults, shared or delegated child-care, and even (if tacitly and with
sharp class distinctions) forms amounting to concubinage. Christian marriages were explicitly surrounded by other forms of kinship even within the
churches, including vowed religious communities and sworn friendships.
At various distances outside the church, there were dynastic alliances and
charitable foster care. Christian marriage was never the only way of making family, especially in the most "traditional" Christian societies.

This late in Christian time, it is easy to forget how much marriage theology has been invention and improvisation in the face of sharp controversies, social shifts, and competing conceptions of family. Christians tend to
take for granted the edifices of marriage, forgetting that they were built
from the ground up and on shifting foundations. The foundations shift
because they stand on unresolved tensions. I singled out just four typical
themes from Christian marriage controversies to underscore disagreements among Christians. I then added another layer of difference in recalling the various Christian and civil institutions that have surrounded marriage and determined both its meaning and its practice. Underneath all
these points of multiplication, down in the shifting foundations, I recognize
older uncertainties. Each of the four topics—calling, jurisdiction, dissol-
ubility, procreation—connects marriage to Christian uncertainties about
time. To say this the other way around: the four topics I selected show
Christian theologians trying to bring marriage's unpredictable time under
control.

Some of the old uncertainties around marriage result from the delay in
Christ's glorious return. As Paul makes clear in 1 Corinthians 7:26–31,
since Jesus is coming back soon and in a period of violent turmoil, Christians do better not to get married. Troubles begin when Jesus does not return as early as expected. Then, according to well-known analyses of
church history, Christians must decide how to live in the meantime, especially in relation to marriage. Some have extended Paul's advice: Christians
should always live in imminent expectation of the eschatological return,
and so they should always avoid marriage. Other theologians have elaborated Paul's concession to those who had to be married. A delayed *eschaton*
is one uncertainty about the time of Christian marriage, but it is not the
most interesting.

If ordinary time may end today, then today may bring decisive judgment on each human life. The individual Christian should (always) live today as if at the end of her or his life. Eschatological Christians should inhabit an accomplished or terminal character, a character for which there is no morally significant tomorrow. Yet a terminal character is not one through which eros can unfold in time. If your present character lives every minute as its last, you are not well suited for marriage. In daily preaching, of course, the eschatological fixity of Christian marital characters are elided. Wedding sermons speak typically of the children to come and a golden sunset for the happy couple, of challenges to be vanquished and mature wisdom to be earned. These clichés do not fit with the more fundamental moral precept that Christian characters should strive urgently to convert a life always at its end. Do not count on raising children and growing old together, the deep precept warns. Live today, in the very hour of your wedding, in the character under which you want God to judge you.

Christian moral thinking is adept at inventing characters around acts. To say this more precisely: Christian theology categorizes acts by attributing them to certain sorts of characters. The rule holds for marriage theology, too. Christian Husband and Christian Wife have been written and rewritten over centuries as characters of different kinds. They have their particular temptations, especially around sexual excess or deviation. So exhortation aimed at the characters wants to fortify them against carnal sin, often by making the characters as unerotic as possible.[9] The descriptions must also fix the characters eschatologically. The unrolling of eros in time, which depends intimately on bodies, on their cycles and ages, must be reduced to a single moment in expectation of the daily apocalypse.

The effort to fix marital characters in time plays through each of the controversies I named and others besides, but it is easiest to see in the apparently opposite topics of indissolubility and procreation. Early versions of the Christian marital characters attempted to stop time quite literally with the strictest version of indissolubility. No matter what life brings, each marital character is defined perpetually in relation to one other. The doctrine refuses to acknowledge the sadly familiar hazards of human life. In marital characters that emphasize the openness of intercourse to procreation, there can be an equivalent refusal to recognize the ordinary consequences of unregulated fertility. Both doctrines have been taught traditionally as matters of trust in God. They understand God to operate in a present that has no future. They conceive marital characters that exist in a perpetually repeated moment. On its unsteady eschatological ground, Christian marriage has to be performed without time.

Old Christian reasoning converges here with the teaching of the new *eschaton.* The erotic characters of gay liberation have an equally paradoxical relation to time, because they are meant to inhabit a "future" imagined as the universal reign of the instant of orgasm. Carl Wittman taught in his manifesto that no liberated relationship could have exclusivity, permanence, or rote performance. Each copulation has to be free—uncommitted, freshly improvised, revolutionary—because each anticipates the collective and perpetual delight that liberation promises to its activists. Whether Christian or liberationist, old or new, eschatological exhortations can disrupt complacency. But the more eschatological they become, the more they can reveal their intrinsic impossibility—and so undo any persuasive effect.

The impossible exhortation to marriage without time has been papered over with more comfortable, more livable versions of Christian marital life. Indeed, the peculiarities of time hidden in Christian marriage characters make it easier to elide the history of Christian marriage theology. The confusions of time around marriage become confusions of time around the "traditions" of marriage theology. Traditional languages are exactly the ones seized by "conservatives" and corrupted by mass marketing. The first task in imagining a different theology of marriage may be to imagine a tradition that is neither static nor vacuous. That kind of tradition has been marginalized in much Christian theology, especially where churches have embraced timeless, universal authority. Even when the authority cites words or reproduces practices from tradition, it treats them as something more like bureaucratic code. Rethinking the foundations and possibilities of Christian marriage theology will mean resisting this model of authority—and not just because it is a very contemporary model of managerial government. Until churches can rid themselves of the fantasy that the best Christian teaching is accomplished by universal bureaucracy, they will have little sense of how to recover discarded social forms or to invent new ones. Much less will they be able to confront the contradictory layers in Christian marriage characters, the extent to which eschatological fixity has been papered over by more amenable depictions of marital time.

Lesbian and gay Christian theologies have played a role in recovering the layers of tradition, despite the strident claims that they are outrageous rebellion against tradition or the friendly suggestions that they are the latest fad for those with exotic tastes. If you look at their accomplishments, you will see the opposite. Some of the most important works on queer Christianity are superb efforts to recover parts of the tradition in all their local, embodied particularity. Think how much more richly one can now remember the history of scriptural exegesis, the "development" of moral theology, or the elaboration of marriage because of efforts by self-identified lesbian and gay Christians who devoted themselves to theological scholarship. Boswell, Brooten, and Bray—to stick only with the B's—restore a sense of Christian relationships in their lived complexity.[10] More constructive theological writers, such as Rogers, have retrieved the most "traditional" theological doctrines as patterns for same-sex relationship.[11]

Lesbian and gay theologies have also exhibited two structural problems in any encounter between queer theory (or queer lives) and a "Christian theology of marriage." The first is that Christian disagreements about marriage have generated and been reinforced by denominational divisions. Because there is no single Christian tradition about marriage, there can be no *lingua franca* for giving a neutral account. What then should a lesbian or gay theology do? Does each theologian enter into the marriage theology of her or his original or most familiar denomination and set to work there? Is the first task to analyze the particular genealogy of a current denominational position, to uncover the exclusions and the fantasies needed to make it seem coherent? Lesbian and gay theologies would then be divorced from one another along the prevailing denominational lines. Or is the first task rather to find some neutral ground on which all lesbian and gay theologies could get together in order to construct an alternative to the prevailing denominational accounts? Their construction would then be either a new denomination or an incoherent assembly of denominational bits. Even on the claim that being queer should outweigh being a Christian of a certain species, queer Christians cannot claim to have a generic Christian theology.

Like lesbian and gay churchgoers, lesbian and gay theologies have improvised charmingly in the face of Christian disunity. Many congregations of the Metropolitan Community Churches are the ecumenical movement in miniature. With tolerance and mutual forbearance, those raised Pentecostal or Evangelical share the pew with those raised Presbyterian or Roman Catholic. In the same way, lesbian and gay theologies have made for themselves a sphere of ecumenical speech in which all authorities somehow count, and no denominational claims are pressed too hard. Unfortunately, this kind of speech can only go so far before it must repeat itself. It falters not for want of congeniality, but for want of specificity.[12] You cannot talk long about Christian teachings on marriage without having to enter into denominations and their competing claims on scriptural or other authorities. Undifferentiated marriage theology has no home.

The second structural problem for staging an encounter between queer theory (or queer lives) and Christian theology arises from the characters in play. If Christian moral theologies have invented innumerable characters around sexual acts, and then reinforced them liturgically, they have been reluctant to recognize them as characters, that is, as historically limited and quite partial performances. Within Christian marriage theology especially, the characters have been treated as natural facts, reinforced in their fixity by the demand that marriage stand on the edge of time, outside of time. The approved characters in Christian marriage have been determined (and overdetermined) by dozens of factors, only partly theological or liturgical. While I don't reduce the factors to some single explanation in terms of time, I find it significant that time is denied in so many marriage theologies. The denial is particularly significant for any conversation with queer theory, which holds as a principal tenet that erotic characters can only be performed in time. How do you stage a conversation between accounts that encourage the performance of eros through dissident, variable characters and accounts that deny eros by trying to lock the only approved sexual characters into timeless marriage?

You cannot stage an encounter between queer lives and the Christian doctrine of marriage—so long as you phrase it in just those terms. The phrasing assumes that there is a single Christian doctrine, that it is distinctively Christian, that it can be separated from the alternate or competing social arrangements of various church epochs, and so on. It further assumes—and this is the most telling point—that Christian marriage theologies have a local gap or failure just at the point of same-sex unions. Many Christian traditions do contain nasty condemnations of same-sex passion or activity. Even where the condemnations are not being pronounced, Christian marriage theology judges queer couples by exclusion. When one is being targeted by such speeches, it is easy to imagine that heterosexual couples have an easier time of it theologically—that they are provided with a comprehensive and consoling theology of marriage. The task of lesbian or gay theology then seems to be imagining Christian marriage teaching without the condemnations. A number of queer theologians have seen through that confusing optimism. The failure of Christian theology to counsel erotic couples is more general. It arises not from a local mistake, but from deeper uncertainties about marriage, its characters, and their time. Same-sex couples are particularly well positioned to suffer these uncertainties, as queer theologians are to recognize them. The urgent question might seem to be, How should queer theology fix the mistakes Christians have made about same-sex relationships? The question soon enough becomes, Why do we expect that there has been a coherent and comprehensive Christian account of any sexual union?

EXPECTING A MARRIAGE THEOLOGY

Remembering the contested history of Christian marrying is one step toward more serious thinking in churches about same-sex unions. Resisting the endless solicitations of the mass images of marriage is another. Performing same-sex unions apart from civil law—even in defiance of civil law—would be a third. The steps lead to more serious engagement with the question, but they do not promise any complete answer or set of answers. On the contrary, the unsteady theological foundations, the complex history, the inevitable encroachment of media, and the perennial engagement with civil politics should remind us that no simple or certain answer is possible.

Unfortunately, much contemporary Christian marriage theology looks like a hunt for certainty, if not for simplicity as well. You can see it plainly in popular presentations of theology—the Christian "self-help" books, radio call-ins, and TV chats. The breezy confidence of their advice cannot be distinguished from the tone of non-Christian shows on the same topics. If anything, the Christian shows are readier to offer quick answers. A tone of certainty often afflicts more official theologies too. The legal firmness of papal documents and the untroubled declarations of the Southern Baptist Convention both suggest that Christian marriage can be prescribed once for all. Here is your tidy answer, now go live it. It will not be enough for Christian theology of marriage to recall its own history or to keep an eye on mass images and the designs of local government unless it can break its own habits of false certainty. Fortunately, other theological habits can be brought into play: there have been innumerable theological warnings against assuming that human language can ever adequately picture the operations of the divine.

Many Christians know these warnings in one form or another. They have read mystical accounts that emphasize the darkness of the intimate encounter with God. They have run across doctrinal assertions that God is radically indescribable and unknowable. They have heard, nearer at hand, the catch-phrases about God's mysterious ways. Whenever things go wrong, Christians are counseled that they cannot presume to understand how God moves in the world. The same counsel should apply when things go right. It is not only misfortune that should be mysterious. The positive or constructive manifestations of divine action are equally obscure. On a consistent theological understanding, human language fails to describe God not just in moments of rapture or tragedy, not only in dramatic conversion or miraculous cure, but in everyday graces.

If divine action is, strictly speaking, indescribable and incomprehensible, then so is the divine action in a blessing or in eliciting and sustaining erotic love. Popular romance finds Cupid mysterious; Christian theology should find God's providence more hidden still. Christians should never expect a complete or certain marriage theology. They should not expect it in general, as an abstract explanation or prescription, and they should not expect it in particular, with regard to their own or any other particular relationship. Theological language feels its limits in abstraction, but never more than when it faces particular lovers who come forward in search of a blessing.

One of the dangers of the theological polemic around same-sex unions is that it pushes all sides toward false certainty. Faced with the dogmatic clarities of the defenders of "traditional" marriage, reformers are easily tempted to offer dogmatic clarities of their own. Something like this has already happened in the cycling quarrels over homosexuality and the Bible. The argument for reconsideration began by raising skillful questions about the assumed meaning of the biblical texts that had been used, for centuries, to condemn same-sex loves. On close reading, the story of Sodom in Genesis turned out not really to justify the theological category of "sodomy." Leviticus 18:22 and 20:13 appeared indeed to punish some (unspecified) act of male-male copulation with the death penalty as a fatal violation of purity, but then many of its other purity prescriptions were ignored by Christians. If Paul mentioned female-female relations in Romans 1, he was not clear whether those relations transgressed by being genital or by being equal. And so on. The tidy list of scriptural indictments fell apart under candid questioning. Then some reformers went further to argue that the Christian Scriptures positively approved modern homosexuality or that they presented certain figures as being themselves gay. The slogan "God hates fags" was answered with the slogan "Jesus was gay."

The two slogans are not comparable in effect or in malice. The first is an act of hate-speech that mobilizes shame to create conditions of violence under which "fags" can be assaulted. To say "Jesus was gay" neither shames nor incites to violence (unless it would be violence against the speaker). It does share with the first slogan a conviction that scriptural evidence underwrites certainties about contemporary sexual identities. The conviction collides with other queer critique—with the effort to remove certainty about "what the Bible says" to changing characters moving through time. The effort to complicate applications of Scripture to the contemporary sexual landscape meets scriptural literalists on its own side. In the heat of polemic, habits of scriptural fundamentalism seize both camps.

More bad habits get replicated in quarrels over same-sex unions. Consider the question of two-tier ceremonies, that is, of reserving marriage to other-sex couples while instituting blessings for same-sex couples. One side in the controversy asserts that while same-sex couples may deserve some sort of recognition in church, they obviously cannot be equated with real marriages. This view is widely expressed, sometimes by queer Christians.[13] The other side in the quarrel then feels impelled to make the counterclaim that same-sex couples are quite as real and deserving of church recognition as other-sex couples. Hence anything less than marriage constitutes a sort of second-class citizenship in the church. The view is just as widely expressed, sometimes by straight-identified allies of queer Christians.[14] A more helpful step, on both sides, would be to ask how Christian marriage has been thought and practiced. How much has Christian theology understood about marriage? Is the history of the rite or its present practice such that other-sex couples should fight without restraint to be included in it? Some of those who want separate union services for same-sex couples do so to denigrate queer love or at least to hold it at arm's length. Should counterargument reply just to their spitefulness, their queasiness? Wouldn't it be better to raise questions about their presumption to understand what marriage is? The provision of a separate rite could also be the provision of a better way.

A decent skepticism about easy scriptural applications or available theologies of erotic relationships is an indispensable prerequisite for talking seriously about same-sex unions. The skepticism should apply equally to opponents and proponents, however differently we might evaluate their motives or their tactics. I believe that those who seek blessings for same-sex unions are right to do so and that their opponents are wrong to oppose them. I also believe that being on the right side of a church controversy is no excuse for bad theology. A theology that claims to know more than it can, about the past or the present, about what marriage has been or what same-sex couples are, is bad theology. Better theology keeps itself in check by negating its own pretensions at every step.

With its pretensions negated, Christian theology might begin to watch for whatever is disclosed of divine operation in the relationships lived before it. Theological discussion could regard the blessing of same-sex unions more as an event to be studied than as a concession to be made. Unions should be recognized, not as an artifact of theology, but as a source for theology—or a rebuke to it. There is an old maxim that marriages are performed by the Christians entering them and only recognized or blessed by the clergy and congregation. The maxim can mean that the partners being blessed are the primary ministers or officiants in the rite, a claim that will be considered below. It can serve just now to remind that divine presence may act primarily in and through the partners in the relationship. Their relationship is where the grace happens and so where the prospects for theological analysis are both most important and most in need of negation.

Theology should attend to the divine presence in same-sex relationships without subordinating itself to the results of psychological or sociological analysis. The "marriage movement" within the Christian churches has produced a flood of studies on the positive effects of lasting heterosexual marriage and the negative effects of deviations from it. The studies are misleading not only in their alleged results, but in their presuppositions. Advocates of social engineering or civil regulation might be content to quantify the benefits of marriage. Can Christian theology be quite so quick to find contentment in quantification? Are the results of standardized surveys really such good indicators of divine causalities in the world? But if the divine activity in the actual erotic relationship ought to be at the center of Christian theology's attention in disputes over marriage, how is theology to get at the activity if not through surveys and empirical studies? This question may look like the beginning of a debate about the usefulness for Christian theology of empirical sociology or psychology as currently practiced, but it is in fact the more arduous question about theology's relation to the singular lives that it wants to describe or (more commonly) to direct. The question is not addressed by replying that theology should skip over surveys or statistics to deal with the raw material of "experience." Field notes or recorded life histories will present, in another form, exactly the same challenges for theological method. The challenges concern the problem of representing human lives, especially when the lives are assumed to show signs of more-than-human agency.

Let me show this by returning to Yip's 1993 study of 68 gay couples in which both partners were Christian, and the relationship had lasted longer than a year.[15] Yip's stories are more interesting than his grids, so the work is best read by pushing past the quantitative apparatus and toward the quotations from the interviews. Yet the stories can also be unsatisfying. Yip's chapter on "Spirituality and Sexuality" provides extensive quotations. Some of them are not directly on point: they concern the stages of self-understanding as a gay Christian, the slow and painful process of coming to terms with sexuality in relation to faith. When Yip turns to the role of Christianity in male-male relationships, the quoted remarks are sometimes beautiful—and never more so than when they show the poverty of the available languages for describing divine presence in a relationship. Several of Yip's interlocutors say that sharing prayer is important to their relationship. For some, it is joint Eucharist celebration; for others, private prayer and Bible study.[16] Other interlocutors stress that shared Christian belief produces a common ethical commitment or practice.[17] The most insistent religious claim in the accounts, at least as Yip edits them, is that the relationship offers a direct "experience" of the divine that supersedes any contrary church teaching. Sometimes the experience is described with one or another detail. It can be specific help received in prayer or added generosity in service (Neil, 109; Robert, 108–9). More often, however, the spiritual experience is the persistence of a loving relationship (Calvin, 109; Robert, 111).

There are several ways to interpret the absence of more coherent or extended articulation of the divine presence in these Christian relationships. One interpretation excuses the absence by noting that most contemporary Christians, and not just queer ones, become tongue-tied when asked to describe in their own words the holiness of their personal relationships. Scraps of official theological formulations appear here and there in Yip's records, especially when the respondent is an ordained minister, but not one of the quoted responses falls back on existing church scripts. This is the more remarkable since various Christian traditions provide elaborate patterns for explaining one's intimate relationships, and many of the scripts are designed to be performed, with more or less feeling, as if they were simple autobiographical description. Of course, the ready scripts typically do not discuss erotic life in any detail, and queer Christian couples are singled out by their erotic lives. These couples fail to speak more fully because they have no ready language or lack the resources for making one. So concludes the first interpretation.

Another interpretation of first-person accounts like those in Yip defends the absence of elaborated theology by arguing that living as a Christian couple, queer or not, doesn't yield distinctively theological discourse. Being a Christian couple is the thoroughly practical business of household chores, family responsibilities, community service, financial justice, and sexual generosity. So the place to look for the Christianity of Yip's couples would be the other chapters where he discusses those topics. This interpretation offers the important reminder that Christianity is not the same as Christian theology. Theologians often mislead themselves by searching for explicit doctrinal content. (This is somewhat like assuming that religion can be only where it is explicitly named.) Of course, something of the reverse must also be true: if theology is not vacuous, its efforts at articulation must add something to Christian living.

The last interpretation of the first-person accounts appreciates the absences as appropriate silence about or before one's Christian life. Christians are commanded to proclaim the Good News, and theology has often taken its command to be that it should double proclamation with reflection or as reflection. Refusing to produce a narrative or even a testimony about divine presence in one's relationships is not quite the same as refusing proclamation — or refusing theology. Refusing testimony can be a reminder of how many tricks memory and self-interest play in the frankest confession. It can reject the flatness of the available languages or genres for talking about Christian lives in relationship. Or it can register the way that divinity fractures human conception. The absences in the first-person accounts rehearsed above might be a recognizable if unplanned response to a divine prompting: be silent rather than trivialize.

The three interpretations together notice that the most Christian part of a Christian relationship often gets left out of telling. They are not an argument against gathering or studying more first-person accounts of Christian couples, whether as "oral history" or as religious testimony. It would be wonderful to have them. Theologians should collect more, as they should attend to the ones we already have. More accounts might help them hear better how the performance of queer character is now conceived as Christian, especially because many existing anthologies about same-sex couples minimize or omit religious issues in favor of political or sentimental ones. But theologians soon have to admit what the few collections specifically concerned with Christian couples, such as Yip's, make clear: the testimonies of Christian couples offer little help to a constructive theology of blessed unions in traditional form — or even to an understanding of how living a union might be motivated by underlying religious attitudes or practices.[18] They seem inept at representing religious self-understandings. If the testimonies are not cases to be judged on dogmatic principles, they are also not data to be summed in tidy generalization. For Christian theology, the lives of same-sex couples are riddles of divine presence to be unriddled with halting, broken words. Attending to the accounts of Christian couples banishes even farther away any sense that theology already knows what happens in them or that it could construct explanations of the sort that most people expect.

What should Christians expect from an accomplished theology of marriage? Is it supposed to guide individual couples in their daily lives? It might be better to leave that to pastoral care or to prayer, private and congregational. Should marriage theology intend to address doubts about the purpose of marriage in Christian life and institutions? Christians already have an arsenal of arguments, for and against marriage, and most do not appreciate the foundational uncertainties in them. Or is the function of a theology of marriage to justify church decisions about who can get married, under what conditions, for which purposes, and at what length? If this is the case, theology serves church law or polity — and may be suspected of serving them cravenly. In churches too decisions are often taken on the hope that justifications can be confected later on. Theology becomes the servant trailing after regulation to tidy its messes.

Before rushing off to refurbish old marriage theologies or to fashion "new" ones of the same kind, queer Christian theologians need to think hard about their function. So much of marriage theology has to be judged useless or violent. Standing this late in Christian time, observers have ample evidence of the accomplishments of theological exhortations. Christendom is a long experiment in writing and rewriting, preaching and teaching, offering and imposing many theological schemes for Christian marriage. The schemes have existed right alongside continuing failures and abuses—as every call to return to an imagined earlier purity confirms. The same is true of theological progressives: they often take credit for long-term improvements in married life that other theologians actively resisted. The loveliest words about Christian marriage have been used for centuries to justify unlovely marital arrangements. They have authorized, for example, bloody persecution of women who loved women and men who loved men. So it cannot just be a matter of getting words about marriage in a slightly better order, broadcasting them with hipper models and the latest technology, or preaching with more and better-choreographed conviction. The function of marriage theology in the upbuilding of Christian lives has to be rethought—and then its form recreated.

I can say what I mean more vividly by putting it more personally. In recent years, nasty debates about same-sex unions have cycled from churches to legislatures or civil courts and then back again. Attacks on unions, in churches or in the public square, rely more and more on appeals to versions of Christianity. They cite the Scriptures and call forth the ghosts of Christendom. When the attacks are loudest, or when I get too high a dose of them, I find it almost unbearable to go to church. This is not because my congregation engages in the attacks. On the contrary, I am lucky enough to live near a splendid Episcopal parish that honors its queer members in their vocations and in their unions. But even within that nurturing congregation I find that the words of liturgy, homily, and Scripture can be poisoned by their use in debate. I am like a child who was always spanked to the accompaniment of Bible verses. I know that the words did not cause the spanking, but whenever I hear them, I feel the blows.

The corruption of Christian language by violent use cannot be remedied only by trying to rebut the use or to balance it with affirmation. The theologian's response must be more radical. The pretense that violence can capture God through language must be dismantled. Theological tradition offers many tools for the work. I have been using them throughout this chapter—in retrievals of "negative theology," in reflections on the necessary failures of language before human lives, and so on. My hope for a useful theology of marriage lies with those tools, because only they can address the abuse of Christian language that violent polemic about unions performs of necessity.

For me, marriage theology becomes useful by refusing to be complete. I conceive it as a constant reminder of the folly of complete explanations of marriage. If churches need marriage regulations, let them draft and amend them on admittedly prudential grounds, without invoking theology. Theology should be kept in reserve to check the tyranny of regulation — or private self-deception. It usefully deploys a series of analogies between marriage and other points of doctrine, including spiritual discipline, apostolic community, or Trinitarian relations. The point of the analogies is precisely to prevent marriage theology from ever being settled. You think you understand marriage? You might as well pretend to understand the relation of Christ to the church!

My idealized marriage theology would prevent persons from settling too quickly on any account of their own lives, especially on accounts taken from campaign shouting, church chatter, or the sibilant seductions of the marketplace. It would do this by recalling as often as necessary how difficult it is to tell what divine agency might look like in erotically coupled lives. Theology's favored form would not be the predictable saint's hagiography, but the fractured accounts of the most improbable saints. Marital theology for same-sex couples would do its work by dwelling on interlaced accounts of unions from the margins of Christianity — indeed, from territory considered to be anti-Christian. Christian accounts have too often tidied up complexity by imposing theological explanations. They pretend already to have rendered lives whole. Theology would do better to look where it cannot yet recognize itself.

Consider, for example, the overlapping texts and artifacts for the circle of friends and lovers around the painter, Pavel Tchelitchev. The cluster of overlapping journals and engaged biographies, of paintings and art photographs, discloses features in these male-male relationships to multiple points of view. It sets high standards for the representation of human loves, queer or not. At the eccentric center of the cluster of printed sources, place Parker Tyler's self-observing biography of Tchelitchev.[19] The book knots and unknots prose as it struggles or plays with memories. It collects photographs of the man, his circle, and his works, including snapshots of his lovers and the images he made from them. Alongside Tyler's book should go the edited diaries of Tchelitchev's last lover, Charles Henri Ford, and of his longtime friend and supporter, Glenway Westcott.[20] One could add the appreciation by Lincoln Kirstein, but also several portraits of Tchelitchev "at work" by George Platt Lynes.[21] And so on. These are merely some of the published materials that depict a single nexus of erotic relations among men.

On what claim of authority does marriage theology override such complexity in favor of its own simple-minded generalizations? There can be no appeal to the simplicity of the Gospels. They are notoriously not a marriage theology nor, indeed, a detailed moral code of any kind. They are contradictory stories studded with paradoxical aphorisms. Every theology that is not written as a life told four ways already departs from the most authoritative model for Christian writing. Nor can the tedious prescriptions or empty exhortations of marriage theology be excused by arguing that theological writing cannot always be as artful as the examples mentioned above. Why not? So far as a theology of marriage claims to rise above the content of "sinful" liaisons, must it not also supersede them in form? To conclude otherwise is to set the bar for theology suspiciously low. I suggest instead that a convincing Christian theology of relationships would insist that as many voices as possible be invited to describe a given love as artfully as possible. It would then remember how those accounts are bounded and supplemented by nonverbal records. And so on. The first exercise for a theology of marriage is to experiment with the possibilities for representing loves—so that it can know what they might do and what they can never do. A new theology that clings to the standard certainties or that refuses time in other familiar ways is not new. It is also not useful—at least, to Christian ends. A useful theology of eros in time needs a new form.

My idealizing observations are not so much a prescription for a theology-to-come as they are reasons why marriage theology cannot meet the expectations regularly brought to it. The lesson applies with extra emphasis to any theology of same-sex unions. Christian traditions do not offer ready languages for praising same-sex eros; they offer many languages for condemning or belittling it, whether directly or by obvious implication. Again, Christian art has few images of same-sex desire that are not images from Hell. It is easy to understand, then, why so many rush to make consoling languages and to create enticing images of a kind of erotic love that has been so maligned, so smeared in Christian history. Yet the rush to representation cannot overcome the limits of representation. In some churches, Christians may be permitted to write more truthfully about same-sex couples now than in the past, but they are never going to be able to write about them with satisfying completeness or sure transparency. The coded or camped representations of earlier forms of homoerotic Christianity offer helpful reminders again. When homoerotic desire was able to survive in churches past, it did so by maintaining secrecy or irony that could avoid violent notice. The present liberty to speak, even if it were less fragile than it now is, cannot escape the need for some secrecy and much irony. Secrecy and irony are the condition of any human representation of the divine—perhaps especially of divine action in human erotic desire. Desire is, after all, the point at which Christian theology finds human beings most intimately connected with the divine in this life—and the point at which it stumbles badly over time.

One way to keep from stumbling is to look at a particular time. I mean a moment in time, not an eschatological "moment" at the end of time or an equally eschatological inauguration of a future conceived as a single moment of bliss. Can anything useful be said about what blessing a same-sex union actually does? Approach the question not by assuming that it can be answered, but by scrutinizing the scattered answer-fragments spoken by those who seek blessing. Their fragments have to be read in the register of desire and possibility, not of fulfillment and actuality.

SAYING WHAT A BLESSING DOES

Debates about the effects of a wedding are almost as old as Christian debates about marriage. I will not summarize them or decide them. Instead, I will represent a range of possible descriptions for them. There are many things such a blessing might do for the churches or the larger society. For the moment, my attention is, as it often has been traditionally, on the couple as the recipients of a public blessing in church. How to speak about what happens for them, in them, to them?

The religious expectation of the rite is often enough the last or least articulate thing in a couple's discussion. Pastors complain of this and the wedding industry counts on it. The religious expectations are particularly covered over for same-sex couples, where the ceremony often comes later on in a relationship. It typically marks something other than the founding of a household or the joining of dynasties. (It is more like a confirmation than a baptism.) Especially when marriage is viewed as something done by the couple rather than by the minister or congregation, the couple would already seem to have done the marriage in an established relationship. What could a blessing add?

Answers offered by couples or their pastors list a variety of reasons for seeking a blessing. One of the most common is that a blessing ceremony and its attendant meal or party celebrate what the relationship has been until now—a sort of anniversary gathering centered on renewal of vows. Some couples do in fact tie the blessing of a union to one of their anniversaries, however they want to calculate it. Thanksgiving and rededication are eminently Christian motives. They are often at the heart of church celebrations of anniversaries for other-sex married couples. Celebrating the relationship is also a motive named when one of the partners is near death. The aim is not just to have a party. The couple wants to give thanks for what has been before it is too late to do so in this world, as Christians say.

It is rarer to hear same-sex couples speak of a blessing rite as enabling a relationship to take place. Some do describe it as marking the return to religious practice for one or both partners. The rite becomes a way of reconciling with God, not so much over same-sex desire as over the abandonment of religious practice. Same-sex couples will also seek a blessing because a child or children have entered their lives. The blessing becomes a commitment to religious practice for the whole family. None of these is quite the same as the view that a marriage founds or establishes either the couple or its family, much less that it authorizes sexual activity. I have never heard a gay couple speak of waiting until they were blessed to have sex—except as a joke.

Another cluster of religious motives for seeking a blessing, also common in my discussions, pushes for public recognition, either by one or another community or (more rarely) by (biological) family. Even a long-term couple of "out" queers may never have declared itself in a public rite or asked so publicly for recognition and support. The couple may live and party together, may do activism as a team and execute interlocking legal documents, and still they have never declared to a large gathering that they are a couple and want help in staying together. The help can be analyzed socially, but it can also be understood as new grace, as a separate ritual effect. In the same way, some couples hope that a church rite will reconcile them with alienated members of the family. A rite of blessing is a way to ask for grace before and from a Christian community; it can also be a gesture of peace to invited relatives. Seeking recognition and support at church can even placate (or notify) one's queer friends. Because same-sex unions are often formed after a long series of other relationships, any particular coupling can seem to friends another link in an endless chain. To underscore the importance of a particular relationship in a rite that puts one's religious practice at stake singles it out for those who might have trouble taking it seriously.

Finally, perhaps less frequently, couples seek a union as an occasion for trying to save their relationship. The effort may come too late. This is certainly one factor in the "union curse," the superstition that the best way to kill a good relationship is by getting it blessed. Some relationships are already dead as they drive up for the ceremony. The self-examination and mutual reflection that ought to be part of preparing for any Christian blessing on the union are good means of assaying the spiritual character of the relationship. One always takes the risk that the examination will end a relation rather than fix it. If it is to be ended, better to do it before the blessing is celebrated rather than have the blessing appear as the cause of the rupture.

I don't want to arbitrate among these four classes of motive for seeking a blessing. The term *blessing* ought to cover them all equally. A blessing is still a blessing whether it celebrates thanks on an anniversary (or near death), reconciles with God, seeks graceful support, or encourages discernment. In view of the plurality of decent motives, it is worth being deliberate about what sort of blessing is being sought and for what reason. Given larger societal confusions, it may be imperative. Weddings function in American life as the great rite of sentiment. Like Christmas, they can accomplish untold miracles. A wedding (or is it Christmas?) cures flagging love, melts cruel hearts, mends warring families, restores the impotent or the frigid, and brings a shower of tasteful gifts. To resist the damaging mythology, a little deliberation about the blessing sought is required. A blessing may do more than is asked or expected, but it will not do what the movies promise.

Stripped of wedding mythology, opened to a range of ritual purposes, a blessing on a union can seem very different from "traditional" Christian marriage. After all, if Christian marriage was not exactly magical, it was supposed to mark a decisive change of status that authorized new (sexual) activities and established a new family. The contrast is much too tidy. Contemporary American Christians, even in the most "conservative" churches, use marriage for all the motives ascribed to a blessing. Couples who have long cohabited will marry on a significant anniversary or when one is diagnosed with a terminal condition. They marry for the sake of their children or to make gestures of peace toward family. Marriage is a last resort before breaking up, as marriage preparation is an occasion for breaking up. Even the "normative" first marriage of young singles is often the recognition of an existing relationship and an established household. The range of contemporary marriage practice in the churches is roughly the range of motives or circumstances for seeking blessings on same-sex unions. It is dishonest to pretend otherwise.

Officially there remains at least one difference between the "traditional" conception of marriage and the conception of blessing. Marriage has been understood, for theological and legal reasons, as a decisive change of status. It is the change from being single to being married. The change has been equated both culturally and theologically with entry into maturity, loss of sexual innocence, and putting on a set of new duties, both in the city and in the church. The change of state in marriage has also seemed to Christian spiritual writers a decisive spiritual step—for many of them, a tragic spiritual loss.

Christian theologies describe the change of status in marriage with dozens of images. The most enduring is the image of the bond that unites the two married partners. In churches with sacramental theologies, the bond stands in contrast to the "character" (now in a technical sense) caused by other central rites. For these theologies, three rites that confer agency in worship—baptism, confirmation, and ordination—imprint a permanent "character" on the soul. The character empowers a believer to conduct prayers and rites. Marriage, by contrast, does not imprint a character on a person; it creates a bond between persons. The simplified version of the contrast between bond and character can clarify reports about the effects of blessings on same-sex couples.

Same-sex couples disagree when they describe how a blessing on their union has changed them. Some Christian couples joke about "making it legal" or "getting right with God," about the "wedding night" and its peculiar morning after. Their accounts refer to the rite as a chronological marker, a date against which a relationship's larger progress (or regress) can be measured. The day itself may seem particularly memorable or catastrophic, but it is one day among others in the shared history. These couples report their union ceremony neither as a decisive change of character nor as the making of a new bond. Indeed, it seems in many narrations to matter less for status than a graduation or a significant shift in professional employment. Many gay couples retell their coming out as a much more decisive change of status than a blessing on their union.

Other queer Christian couples do report being surprised at how much difference they felt in the bond after its blessing. The change is attributable in some cases to the fact that the religious ceremony was linked to a change in legal arrangements, either by a civil ceremony (where permitted) or by the execution of legal documents (interlocking wills and powers of attorney). For other couples who are surprised by the effect of a blessing, the importance of the rite lies in its capping a process of discernment and (re)commitment to the union. None of these reports posits the imprinting of a new character. Couples who report surprise at the power of the blessing are not describing the creation of a new spiritual identity. For that matter, the bond after the blessing may be understood not as a new creation, but as a strengthened or enriched form of the relation already there. For these couples too, the deeper rites are the rites of character, including both Christian baptism and coming out.

Heterosexual Christians sometimes narrate the effect of marriage much more emphatically, as the assumption of a new identity on analogy to baptism. Passing from the quasi-metaphysical status of single to married appears as a giant stride—or, rather, a second giant stride after the stride from sin to salvation. Only rarely have I heard such language used by same-sex couples, and in those cases I thought I was hearing echoes of transposed marriage theology. For both straight and queer couples, I strongly suspect that marriage gets described as a change of character only when the effects of church blessing or recognition are confused with a host of other effects.

The change of status is not sanctification brought by blessing, it is a list of psychological, social, and legal entailments now pegged to the performance of a church rite. If one could separate the experience of a Christian wedding from its legal effects and its sexual permissions, if one could bracket off social approbation and material gains or losses, where would one locate the decisive change of status? If "traditional" church weddings of other-sex couples were shorn of legal and economic effect, how would those couples describe the effects of their being blessed? As it has been conceived, the change of status embodies maximum social regulation. It offers the firmest resistance to the course of eros in time. Emphasizing marriage as a change of status has many social uses. Christian theology finds it useful to rely on the emphasis the more it commits itself to indissolubility. The two characters of husband and wife are defined as forever interlocked. The grace of their union is then read only as support for that permanent dyad, rather than as the gift of eros disclosed through time.

So far as same-sex couples have been compelled to try to give something other than an indissolubly linked account of their expectations or their experiences in blessing, they are further along toward discovering the difficulties of saying what blessings do just as blessings. For all Christian couples, queer or not, two limits circumscribe speaking about the spiritual effects of a blessing. The first has to do with knowing how to recognize and then narrate divine or spiritual agency in one's experience. The second has to do with voicing religious sentiments in shared, "secular" speech. The first difficulty is notorious in mystical writing, as I have said, where the failure of language and the possibility of self-deception lurk at the end of every line. The second is notorious in American public exchange, where religion or "spirituality" is essentially private and so frequently embarrassing. Between the two, any queer couple of Americans may find itself reduced to utter silence when asked to describe what a blessing has done or might do. Official descriptions of a change in status can be learned. When testimonies to the idiosyncrasies of grace are learned, they can also be feigned.

For different reasons, I don't want to wish away the two limits on speech about blessings. I underscore them in opposition to the image of change in status. By refusing to concentrate on the blessing of a union as a decisive change of status, Christian theology of relationships might be able to attend better to what the blessing always actually is—namely, a ritual. The important thing may be not what the blessing does, but what the blessing is. Its principal effect on the relationship, the surrounding families and communities, may be not result from a legal or magical change of character, but from a ritual enactment, an event. The ritual responds to time by recognizing that desire in the present pulls forward. It points not to an eschatological moment or to a golden sunset some decades hence. The ritual of blessing gestures toward a future of moments animated by pulling desire. The principal usefulness of theology may be to strip away a host of fictions and confusions in order to assist this motion, to frame it as a gesture toward the enactment of desire as continuing character. If so, the best theology of marriage assists an event. As their fragmentary accounts suggest, same-sex couples seek unions not in order to subscribe to a nonexistent theology of marriage as their estate, but to perform a liturgy of their erotic characters.

CHAPTER FIVE

The Wedding and Its Attendants

⤨

After the planning, the bills, the legal arrangements, and the family feuds; before the banquet, the drunken dancing, the stacking of gifts, and the convalescent honeymoon, here comes the wedding. Whatever else it might be, for Christians a church wedding is supposed to be a religious ritual. The ritual, like most Christian rituals in America, is often lost to anticipation or aftermath. Christmas, which ought liturgically to begin on the eve of December 25, ends some days before then with disgusted overexposure. A wedding too can become planning and paying, not praying. Still, if curiously, the ritual charge of weddings is deeply required, even when it is covered over with a kind of embarrassment by surrounding fuss.

Christian churches with long genealogies now bless same-sex unions.[1] The blessings are acts of public prayer. For most participants the public character is indispensable. However exactly it is conceived, as miraculous transformation or ratification of tested love, as enacting a sacrament or sealing a contract, the blessing is an act on behalf of a church or before a church. It occurs within the cycle of a community's public celebration. It takes its place within a history of corporate worship. For many churches, especially but not exclusively the ones that used to be called "liturgical," to have a place in the history is to enter a liturgical genealogy. The genealogy serves various functions: it establishes authenticity or legitimacy, but it also enriches or challenges prevailing tastes. When a blessing for same-sex unions tries to enter into a liturgical genealogy, to take its place there, it needs to find ancestors, to argue from authorizing precedents. Or so it has appeared to many.

For others, the challenge has been to write utterly new liturgies in place of the obviously decadent liturgies of old. Already in 1973, an author in the magazine of the Metropolitan Community Church (MCC) in San Francisco was exhorting his readers to innovate: "Cast the chains of custom aside! Let imagination flow! Liberate your thoughts. Dare to attempt variation. . . . Remember, you are commemorating a joyful bond and not a staid, conventional turkey trot designed to produce more children and Gross National Product."[2]

Efforts to retrieve genealogies or to invent something "new" both suppose that there is a settled liturgy or set of ritual customs for Christian weddings. Christians do now have a surfeit of wedding liturgies and "traditions," but it would be a mistake to imagine that they are somehow intrinsic to Christianity—that they have always formed part of it. One of the oddest features about the history of Christian weddings is how late they developed. Some early Christian communities may have performed something like a Jewish blessing, but as a domestic liturgy. Other communities left the ritual to civil officiants and required only that the couple observe Christian moral precepts. Before the fourth century, there is no compelling evidence of marriage in front of the church or in a distinctively Christian ritual.[3] When the evidence appears, it shows a practice of nuptial blessing that combined Jewish and Roman or other ethnic elements. To find a surviving Latin text for a nuptial Mass—a wedding celebrated in connection with the Eucharist—you have to wait until the seventh century. Even then, this kind of wedding was often restricted to Christians who had never married before and who were virgins. Other Christians had to be married in other ways. Near the end of the first thousand years of the Christian era in the West, a full "church wedding," a nuptial mass before the congregation, was more a privilege or special recognition than a requirement for a valid marriage.

No historical evidence supports the claim that there was a distinctive ritual of Christian marriage from the early church on—much less that such a ritual was practiced or instituted by Jesus. The wedding that Jesus attended in Cana, so often cited as precedent by later theologians, was a Jewish wedding celebrated in a home (John 2:1–11). If Jesus approved anything marital by attending, it would have been Jewish wedding customs. The marriages among Christians that Paul accepts, but advises against in 1 Corinthians 7 are Jewish or civic. The New Testament, wary of marriage, is not interested in writing wedding services. The distance between doctrine and rite carries through the slow development of Christian nuptial liturgies. Influential patristic treatises on marriage among Christians, such as Augustine's *On the Marital Good,* do not quote liturgical texts or use Christian ritual practices as evidence for their arguments.[4] In the last thousand years, of course, Christian churches have proliferated both marriage theologies and wedding liturgies. Present disputes cannot let that great wall of texts hide what lies behind it: an equally long period in which "Christian wedding" was either an oxymoron or a nonchurch wedding between Christians.

Liturgical genealogies and revolutionary improvisations both contend again this odd history. The slow, patchy, always mixed development of Christian weddings can embolden both genealogists and revolutionaries. If Christianity had a long period in which it experimented with various arrangements for uniting Christian couples, why not claim a similar freedom now? It might be the freedom to retrieve alternate or parallel rites excluded from official liturgical history or the freedom to start new experiments. There is freedom to be taken, but I find myself more interested in another implication of the liturgical history. If during centuries, Christian marriages were performed elsewhere, with nonchurch rites and legal arrangements, how might we conceive the Christian function of a wedding ritual? Should it replace or absorb the ethnic and legal functions? Should it correct or criticize them? Pursuing these questions, you will topple opposite assumptions about the relation of Christian liturgy to marriage theology. The first assumption is that churches have a moral theology of erotic relationship and then write up rituals to reflect it. The second assumption is that churches develop liturgies for erotic relationships from which a coherent moral theology can be read off. Both assumptions are false. The actual connections between liturgy and moral teaching are much messier and so better suited to express divine action in eros.

RETRIEVING RITES

Same-sex couples in Christian cultures have used existing wedding rites, parallel rites, or variations on both to bless their unions. The wide inference is justified because the evidence is so scattered. Despite the best efforts of various church bureaucracies to prevent or punish unions, despite efforts to prevent records from being kept or to confuse records that were, scraps of evidence for same-sex unions survive from many centuries and countries. The scraps gain added importance from more recent American evidence (including oral history). Many lesbians and gay men have heard stories from sixty or seventy years ago of ceremonies performed in secret by Christian priests and ministers. Many know couples that celebrated unions in renegade churches or communities thirty or forty years ago. Other couples went to important Christian sites and performed private rites there, sometimes during standard liturgies.[5] Then there were the "drag" or parody weddings performed at various places and various times—sometimes, in the Texas of my childhood, at Methodist church fund-raisers.

The parodies I remember from childhood churches were meant to be funny because, *of course,* men did not love men or desire them. To have an all-male wedding, with half the group dressed as women, was much like taking a pauper and putting a pasteboard crown on him. It was a carnival's inversion of the natural order. Gay men performed similar parodies—with shadowed humor. Ricardo Brown writes of a "wedding" at a house on Lake Minnetonka in the 1940s.[6] One man performed a bridesmaid as Bette Davis and managed to upstage everyone else—at least in producing comic effects. The "minister" claimed authority to preside because one of his uncles was a priest. "In all the commotion, the screaming, the hugging, the laughter, the loud music on the record player, only the groom looked subdued. He looked wistful, even rather tragic, anxious for his bride and bravely determined to make the best of things." The ceremony is a parody, a "kicky" weekend party game—and it is the wistful, even "tragic" expression of a love that has no public rites. The same can be said of star-crossed male and female lovers, like Romeo and Juliet. Indeed, the story of those unlucky teenagers is easily inhabited by queer sensibility. What is the private marriage scene of *West Side Story* but the homoerotic inhabitation of Romeo and Juliet? Its magic worked even at a distance—say, to rescue queer boys trapped in an oppressive parochial school's music class.[7]

Regular clergy of disapproving denominations performed secret unions in homes or locked churches. Renegades or clergy of dissenting groups presided over more public rites. These Christian blessings go a long way back and leave their traces in various forms. Montaigne writes of a criminal ceremony at Rome in 1578. Two Portuguese "married, man to man, at Mass, using the same ceremonies that we do for our marriages, taking their communion together, reading the same wedding Gospel."[8] Some centuries later, in the early 1930s, a young gay man newly arrived in Washington was invited to attend "a lesbian wedding at the home of a minister from one of the city's more 'prominent congregations.'"[9] In 1945, a Roman Catholic seminarian declared himself in favor of pastoral care for homosexuals. George Hyde had then to leave, of course, and so he joined with queer laity who had been denied communion to establish in Atlanta the "Church of the Holy Eucharist."[10] Whether Hyde himself performed same-sex marriages, they were certainly celebrated at a successor congregation, the Church of the Beloved Disciple in Manhattan—which figures prominently in Patricia Nell Warren's love story, *The Front Runner.*[11] Other urban churches, affiliated with mainstream denominations, performed unions in secret. In Michael Arditti's *Easter,* set in present-day London, two women are joined by an Anglican priest behind the locked doors of a parish chapel. Earlier that day, one of them had been married legally in the parish to a gay man, for immigration reasons.[12] There is a carefully guarded history of the use of marriage rites for same-sex couples, which broke into the open some decades back within major denominations. In the spring of 1971, the *San Francisco Chronicle* was reporting on a "covenant" ceremony at Glide Memorial Church presided over by the Rev. Lloyd Wake.[13] The two grooms, dressed in white kaftans, promised "to live together, and love, honor and cherish each other." Wake claimed to have performed half a dozen such rites before this one. By 1977, the *New York Times* was reporting on "covenant services" performed by Paul Abdels, pastor of Washington Square Methodist church. It described the events as "coming close to the marriage ceremony without using the words."[14] In published accounts of more recent ceremonies, there can be a studied ambiguity about the openness of participating clergy. One man describes his 1987 union in a rented bar in New York's Chelsea: "A real priest accepted our vows."[15] Context leads the reader to think that the priest was Roman Catholic. Did the archbishop know?

Impulses to retrieve older rites for contemporary liturgical use have no interest in secrecy or parody. They claim legitimate parentage by arguing a decent genealogy. (Recall Wilde's *Importance of Being Earnest:* you need a genealogy to make a good match.) The argument has so far taken two rather different forms. The first form, the better known and more scandalous, contends that Christian churches approved rites that amounted to same-sex weddings. The second form, the more plausible, remembers that Christian churches offered other kinship rites to bind members of the same sex in affection, if not in copulation. The first argument promotes simple retrieval of those rites into present circumstances. The second exhorts Christians to recall alternate kinship rites in order to correct their exaggerated concern with sexual relations. I have spoken of two arguments, but I am actually thinking of two books. Although neither book can be reduced to the arguments I extract from them, each can illustrate forms of argument. The two books share common ground, but they come at it with different purposes.

The famous illustration of the first argument is John Boswell's *Same-Sex Unions in Pre-Modern Europe.*[16] Its necessarily rushed publication set forth fragments of three different monographs.[17] The first paints with thick strokes a diorama of friendship and marriage in Greco-Latin antiquity and the early Christian church. It does much to unsettle assumptions about the place of marriage among relations of affection. The second fragment reinterprets a Byzantine and Slavic liturgical rite, called in Greek *adelphopoiēsis,* which had been understood before Boswell as a rite for establishing spiritual sisterhood or brotherhood. For the third fragment, Boswell tries to connect scattered mentions in medieval Byzantine, Slavic, and Latin sources to give some sense of the practice of the rite. I concentrate only on the second fragment, which is the cause and centerpiece of Boswell's project: the eastern Christian rite of *adelphopoiēsis*.

Boswell did not discover the rite. He first read a badly mangled version of it in a standard liturgical collection, Goar's often reprinted *Euchologion* (originally published in 1647).[18] Boswell did much to provide better versions of the rite, but his original contribution was to reinterpret it as functionally a same-sex wedding in certain times and places. Boswell performs the reinterpretation by interrogating the ceremony with three new questions (188). First, he asks, "Does it solemnize a personal commitment as opposed to a religious, political, or family union?" Boswell replies at once, "The answer to this is unequivocally yes." Why? "It is unmistakably a voluntary, emotional union of two persons (always two: never more)." Boswell's next question is whether the ceremony celebrated "a relationship between two men or two women that was (or became) sexual?" Boswell answers: "Probably, sometimes, but this is obviously a difficult question to answer about the past, since participants cannot be interrogated" (189). Then the third question, the most important: "Was [the ceremony] a marriage?" Boswell answers: "According to the modern conception—i.e., a permanent emotional union acknowledged in some way by the community—[*adelphopoiēsis*] was unequivocally a marriage" (190).

Much energy has been spent rebutting Boswell's answers to these questions. So, for example, there is evidence that *adelphopoiēsis* was performed under conditions that we would not typically call "voluntary" and that it was embedded within ceremonies of group union. Again, to answer that *adelphopoiēsis* is "unequivocally" marriage is to equivocate on some obvious features of the texts for the two rites. The rite of *adelphopoiēsis* is not identical to the eastern Christian rites of marriage. If it were the same, it would be redundant. In fact, the texts for the two rites do not much resemble each other. Boswell's best evidence for their resemblance depends upon the debatable evidence of a single manuscript.[19] And so on. Of course, Boswell's claims were also caricatured, especially in the press. Beginning with some panels of the comic strip "Doonesbury," the buzz reduced Boswell to saying that the Roman Catholic church or unspecified, ancient Christian bodies had married same-sex couples over centuries.[20] Even when Boswell is being most emphatic in the book, his claim is actually more nuanced than that.

In the end, it is less interesting to rebut Boswell's answers than to examine his questions. Consider the first. How to judge whether a ceremony solemnizes a personal commitment? By interpreting the letter of the liturgical texts? You would struggle to translate terms like "personal" and "commitment" into the language of the Byzantine rite. There is much less chance of connecting them with hypotheses about how the ceremony was "meant" to be used. Who is presumed to have the intention, and how is its tenor to be established? Official intentions about liturgical rites are typically established by reference to rubrics, to canon law in its various forms, and to related church records. Boswell is more interested in how the ceremony was used or viewed contextually, in its actual performances. Is his question then a statistical one about the opinions of some, many, most observers? There is no basis for a statistical answer. Or should it be taken as a question about what participants "felt" in one or more particular cases? No first-person descriptions by observers or participants in the rite are known to survive.

Turn to Boswell's second question, which asks about possible sexual relations between persons joined by the rite. Boswell regrets that they cannot be "interrogated." Even if they could be, the interrogator would need cunning to assess the honesty and completeness of their answers about sexual behavior. After all, reasonable doubts may be entertained about the reliability of the latest sex surveys in America—or about how people recall and represent their sexual acts even in intimate conversation. Moreover, if some or many couples bound by *adelphopoiēsis* were having sexual relations, what would that imply about the rite? Perhaps couples sometimes used it as a cover for their homoerotic activity. The same could be said of heterosexual Christian marriages or religious profession in many times and countries. Marriage vows and vows of chastity have been used regularly enough by Christians that many would now call "lesbian" or "gay" as rites through which they could secure erotic lives that were hardly envisioned by the rubrics.

Boswell admits that Byzantine theologians would never have consented to view *adelphopoiēsis* as marriage. Hence the eastern churches could never be said to have approved or blessed homosexual marriages "unequivocally." In a crucial passage, he allows himself to say only that *adelphopoiēsis* "most likely signified a marriage in the eyes of most ordinary Christians" (191). But the "ordinary Christians" have just been described as constituting "a mostly illiterate . . . community" unconcerned with "theological or canonistic niceties" (191). How then to understand, much less recover, the meanings discovered by their eyes? Boswell has an important point to make about the many ways in which liturgies mean. Deeply suspicious of repressive or irrelevant discourses in churchly elites, he seeks to restore the experience of the majority. The problem is that he must then presume not only direct access to long-dead participants and observers, but an essential sameness between their experience and our own. The rite signified a marriage to them—according to "the modern conception [of marriage]—i.e., a permanent emotional union acknowledged in some way by the community." It is as if Boswell were thinking to himself, "Given what my likely readers probably think of marriage, they might well call the relationship created by certain performances of *adelphopoiēsis* a 'marriage.'" Of course, the "modern conception" that Boswell has generalized is not specifically religious, much less Christian. Moreover, appealing to some "modern conception" is very different from Boswell's historical claim that some, many, or most "ordinary Christians" who observed the rite at some remote time past would have regarded it as a "marriage"—presumably according to their notion of marriage and not according to the "modern conception." The first argument hinges on universalizing a dilute (and secular?) "conception" of marriage. The second requires us to imagine what a deeply religious, if also untutored Christian majority might have judged a "marriage" in medieval Byzantium or the Slavic kingdoms.

Contemporary liturgists worry regularly about where the signification of a rite is to be located, as they wonder whether it can be specified and contained. Even on the textual level—before one gets to questions of ritual performance or the actions of the Holy Spirit—the signification of a liturgy cannot be reduced to any literal paraphrase. Christian liturgy is largely a poetry of scriptural citation. Its poetic effects borrow from the broader range of effects in the Christian Scriptures. An ancient belief holds that the Christian Bible speaks in all human genres, in every kind of voice. To read the Scriptures is to read texts that perform a singular polyphony— the full range of styles on the literal line, with three or four or five lines of "spiritual" meaning above. Liturgy relies on this polyphony to create its own effects of signification. It produces them not as sealed artifacts, but as invocations or solicitations of divine action. It cites or quotes scriptural poetry to put it in the service of eschatological gestures, gestures at what Christians regard as the boundary between the mundane and the inevitably disrupting divine.[21]

Boswell's position as a liturgical Christian writing for lesbian and gay believers twists the knot of these methodological questions. Boswell hoped that his historical retrieval would help contemporary lesbian and gay believers. For example, he anticipated a liturgical edition of the recovered rite of *adelphopoiēsis* for use by contemporary same-sex couples. Of course, after publication of the scholarly book, and beyond Boswell's intention, some of his motifs have been widely commercialized—in medallions and greeting cards of Sergius and Bacchus, "patron saints of same-sex unions."[22] The merchandising shows the uneasy relation between history and worship. Sometimes Boswell writes as if a sociohistorically demonstrable fact about the significance of a past liturgy were an immediately compelling liturgical precedent for modern believers.[23] Indeed, his arguments about the perceived significations of liturgy imply a certain theology of liturgy in which the people's practice of a rite determines its essential meaning. His book enacts a hope for church reform in the present by persuading queer Christians to retrieve (genealogically authorized) ritual meanings against official disapproval. Retrieval of a de facto liturgy of same-sex marriage becomes the best calculated rebellion. That is the sort of view of liturgy a medievalist is likely to find congenial. But is it a sufficient understanding of either liturgical retrieval or liturgical genealogy?

The second argument I abstract urges not the retrieval of a liturgy, but the recollection that same-sex couples in Christian history had well established alternatives for blessing their affection. I take Alan Bray's *The Friend* as illustration, though I confess that I will simplify it (as I simplified Boswell) so that an argument can stand out.[24] On one reading, Bray's book is a series of case studies of English friendships from the high Middle Ages into the nineteenth century. It traces, on another reading, a sequence of Christian, same-sex couples whose "friendship" was either memorialized by church monuments or blessed with church rites. Bray intended both readings and thought that the first would add force to the second. His argument was that retrieving a lost notion of public friendship would allow modern Christians to see new possibilities in their ecclesiastical genealogies.

The evidence Bray deploys for the argument is enormously rich. It reaches, in a remarkable span, from a monument at Constantinople of two crusaders kissing to the grave that John Henry Newman explicitly willed to share with Ambrose St. John "on a hillside looking out cross Warwickshire" (288). The consideration of Newman ends with this paragraph, which is the last of the book's body:

> As in our own time the permafrost of modernity has at last begun to melt— and a more determinedly pluralistic world has bounded back into an often troubling life—the world we are seeing is not a strange new world, revealed as the glaciers draw back, but a strange *old* world: kinship, locality, embodiment, domesticity, affect. All of these things, but I would want to add that at times we are seeing them in something as actual—and as tangible—as the tomb of two friends buried in an English parish church. We did not see these tombs because they did not signify, but they are beginning to signify again. (306)

Bray's contrast between the modern and the premodern intends to forestall any appeal to a "modern conception" of either erotic relationship or friendship in interpreting the couples he considers. Here his strategy seems the opposite of Boswell's. What the vowed friends had was precisely neither a modern homoerotic relationship nor a modern friendship. Their bond cannot fall under any "modern notion." They lived a vanished species of friendship that was intrinsically public because caught up in a dense kinship, "family" in a quite extended sense.[25] They were permitted an ambiguous silence around the sexual, so that they could deploy the language of passionate love without automatically provoking suspicion of unnatural lechery. The suspicions provoked in highly visible or notoriously criminal cases show how many other cases passed without social comment. After all, and as Bray rightly stresses, the monuments to friendship that concern him were placed prominently in spaces of Christian worship. If we moderns have overlooked them, the fault was in us, not in their deliberate iconography.

The public monuments have their parallel in public worship, in a liturgical or paraliturgical rite used to swear such a friendship. The ceremony often began with an exchange of rings, usually on the porch of the church, but it culminated inside, in an act of shared communion.[26] Shared communion and the exchange of rings were employed not only in weddings, but in a variety of ceremonies for establishing alliance, patronage, and other forms of fictive kinship, as we now call it. To speak of "fictive kinship" is already to adopt an impoverished modern notion. The forgotten ritual of friendship was a way of uniting persons, families, and fortunes. It was sealed at the communion rail because that was the perfect degree of kinship: incorporation into the one body of the Lord.[27] Rites for swearing Christian friendship were linked to traditional forms for celebrating marriage, but they were neither imitations of marriage nor parasitic upon it. They were, alongside marriage, elements in a larger ritual system that fostered many kinds of affectionate relation.

In Bray's account, the ritual system was connected to fundamental Christian beliefs about a community linking earth to heaven. Rites of friendship were charged with creedal formulations and sacramental energies. They were subordinated to redemptive ends. Bray's book tries to maintain the same relations and subordinations even in its microhistories. A reader sees this already in the choice of funerary monuments as the linking device. She can feel it as well in the book's hortatory character, which culminates in that last paragraph, but builds throughout. Bray pieces together a ceramic mural of evidence for the meanings of friendship in particular Christian communities, to particular pairs of friends.

In its emphasis on the details of the old friendships, in its exacting interpretation of funerary monuments and family relations, Alan Bray's book may strike some readers as a charming, impotent antiquarianism. They would be mistaken. *The Friend* places antiquarian curiosity in the service of church reform — puts it in service not only elegantly, but quite traditionally. Bray resituates ethical questions about sex within friendship, as "a larger frame of reference that lay *outside* the good of the individuals for whom friendship was made" (6). Bray's recovered friendship "overflow[s]" the contemporary preoccupation with sex (7). "There is, of course, no return now to the friendship of traditional society, but the ethics of friendship have an archaeology . . . that can be recovered; and if this book in some measure helps to explain and find ways of transcending the ethical problems raised by friendship in a diverse world, it will have served its purpose" (8).[28]

Bray's purpose assumes that liturgical genealogies can still persuade— that there is still force in the appeal to liturgical and ecclesial descent. He displays the old rites and monuments of church-blessed friendship because he believes that they still command some respect. Bray's effort to restore the broken genealogy of Christian friendship projects that genealogy into the future. When Bray imagines Christians reinhabiting the older forms of friendship, experimenting with them, giving them content, using them to escape from the dark corridors in which the churches have tried to trap same-sex love—when he does this, he supposes that contemporary Christians will choose to make just these experiments before trying others. He believes that the forms have a claim on some Christians (at least) because they come from an ecclesial genealogy.

Bray may share with Boswell a certain churchly nostalgia—a longing for a Christianity Past in which liturgy guided imagination. This nostalgia shapes Boswell's earlier *Christianity, Social Tolerance, and Homosexuality*. It is more grandly and perhaps more desperately the form of Boswell's last, incomplete book on unions. Before Boswell, one can find the nostalgia latent in Derrick Sherwin Bailey's *Homosexuality and the Western Christian Tradition*.[29] Indeed, any effort to reinterpret one or another period of church history as favorable to same-sex desire (or at least less violently opposed) may solicit nostalgia. In the same way that same-sex desires can be projected onto exotic foreigners, so too they can be cast back on remote ancestors. "Once upon a time, there was more ambiguity and more variety in blessing Christian relationships. Once upon a time, churches had other ways to talk about our loves—ways that did not search obsessively for genital contact or impure thoughts. Once upon a time . . ." Does potent nostalgia yield convincing genealogical arguments?

Bray's nostalgia is not simply Boswell's. It differs not only in historical nuance, but also in being more persistently tentative. Contemporary Christians have no possibility, Bray admits, for restoring traditional friendship and its erotic ambiguities. Churchgoers should not rush to print up copies of the shared communion service for distribution next Sunday. Bray reminds his readers of the so-far-invisible monuments in order to call for *experiments* with different ways of conceiving the erotic in same-sex rela-tions. The call is graciously made without prescriptions. Bray does not think that he has established a fact that imposes itself as proof on late mod-ern believers. His genealogy exercises an attraction, like the gentle famil-iarity of a countryside church. The old rites have left traces in those churches. The traces are not proofs, not aggressive precedents. For Bray, they beckon to late modern couples of the same sex as friendly predeces-sors. I find their gestures charming, but also misleading—and precisely as wistful longing.

ARGUING FROM LITURGICAL GENEALOGIES

Two arguments about liturgical precedents for same-sex unions play upon what looks like nostalgia. We might well ask, then, whether the arguments slip when they take up liturgical genealogies. In fact, they suggest several slips, if they do not commit them in any obvious way. One is a presentist mistake of assuming that the range of human relations is more or less con-stant throughout history, so that the genealogist's task is merely to recover applicable texts in eras past. The texts will have something to say about ex-actly the sort of relationship contemporary Christians see before them. To find genealogical precedents for blessing same-sex unions, they need only look back to earlier Christian marriage rites or to rites that run alongside them. Yet the prior question is how a Christian identifies which earlier rites might be pertinent. In the present, same-sex unions are blessed for dis-parate reasons—to inaugurate a new relationship, to celebrate the an-niversary of an established one, to mark an undertaking or return to Chris-tian practice, to prepare for the death of one or both partners, and so on. A Christian reformer could look for liturgical antecedents not only in wed-ding or friendship rites, but in confirmation, confession or reconciliation, and anointing of the sick. Like contemporary heterosexual weddings, the blessing of same-sex unions is an umbrella sheltering a number of ritual motives that were sometimes broken out into diverse rites for older churches. Since marriage is now the arch-rite of sentiment, there is the temptation to spy it whenever tender feelings are called to do their work.

Even when a reformer wishes to construct a genealogy for only one or two of those motives—the ones she imagines most closely analogous to her notion of traditional marriage—she immediately risks another slip. To illustrate it, I jump over the ambiguities of historical evidence to imagine two scenarios that test the project of arguing from a liturgical genealogy. Much criticism has focused on details of scattered evidence in Boswell and others. What happens when we imagine the existence of much better evidence?[30]

The first scenario: Imagine that there were convincing attestation of an early Christian rite that recognized or created an exclusive bond of same-sex affection, where "exclusive" meant that the partners could neither enter into another such a bond nor be married in the church without dissolving their sworn friendship. Boswell argues that the rite of *adelphopoiēsis* was sometimes like this, and Bray may hope for something like it in future experiments with vowed friendship. Would this sort of case be an adequate precedent for blessing same-sex unions? No, unless the sexual issue were explicitly resolved. Certainly too much contemporary discussion is dominated by erotic obsessions that flow from the overarching regime of sexuality. To complain of that is not to say that we can escape just by closing our eyes and clicking our heels. Convincing historical evidence of an exclusive friendship rite without erotic specification would not authorize blessing same-sex unions that are presumed or proclaimed to be sexual. The ambiguity of the evidence would be trumped by explicit condemnations of same-sex desire elsewhere in the approved traditions.

In a different form, this difficulty affects all genealogical arguments for blessing contemporary lesbian or gay relationships. The diligent searcher can find rites with interesting ambiguities or rites that were probably used to cover same-sex erotic activity (though the "probably" will be vexed), but finding them does not warrant blessing highly eroticized present-day relationships between queers. The explicitness of hypersexed characters does not cohere with the ambiguities or enforced discretion of the preserved rites. You could invoke them as genealogical warrant only for a relationship built around ambiguities and enforced discretion, not for an "out" lesbian or gay relationship. Of course, the same objection applies to contemporary heterosexual relations—a point to which I shall return. I stress now that rites for blessing ambiguous relations cannot be retrieved to bless a relationship that has been deliberately, publicly, even painfully disambiguated. Reticent rites would work only for a future in which the genie of sexuality had been put back in the bottle.

The second scenario: Imagine simultaneous discoveries that widely scattered Christian communities had performed marriages for both other-sex and same-sex couples. Would this be, at last, an adequate precedent for blessing same-sex unions in the present? I am less sure about the answer to this hypothetical case. The discovery might in fact persuade some churchgoers to support blessings. For many others, it would prove that all of those communities were not really Christian—or that the cited evidence, no matter how scientifically convincing, had been forged or falsified (like dinosaur bones). Still others might dismiss the evidence as a sign that all human institutions, including the early church, bear the marks of sin. The more startling the challenge, the more devices for managing it are already in place. The management of liturgical genealogies is, after all, a venerable theological task.

I conclude that no imaginable liturgical discovery will automatically produce widespread conviction of the legitimacy of blessing same-sex unions. I am not complaining about how little importance churchly debates give to historical evidence or diagnosing the role that present politics plays in the construction of accounts of the past. The more important point is that there are limits intrinsic to the construction of any liturgical genealogy, including limits on the role of liturgy in arguments about legitimate sexual relations. After all, the discovery that early and widely scattered Christian communities had performed marriages for both other-sex and same-sex couples would significantly alter our standard histories of Christian heterosexuality. Modern Christians have no early marriage rites from churches in the west. They have no elaborate early theologies of marriage as a sacrament. What they have is the slow, patchy development of various accommodations to civil regimes and their notions of gender relations, kinship, and proper weddings.

Same-sex unions cannot be forced to produce what no other rite really has. The churches' present practice of Christian marriage between *other-sex* couples is not authorized by a liturgical genealogy that goes back to the beginning. There is as much churchly amnesia about weddings as about marriages. The staunchest advocates of "traditional" Christian marriage typically defend a notion not more than 150 years old. Their defenses forget not just recent changes in gender relations, family structures, and household economy, but recent reversals in church teachings on marriage preparation, family planning, and annulment or divorce. Similar changes, if less studied ones, have occurred in most Christian marriage liturgies, however customary some of their phrases sound. Taken as a whole—with music, sermon, and nonrubrical additions or alterations—most contemporary marriage liturgies can be said to quote earlier rites without enacting them. They are as much innovations, historically speaking, as the last century's blessings for same-sex unions. If Christian reformers begin with the assumption that same-sex unions must justify themselves by unrolling a liturgical pedigree, they ignore the very short genealogy for present liturgies of *other-sex* unions.

The creativity and the hazards of liturgical reform should be fresh in the minds of many Christians. They have lived through sweeping and sometimes brutal changes in their ways of worship. Or perhaps the tumult of the changes has led to their repression. Many churchgoers seem to have forgotten that Roman Catholics recently prayed together in Latin or that Episcopalians warred over the 1928 prayer book before they picked fights over honestly gay bishops. Quarrels generated by the reform of liturgical texts, including hot quarrels over seemingly minor rubrics, often forget as well the conditions for the performance of liturgy. Polemic about liturgy shoves out of sight the facts of liturgy in time. Each performance, as Judith Butler ceaselessly reminds us, is both a citation and a variation. Any particular Eucharist cites the liturgical norms of a particular community (as it cites the Last Supper), but it also works variations on them. Any particular Eucharist *situates* the liturgical norms anew—in the particular personnel and their performances, in musical and visual contexts, of course, but also in social and political circumstances. Christian reformers need to look beyond the norms, then, as both Boswell and Bray argued, but not in the direction of social history or lost patterns of kinship. They need to look beyond them because of how liturgy has its existence. Once reformers look outside the instructions and the prescribed texts, they will see not only the varied contexts for particular performances, but the salient liturgical fact—that any liturgy, as text or performance, necessarily fails to represent what it enacts.

The motley history of Christian weddings is united by the effort to sacralize existing civil rites—followed, of course, by efforts to desacralize or resacralize them differently. For generations, part of sacralizing has been standardizing within both church law and moral theology. Reducing wedding rites to a legalized moral theology has persistently ignored the celebration of Christian marriage as a blessing—that is, as a liturgical act, as a prayer. The project of standardizing weddings should be the first issue in any debate about blessing same-sex unions. To say this positively: advocates of same-sex blessings will gain most theologically by refusing to play the game of constructing standard liturgical genealogies. They will remind themselves—and those willing to listen to them—that the history of Christian worship has been too often a flight into manageable superficiality.

If Christian blessings on unions do nothing but acknowledge or accessorize civil unions, then Christian liturgy, with or without its history, is reduced to decoration or supplementary social control. If, on the contrary, Christian blessings on unions call down causes essentially different from the civil—if they do something more than ratify the local etiquette—then the history of Christian liturgy might indeed be helpful, so long as it is allowed to be what it is. For believers, liturgy ought to be an incomplete register of traces of eschatological gestures. Unbelievers should admit the aspiration if they deny the fact. Remembering this much, both believers and unbelievers may also be led to remember that what a liturgy of blessing is supposed to do eludes any description of it, much more any paraphrase. The words and actions of a blessing are not supposed to be adequate representations of their effects.

INVENTING RITES

The opposite of retrieving rites for blessing unions is inventing them. Invention is particularly attractive in a culture that makes erotic passion the particular (the only?) preserve of freedom. Idiosyncratic vows, eccentric ceremonies, and "unique" settings mark many American weddings, not just the unions of same-sex couples. Indeed, the same exhortations to be creative in composing the rite are found in other-sex and same-sex planning books. "It doesn't matter if your approach to your wedding is New Testament or New Age; writing your own ceremony or choosing it from existing ones can be the most rewarding process you go through in getting married. Your ceremony is being held so that you can tell the world, or your world anyway, about what your love means to you and where you want it to take you."[31] "It's a good idea to jot down the parts of the [traditional] ceremony that are most important to you."[32] The first is from a same-sex guide, the second from *Modern Bride* magazine, but the imperative of consumer choice is the same.

Same-sex unions don't have to be another wing on the shopping mall. The demand for creativity in them can be something less tedious than hunting for sizes. It can address the craving for rituals that have power in queer lives—and especially at the point where those lives have been most forcefully excluded from civic or religious ritual. One book of lesbian and gay liturgies puts the point generally: "Merely to transplant heterosexual and heterosexist models of worship will not work."[33] It will not work both because those models don't reflect same-sex lives and because they have been used to persecute same-sex loves. An anthology of lesbian unions says this more specifically: "Lesbians are also creating their own [union] ceremonies, interweaving what is meaningful for them from various traditions with words and images of their own imaginings." Why? "The creation of women's rituals has come to be seen as a way of affirming our own identity, a way of creating our own symbols and traditions."[34] The imperative to make a new ritual that expresses "who we are" can be, for Christian same-sex couples, not only consumerism. It can be the imperative to find a place in Christian worship that has been insistently denied—and not only to same-sex couples.

Crafting liturgies for blessing same-sex couples is, in most denominations and congregations, a process, not a fiat. The process can benefit all members.[35] Deliberating about how to bless same-sex unions has led to more transparent wedding ceremonies for other-sex couples. In many congregations that have liturgies for blessing unions, those liturgies have been used first or more frequently by heterosexual couples that prefer them to the standard wedding service. Where there is no crossing over, discussions around same-sex love and its troubles still raise neglected questions about relationships, families, and church community. At the very least, the process of discussing unions means that marriages can no longer be taken lightly as fixtures of Christian life. If the partnership of two women who have been together for years, and kept the congregation going for almost as long, can provoke such serious religious questions, then marriage must be importantly religious.

By now hundreds of religious rites for same-sex unions are in print or on-line. The largest number is Christian or Jewish, but there are examples from many other religious traditions. Among Christian rites, some barely depart from established forms used by male-female couples. Others are almost wholly invented—though these too are not so different from the more experimental rites used occasionally to marry women to men in church. Some of the published Christian rites are composed by particular couples; others are the work of pastors, theologians, or liturgists. In this summary, I have of course begged the most important question for selection: Which criteria do we apply to determine whether a union rite is Christian or not?

Same-sex unions pose the question in a number of ways. With unions, as with marriages, interreligious difficulties arise. There are Jewish/Christian unions, but also celebrations that unite Christian liturgical elements with symbols, texts, or actions from one or another of the "world" religions. More interesting still are unions that attempt to combine Christian elements with Wiccan, neo-Pagan, or New Age rituals. For example, a text composed by two women for their 1988 celebration in Australia brings together a reading from 1 Corinthians 13, a responsive reading from the Song of Songs, a homily by a (gay) Anglican priest, an adaptation of a Jewish Sabbath blessing, and the gift of a dolphin ring as "a symbol of health and right relationships between people as well as between humans and the creatures and all creation."[36] It can also be unclear whether a rite combines religious or ethnic elements. Two grooms step on the goblets from which they have drunk in a ceremony and are lifted up on chairs at the wedding dance.[37] The acts are explicitly meant to reflect "Jewish heritage." Another union ceremony is "based on the tradition of Kwanzaa," but takes its scriptural readings only from the Christian Bible, offers communion, and paraphrases the Gospel in its final declaration: "Those whom God has joined together, let no one put asunder."[38]

Whether a liturgy is Christian can be asked even where there seem to be no Christian elements or a desire precisely not to be Christian. The union of Dusty and Ali was celebrated in 1984 on a California beach. It was meant to draw "from the Yoruba faith, from matriarchal faith, and a little bit from Sufism." [39] Yet when Ali knelt down in front of the improvised altar, "this real Catholic thing of church and altar hit [Dusty]" (185). Dusty wanted to leave, but Ali persuaded her to stay. Since Ali describes herself as having "very strong roots with my Latina community," the Catholic reference is neither accidental nor trivial (189). Her kneeling in front of an altar to be wed is a citation of Catholic liturgy known to her in her "roots." How to conceive the citation of a central action from Roman Catholic liturgy in a wedding rite that is deliberately not Catholic?

Interreligious eclecticism, the incorporation of "ethnic" elements, and the (involuntary?) repetition or citation of Christian gestures or symbols illustrate some perplexities in dividing Christian from non-Christian union ceremonies. Others arise in trying to analyze rites more clearly aligned with one or another Christian tradition. For example, two women arrange to hold "basically . . . a Catholic wedding ceremony" presided over by an ordained MCC minister.[40] Even though MCC rubrics permit this sort of liturgy to be performed, many other Christians would consider it liturgical theft. Congregations within the Unitarian Universalist Association regularly perform "Services of Union" for members and nonmembers. Many other Christians doubt whether these or other Unitarian services are Christian. What then to say about a union ceremony between two Unitarians celebrated in space rented from a lesbian and gay synagogue, presided over by a professor of philosophy, and beholden to a text in Rosemary Ruether's Women-Church?[41] Again, many Quaker meetings in the United States have adopted "inclusive minutes" that permit same-sex couples to enter into marriage under the meeting's care.[42] Couples united under these minutes go through the traditional discussions with a Clearness Committee and sign traditional vows endorsed by all present.[43] But then some other Christians have long doubted Quaker orthodoxy. And so on. Serious consideration of union ceremonies will encounter not only the puzzles of American coupling, but old divisions among Christians.

Without pretending to settle these questions, and without wanting to dismiss them, I consider three published liturgies for same-sex unions. The liturgies were written specifically for blessing same-sex couples, whether female-female or male-male. The first is a ritual used by Michael Piazza when he was pastor of the MCC's largest church.[44] The second is by Chris Glaser, a gay theologian formed in the Presbyterian church. The third is a ceremony written by Eleanor McLaughlin, an Episcopal priest and spiritual director.[45] I choose the rites precisely because they are recognizably Christian and indeed rather staid. They can show what displacements of meaning or agency happen when same-sex unions are performed using "traditional" materials. I recognize that part of the rhetoric of these three services is apologetic: they mean to show that same-sex couples can have a Christian union. At the same time, and more importantly, they appeal to tradition without claiming to retrieve a lost liturgical genealogy. They show, in other words, the persistence of tradition through invention.

The first ceremony is from the Cathedral of Hope in Dallas. With more than two thousand members, it was the largest congregation in the MCC (until its departure in the summer of 2003) and a large church for any denomination. The ceremony itself is highly traditional, both in its understanding of biblical theology and in the content of its vows. The published liturgy can be divided into six episodes or actions: an opening charge that instructs both congregation and couple; a statement of intent by the couple; their exchange of vows; their exchange of rings, with corresponding vows; a prayer of dedication that calls down a blessing on them; and a pronouncement.

The charge announces that the whole liturgy is "a time for tying a knot in the rope of days," but also "a time for declaring vows and intentions."[46] It vests agency immediately in the couple, who are the first and the principal addressees of the opening text, even if it is labeled "Charge to the Congregation." The officiator says to the couple: "Having found one another and established your relationship, you are here to sanctify it and to give it special significance by celebrating in this holy place." In order to accomplish sanctification, the couple must first resolve to live up to "the Bible's definition of love," which is compiled from a free translation of 1 Corinthians 13, verses 1, 4–8a, and 13 (Statement of Intent). Christian weddings often incorporate this Pauline text by a sleight-of-hand: the *credo* of Romance is imposed on a praise of love in community. That happens here when the conflation of its verses becomes "the Bible's definition of love." The text anchors the statements of intent by the couple. Each is asked to declare that he or she intends to uphold the Pauline ideal, to imitate God in loving, and to "forsake all others and love faithfully so long as you both shall live." Paul's encomium to Christian *agape* is taken to require free, unconditional, and yet restricted (erotic) love for one partner until death.

Permanence and fidelity are underscored again by the vows: "I will love you faithfully through the best and the worst; through the difficult and the easy. Whatever may come, I will always be there . . . so help me God." This recalls the most traditional wedding vow to the ears of English speakers, as its ending repeats the most familiar form of a solemn oath. The officiator refers to it as a "covenant," confirmed when the two partners "pledge" their love with the rings. The officiator prays for God's grace so that the couple "may fulfill the vows that they have pledged this day" (Prayer of Dedication). The officiator then ends by recalling the story of Ruth and Naomi, with the reminder that it was spoken by one woman to another. After quoting "the Apache Ceremony of Love," the officiator ends with a modification of the traditional formula: "By the power that is vested in me by this church, and by the power of your love, I do proclaim that you are partners for life, in the name of God, the Parent, Son, and Holy Spirit" (The Pronouncement). Before giving permission for the couple to embrace, the officiator recalls Scripture a final time: "'What God has joined together, let no one put asunder.'"

Michael Piazza's text implies several notions of agency. The liturgical agency—the agency for performing the rite—is very clearly given to the officiator rather than to the partners. She or he fixes the meaning of the ceremony, proposes the terms to which the couple assents, glosses the exchange of rings, calls down divine grace, and makes the final pronouncement "by the power that is vested in me"—though also, in second place, "by the power of your love." The members of the couple take the vows, but they pray neither for themselves nor for each other beyond the standard phrase "so help me God." Their agency is like the civil agency of the oath and so unlike the sacral agency of the officiator. Their oath, prescribed for them, is as sexually exclusive and ideally permanent as the dourest pastor might wish for heterosexual couples.

The second liturgy I choose, Glaser's "Celebration of Love and Commitment," stands at the opposite end of the range of mainstream Christian services. It is neither so "evangelical" in its handling of the Christian Scriptures nor so prescriptive in its solicitation of promises. Indeed, it begins with a "prophetic defiance" of the churches' ostracism of homoerotic love as it affirms the principle that "our intimate relations are the text of spirituality."[47] The message is reaffirmed in a rewritten hymn, though it is set to an old melody. There are two readings about love from the New Testament, including 1 Corinthians 13. The "vows" are a single text to be read alternately by the couple. The sentences are paradoxical formulations of the couple's love for each other and for God, who loved them first (92). Love for a "lifetime and beyond" is mentioned, as is "fidelity," but neither is promised or explained. The paradoxical structure makes it hard to attach particular meanings to any of the sentences. The closest thing to a vow in the ordinary sense is spoken over the "exchange of tokens," which is marked as optional in the rubrics: "I offer my love over time, praying that our history together will prove fertile for my love to grow . . . " (92). The minister then announces: "In the presence of those who love you, by the power of God's love embodied in your covenant, you are joined, one to another." The congregation acknowledges the couple's "covenant" and commits itself to "embrace them as a couple and as individuals" (93). Communion is optional. The service ends with another rewritten hymn and a blessing from Philippians that calls for rejoicing and confidence in God.

Glaser's liturgy would be recognizable in its hymns, readings, and basic shape to most liberal Protestants. It might even be recognizable as a contemporary variation on traditional wedding forms. Note, then, what Glaser's liturgy does not contain. It does not specify binding promises. If the union is understood as a covenant (which is, indeed, a potent notion in Reformed traditions), the covenant is unspecified as to obligations and duration. The "vows" are written as shared declarations, not individual promises. Spoken in the first person plural, the declarations describe the couple's love: what it is not, what it does, whom it thanks and glorifies. The vows are not performative utterances. There is no sense of executed agency. In fact, it is hard to locate definite agency in this ceremony even when the voices become singular. Speaking individually at the "exchange of tokens," each partner offers love in connection with a petition, namely, that "my love" should grow from "the seed of love we plant today" (92). Is the offering itself the planting? Is the offering the making of the covenant? Immediately thereafter, the minister affirms that the two are joined, but does not "pronounce" or "declare" them so. The most definite agency would seem to be exercised by the congregation, which not only thanks, admires, and honors the couple, but prays for illumination from them and union with them, even as it commits itself to embrace them.

If the agency is diffuse in Glaser's text, so too is the form of relationship being blessed or announced. The "vows" are vague. They could refer to a sexually exclusive, financially merged couple sharing a household until one of them dies—or to a couple with separate domiciles, checking accounts, and sexual liaisons. Vagueness might be inevitable in writing a single liturgy for a range of same-sex relationships, but it can also be a deliberate assertion that the only thing necessary for a Christian union is sharing a paradoxical praise of love before the local assembly.

My last text, McLaughlin's, is Anglican in form and reference. The ceremony opens with an address that calls on "the community" to "witness, celebrate, and support the covenant" of the couple "to live together in lifelong love, friendship, and mutual service with the larger human family."[48] The address connects an act of covenant both with the universal call to sanctification and with pairs of same-sex friends in the Christian Bible, from Jonathan and David to Jesus and John, the beloved disciple. More important, it specifies the purposes and effects of the covenant, which, with its "vows of faithful life together," establishes a new family as a "'Little

Commonwealth,'" a reference to one of Anglicanism's cherished models for marriage (101).[49] The first words from the couple rehearse the language of covenant, but also distribute the agency for the blessing: "We seek a blessing of God, each other, our friends and family, and this community upon our covenant" (101). Friends and family take hold of the distributed agency by sharing anecdotes about the couple. Their storytelling replaces the traditional assent of the congregation. There are no other liturgical formulas by which the congregation or the couple's family and friends express their approval.

Scriptural readings are taken from the Song of Solomon and 1 Corinthians 13. They are expounded, presumably, in the required homily. The couple's statement of intention is performed as an agreement to a series of questions (as in the question and answer of baptismal promises). Here the couple is asked to agree jointly, in the first person plural, to love each other with "heart and soul and mind and body"; to be "loyal, trustworthy, and faithful"; to be vulnerable and nurturing; and to give their "whole and true [selves] to this relationship" (101–2). The partners then recite vows they have written freely and without explicit restriction on content. So too with the exchange of rings. In blessing them, the celebrant says that the rings are reminders of the vows by which the two "pledge themselves to be for and with each other a new family in the midst of the human family" (102). Yet the ring words themselves are written by the couple as they please. This liturgical text constrains the agency it gives to the celebrant, but grants the couple freedom to fashion their own avowals.

The couple is also recognized as having the main agency, with or under God. After affirmations of intent, vows, and exchanges of rings, the celebrant pronounces that the two "have given themselves to each other by solemn vows" and invokes God over them. This pronouncement ends with the traditional warning: "Those whom God has joined and blessed, let no one put asunder" (102). Traditional language is carried forward into the celebrant's blessing: God is asked to give "grace and nurture" to the couple in what is likened to a "birth-giving" (103). The blessing contains many images of fertility and growth, though its imagery is qualified in a concluding rite. The partners are asked to join the flames of individual candles as the celebrant prays: "When two souls that are called to become one flesh choose each other, their streams of light flow together and a single brighter light goes forth from their united being" (103–4).[50] Images of flesh sit uneasily beside those of light, flames, and streams, but the jumbling of images traces an interesting sequence: called to be one flesh, choosing each other, transformed into united being. The actions in the sequence are actions of God and the couple, not of the celebrant or the community.

What can be said of these three rites together, other than that they all include portions of 1 Corinthians 13? Rather little that wouldn't also apply to many heterosexual marriage ceremonies in the American present. The three rites do notice that the couples are of the same sex, though they do so differently: the first and second with reforming and even "prophetic" emphasis, the third only in its list of exemplary scriptural pairs. While the three rites record a moment of change, an epoch in time, they situate it within the growth of a relationship that has both past and future. The third rite does emphasize newness more than the others, especially in its repeated emphasis on the "new family." It is perhaps also most reticent in acknowledging an existing relationship, but even its rubrics call for "anecdotes from that past that connect to the present experience [of the couple] and point toward their future."[51] The three rites might also be distinguished from many heterosexual ceremonies by the theme of the couple as agents of justice in the world—though the first and the third say this more clearly than the second.

There may be other shades of meaning that distinguish the three as rites for same-sex couples, including a particular accent on friendship, but what strikes me in them is how much they are like centrist or liberal rites of heterosexual marriage. The resemblance may be partly strategic. Something can be gained for the acceptance of same-sex unions if the rites look like rites for heterosexual marriage. The resemblance may also be a sort of nostalgia—the desire of some lesbian and gay couples to have a "real" wedding. Still, much of the resemblance may be attributed to a more basic cause: the couples being married by these rites are Christian couples, and so it is hardly surprising that the rites they choose will resemble the rites chosen by other Christian couples who are heterosexual.

The resemblances to heterosexual rites are so strong that it may raise for some readers a question of sacrilegious parody. This is a typical reaction to any dissenting liturgy—a first and automatic dismissal. The charge not only ignores how liturgies grow from the margins, it commits the fundamental mistake of assuming that any liturgy can be other than parody. Recall the blessing given by the Sisters of Perpetual Indulgence at the civil ceremony in San Francisco. In the midst of a political rally, surrounded by ads for liquor companies and glossy magazines, in full view of state legislators and notary publics, while performing their own delicious parody of Christian religion—the Sisters had the audacity to call down a blessing. One way to read this is as an affirmation of what Judith Butler has said for some years: The character of queer identities is disclosed in the deliberate, outrageous parody of what we cannot seem to escape.[52] I would shift the emphasis: any repeated liturgy is a constrained variation on an original that can never be-

come fully present. Each Eucharistic memorial recalls what it cannot exactly recreate—or recreates only as a duplication of an absolutely singular
original. So too with Christian marriage rites and their citations, not only
of scriptural couples or events (the wedding feast at Cana), but of endlessly
multiplying analogies between human relations and relations of the human
to the divine. Before there was drag, there was Christian liturgy—which is
always a parody of its own incapacity to accomplish what it intends.

My disclaimer highlights another common feature of the liturgies just
analyzed: their confidence. They suffer no hesitation, much less any radical
doubt over their liturgical efficacy. Explanations for confidence could be
found in their apologetic intent or in the relentlessly upbeat tone of most
wedding rituals, straight or queer. Who wants ritual nuance at a wedding?
Still the positive, literal tone of the analyzed rites is linked to something
more remarkable: the absence of camp in them, the lack of that polyphonic
irony that is supposed to be the hallmark of gay male performance (if not of
queer performance simply). The three liturgies do not interrogate or challenge the characters coming for blessing, the characters that make possible
the specificity of the love being blessed. They do not try to reflect the paradoxes of (queer) eros in (heteronormative) time. They do not mock themselves, play with their own ritual pretensions.

Perhaps the particular rites don't need to invoke queer performance.
After all, their staid celebration cannot conceal their context. They occur
within a much larger cycle of ritual—and precisely not a rainbow church
calendar or a restored liturgical genealogy.

OTHER RITES, OTHER NIGHTS

Since weddings are supposed to be unique events, "your special day," a decisive change of social status, it is easy to forget that they fall for any Christian within a cycle of rites. The cycle runs from baptism to burial through
others specified by one's tradition. The rites differ in kind. Christians have
distinguished between repeatable and unrepeatable rites or between rites of
ordinary adult practice and rites of the life-cycle. Life-cycle rites tend to be
unrepeatable. Once validly performed, baptism cannot be done again. It is
the classic example of a decisive event in any Christian's biography—a step
from one kind of life to another. The same has held true for confirmation
(when separately administered) and ordination. The Eucharist, by contrast,
is an eminently repeatable rite, though its first reception (First Communion) is also a way-marker for some Christian groups. Ritual penance or
reconciliation was, in some early churches, not easily repeatable; in modern practice, it has been commended as a weekly habit, though its first instance remains for some a life-stage. Marriage itself has gone from being

rarely repeatable to conditionally repeatable to easily repeatable. A succession of marriages can mark the stages of a modern Christian life as much as any other ritual practice. Whether first or third or fifth, though, a Christian wedding takes its place in the larger cycle of rites, just as its particular date falls somewhere in the cycle of the liturgical year. On a minimal church calendar, a June wedding still falls between Easter and Christmas. In a particular local church, it falls after the last funeral and before the next baptism.

For queer Christians, a marriage falls into another cycle of rites. Some have been accepted by churches and others have parallels in them, but they were not originally church rites (any more than marriage was). They are the great mysteries of modern "homosexual identity." Coming out is the clearest example. This hallmark of gay liberation has something in common both with baptism and with the testimony of conversion. When you come out, you take on a new name, but you also tell the story of your deliverance. It is in some sense a repeatable rite, since it is never fully accomplished. Still its first time has a notable poignancy and is incorporated into later tellings of the story. Some Christian liturgists have written texts for it, though most still do not envision that it will be performed in church.[53] Coming out is, even among queer Christians, still celebrated outside churches and often despite them.

Other queer liturgies occupy intermediate spaces. These days, funerals for queer Christians are performed in some Christian churches without dissimulation or embarrassment. The community's grief has moved within particular church walls. In other churches, silence still rules. The "biological family" of an adult lesbian long estranged from them can still specify that the funeral make no mention of her "lifestyle" or her partner of many years. Some churches still refuse to admit out loud that the deceased died of AIDS. Just a few years back, many more churches kept such ritual silence. For the 1980s and at least the first half of the 1990s, the most frequent gay liturgy seemed the memorial service. Its imperatives—its acts of remembrance and incorporation, of blessing and sending—are still needed. The same is true, of course, of many union celebrations between queer Christians. Long before most churches would dream of blessing them, they were celebrated not in private, but in community—with friends, ex-lovers, fellow revelers. Queer Christians have their own rites and so their own ritual time.

Queer liturgies in general and same-sex weddings most particularly should be regarded as points of serious liturgical innovation. The innovation raises fresh questions about what liturgies are, how they mean, and what social reforms they can produce. Particularly useful here is the category of "emerging rites" now adopted by some Christian liturgists. The cat-

egory has a number of features. I underscore three: emerging rituals establish group membership without shared belief; they emerge from "family"
rites rather than producing them; and they constitute acts of social reform.[54] Together the three points interpret the need for innovation in
same-sex ceremonies for Christians as something other than the power of
purchase or the tickle of novelty for novelty's sake.

Many same-sex union ceremonies invoke a particular church tradition,
but they also call up the generations of lesbians and gay men who were denied any public recognition of their unions, unless it was in criminal court.
The narrative of shared struggle constitutes a group without anything so
definite as a creed. A highly sentimental version of group membership is
depicted in the union ceremony that completes the television anthology
Common Ground. Viewers not only hear about, but actually see the queer
foremothers and forefathers: they sit together in a back row for the service.[55] The vignette can be faulted for suggesting that same-sex unions of a
religiously ambiguous but WASP-standard form are the culmination of the
whole movement for lesbian and gay civil rights. It cannot be faulted for
misrepresenting the impulse to group memory in many rites of blessing.

Christian union ceremonies do often come after family rituals rather
than before them. The family rituals may be Christian, ethnic, or private
rites of the couple's families of origin, but they may also be the rituals of
lesbian and gay lives. Lesbian rituals, as noted, have been nourished by a
number of sources. Their influence can be felt at many unions of Christian
women. The same is true, if more diffusely, for gay men. There have been
groups of gay ritual specialists for several decades, including the Sisters of
Perpetual Indulgence and the Radical Faeries. Their rites draw liberally
from drag or camp traditions, from neopaganism, and from real or imagined ceremonies of male "bonding."[56]

Contemporary Christian unions are "emerging rituals" in a third way:
they aspire to be acts of social reform. A note of defiance or rebuke is often heard in them. Legal or churchly injustices are named and then
rectified, so far as they can be by rite. Coming together out of the lonely
diaspora of queer childhood and adolescence, the participants declare a minority love against a hetero-norm that is the bedrock under so many daily
assumptions and grand institutions. Even if queer women and men were
much further along the road to civic equality or church acceptance, same-
sex unions would remain acts of protest against the assumption that queer
couples need to be *given* equality as a liberal concession or to be *welcomed* as
if for the first time.

For marginalized groups, deeply consoling ritual often exists without
cultic authority. Emerging rituals spread rapidly and continue steadily

without an elaborate priesthood, much less an endowed hierarchy. They flourish in the absence of a fixed place, expensive costumes, or uniform texts. Nathan Mitchell illustrates the point beautifully from Alcoholics Anonymous meetings.[57] Some people depend on the rites of AA much more immediately for their well-being than most Christians seem to depend on the weekly Eucharist or service. Emerging ritual works powerfully in AA even as it floats free of most of the establishment that Christian worship often supposes to be required. It shows how sanctifying disestablished liturgy can be for those who are themselves outside establishment. But it may also remind us that unsettled liturgy accomplishes more because it makes fewer claims to capture ritual effects. Many regular worshippers depend on the familiarity and antiquity of their liturgical forms. Settled texts or rubrics certainly can be insignia of tribal identity. They offer reassurance of continuity. I am less convinced that tribal insignia and assured continuity are the highest aims of Christian worship. Fragmentation is a surer instrument of redemption.

The "emerging liturgies" of queer Christian life are not exhausted by rites of coming out, union, and funeral or memorial. Life-cycle rites for queer Christians take place alongside other events and on a growing alternate calendar. For many queer Christians, the other rites include fierce ceremonies at the dance club, dyke bar, bathhouse, or music festival; the intimate exchange of support groups; the loud declaration of the rally or the protest action. The alternate ritual calendar centers on the Pride march, often loosely tied to the date of Stonewall, but there are other festivals: Halloween, of course, and New Year's Eve, or now Valentine's Day and National Coming Out Day. Gay men may celebrate the great feasts that mark off summer and its danced pleasures: Memorial Day, July 4th, Labor Day. Beyond them, for those of strict liturgical observance, the years is punctuated by Circuit parties. Radical Faeries observe Samhain and Beltane. The Saturday before many Pride parades is Dyke March.

These celebrations should not be denigrated as somehow unreal. "A collective social practice exalting joy, desire, and liberation becomes known as a 'gay pride parade.' How does our choice of words collapse complexity and trivialize our gatherings? How do the limitations of diction make pedestrian these core spiritual convergences?"[58] Some of the choice of diction is sexual shame before outsiders—a desire not to be entirely frank about how exactly we conduct our lives. For queer Christians, there may be as well the desire to distinguish sharply between religious rites and "social" ones, between the real rites of church and counterfeit rites outside. For many, Christian or not, there is a reluctance to admit how powerful the "secular" rites really are.

The annual trip to a big Pride parade can be an important pilgrimage. The effort and expense it requires, the buoyant healing it provides, the shape it gives to the rest of the year—I cannot distinguish these from the pilgrimages I observed as a boy living next to a major Marian shrine in Mexico. I am neither surprised nor offended, then, by the tendency to describe queer parades or dances in religious terms. Take the language of the large gay dance clubs. The DJs, leaders of these "rites," hope to be "worshipped." "Divas" sing Gospel lines that pierce heavenward from a tribal bass. ("Diva" entered gay slang with the opera queens, who knew that it meant divine.) Then, at the appointed hour, at the liturgically appropriate time, bodies of the gym "gods" materialize on the floor. The bodies are flawless as temple marbles, immortal, untouchable—except briefly by other gods and then under threatening taboos. When the dance falls on a great day of the liturgical calendar—say, Pride weekend—it will take a special name (like "Mass") and require smaller parties as processional and recessional.

Is it offensive to use religious language in these cases? Or would it be more offensive not to do so? Queer Christians may worry that the rites outside church are too powerfully sustaining. The fear is not so much that Pride will cheapen religion as that Pride has already overtaken religion. The weekend of Pride in the Castro is most like what older Christians meant by holiday: a day for suspending ordinary schedules, costumes, codes, and proprieties. Traffic stops. Groups dance in the streets. The mood shifts, whirls, in the suspension of ordinary time. Christian holidays used to be like this in many American cities. They are not now. The dual character of queer Christians discloses what other Christians may learn in other ways: the "emerging liturgies" in our several communities are often the most powerful liturgies for Christian lives.

For me, worry about the power of alternate rites leads not to restricting or suppressing them, but to discovering what they have that many Christian liturgies lack. Nothing is gained by exchanging a lively rite of union outside church walls for a pale wedding within. Keep both—or use the lessons of the lively rite to fortify its pale sibling. Best of all, bring whatever practices of camp remain in queer rites through the church doors. All Christian liturgy camps grace. It does so best, most powerfully, when it does so with some self-awareness. Explicitly camped liturgy can be immensely serious—precisely because it never takes itself too seriously. It invokes powers that it doesn't try to contain or control. Invoking the powers around an erotic relation reminds the participants of the uncertainties of eros in time. Consciously camped liturgy is an event of dangerous futures.

CHAPTER SIX

Afterward; or, Out of Bounds

⥂

F. O. Matthiessen must acknowledge his lover's infidelity. Russell Cheney has written to confess (or record?) having "given himself" to a former lover while on a trip back to New York.[1] Matthiessen responds: "I suppose that an outsider given the actual cold facts of the case couldn't understand how this could leave the wholeness of our union unblemished, and right there is just the supreme overpowering joy: that we know that no matter what happens we belong to each other. . . . It seems to me that the most significant thing revealed by this situation with Malcom [the ex-lover] is the truth of the statement that you can give the supreme expression of your body only to the man you love."[2]

A male-male couple confronts what is alleged to be the most disruptive and yet most common threat to their common life: sexual "infidelity." Matthiessen's gentle, hopeful reply picks up some common notions about gay married life. Gay relationships are not like straight ones. They are more candid about sexual matters and more tolerant of them. They are impetuous, fluid, and yet also intense and magically committed. The magic renders infidelity impossible. The body can be given to another man only in a phantom act, a simulated copulation, because the heart has already been handed over to the lover.

On first hearing, Matthiessen's metaphysics of the couple stands out from current clichés of gay gossip as naive. Many gay men suspect or accuse each other of being really unfaithful, and they regularly tell stories of separating because of it. They import the whole vocabulary of straight adultery, along with a quantity of country/western ballads. Gay men "cheat" on each other. They "sneak around," "fool around," fall into "lying," "cross the tracks" to the other side of town, keep "love nests," even have "another 'woman.'" Or so some of them complain to each other in bars, gyms, and coffee houses. Where is Matthiessen's impossibility of infidelity? These clichés of gay gossip conflate moral condemnations in just the ways that prevailing uses of *infidelity* do. To have genital contact with someone other than your partner makes you unfaithful. You betray not only your bodily bond (which is what kind of entity?), but also your plighted troth, your sworn honor. In the samples of gossip, infidelity is all too possible; it is common enough to motivate a whole vocabulary of invective.

In other talk, less malicious than some gossip, gay commonplaces acknowledge with Matthiessen two principles. First, gay relationships are supposed to distinguish sex from love better than straight relationships. Second, gay relationships are imagined as more negotiable than standard marriages. Combining the principles yields a subcultural expectation that partners can choose to be committed in love through a variety of sexual events or arrangements. "Fidelity" can be negotiated to have different meanings— even while the impulse to invective remains in the broken-hearted.

The commonplace that gay relationships have negotiable sexual boundaries impels many Christians to deny them the name of marriage. The distinguishing feature of Christian marriage is, for many, a strict sexual exclusivity between two and only two partners—at least according to the ideal. Conversely, the long history of Christian discourse on sex can be told as a story of making marriage into the only safe place to house it. There is a double bond between marriage and sexual exclusivity. Marriage requires "forsaking all others" for one sexual partner, and marriage is the only place for approved sexual activity. When gay relationships seem to hedge on sexual exclusivity, they appear to violate both the explicit commandment against adultery and the equally basic impulse to quarantine all sex by locking it within marriage.

After Christian theology restricts sex to marriage, it restricts sex within marriage. Typical theological justifications of marriage have hardly given general license for sex, that is, "marital acts." Most Christian theologians have shared the conviction that marriage provides only a limited justification for sexual intercourse. Certainly they have provided no justification for the pursuit of sexual pleasure in its own right. In many ways, the theology of Christian marriage has tried to promote sex without eroticism. It has wanted both to limit the kinds of sex that married Christians could have and to extend a means of surveillance or accountability into their sexual activity. When same-sex relationships generally and male-male relations particularly are conceived as incitements to unregulated sex, to the pursuit of eros for its own sake, they seem in their essence to contradict Christian marriage—or, rather, its idealized poster-images. The alleged contradiction can become the revealing churchly argument that same-sex copulation must be condemned precisely because everyone knows that it is more pleasurable than other-sex copulation. Men know best how to give pleasure to men, women to women. Good Christians must repress homoerotic recruiting because one taste of those intoxications shows how insipid are the satisfactions of the (heterosexual) marriage bed. Homosexual acts threaten Christian marriage, the argument tacitly supposes, because they show up the unerotic sex authorized by proper church weddings.

A contradiction between gay clichés and church ideals lies near the center of quarrels over blessing same-sex unions. It helps to explain, for example, the resentment that so many church leaders betray when talking about gay couples. If straight couples have to pay the price of sexual exclusivity in order to get married—that is, to have any approved sex at all—shouldn't gay couples have to pay too? Indeed, shouldn't gay couples have to pay a steeper price, since their sexual desire looks to be particularly undisciplined? "Liberal" Christians who want to include same-sex couples in the compact of Christian marriage can fall into this reasoning: We'll let you in, but only to the strictest, most old-fashioned model of marriage, a model that many of us know to be unrealistic and judge to be undesirable. When you give clothes to the poor, you tend to give the ones that no longer fit or have fallen far out of fashion. So too when marriage is donated to "the poor homosexuals."

The collision between gay imagination and the logic of churchly debates over exclusion and inclusion reveals the naïveté of a certain strategy in reformist theological ethics, the strategy of getting same-sex desire recognized by subsuming it under the approval granted sex in marriage. Only marriage-like sex need apply for theological endorsement, and all questions about the meaning of marriage, except for the question of genital configuration, must be suspended. The naïveté, to stick with that word, is accepted or encouraged by those who know better about both marriages and same-sex relationships. But such an obvious collision between perceptions of promiscuity in gay couples and the Christian principle that sex be restricted to nonadulterous, binary marriages cannot be kept silent long. It should be brought into speech earlier rather than later—and without slipping into other sorts of simplifications. I can point out three of these slippery theological slopes.

One slip is between *cliché or ideal and reality*. I have so far reported commonplaces and ideals precisely because I have not wanted to pretend that anyone could begin straightaway with the *facts* about sexual activities for gay couples or straight ones. Unsuspecting partners are not the only ones kept in the dark.[3] Sex surveys seem often to count boasts and wishes rather than felt desires or committed actions. Public conversations are regulated by other concerns. For example, good politics now requires that gay men hide nonexclusive or multipartner relationships from public view for the success of the movement. The same might be said of domestic partner benefits, which require the presentation of a stable, identifiable dyad as the condition for an award.[4] Of course, the same is anciently true of straight marriages. Whatever goes on behind closed doors, the façade of the contented couple has to be maintained in order to keep economic benefits, social standing, and the approval of relatives. We cannot think about sexual exclusivity by contrasting the "facts" of gay promiscuity with the "facts" of straight monogamy, since we hardly know either and because we are accustomed to conceal both.

Powerful mythologies produce another slip in thinking about sexual exclusivity. To picture male-male relationships that are deliberately nonexclusive is to provoke some of the most violent stereotypes about gay men and their promiscuity. The stereotypes not only denigrate gay men, they diagnose them and police them, they treat them and punish them. Because gay men cannot be trusted to seal their sexual impulses into an airtight marriage, they must be pathological, antisocial, and menacing. They should be denied jobs, put in jail, or ordered to the clinic for castration. It is probably impossible for someone of my generation, gay or straight, to overcome these prejudices entirely — or to forget their dreadful consequences for lives. Debate must keep them in view without ever endorsing them.

A final slip around exclusivity imagines that sex is the *only or principal issue in living gay relationships.* Sex dominates so many public discourses that any speech about sex risks reinforcing its hegemony. The risk is greater with male-male sex, since "gay" as a category enshrines sex with extraordinary prominence. The risk has to be run because sex is so useful an index to the differences between views of straight marriages and gay unions. But the index is a dichotomy that obscures many other scales: not only the relative importance of sex in the relationships, but also how they are renegotiated once begun, how they fit into family schemes, and how they are related to procreation.

With these slips in view, I take up sexual exclusivity as a point of collision between gay clichés and churchly idealizations. The collision presents more principles to be interrogated and more suppressed history to be retrieved. It also discloses another battle of the gods — now as (what else?) competing notions of the Christian God.

PATRIARCHAL GHOSTS

Opponents of same-sex unions try to prevent their legal recognition by en-
shrining a definition of marriage. In the Judeo-Christian tradition, they
proclaim, marriage has always been the union of one man with one woman.
Of course, they are plainly wrong. To claim that marriage is by nature the
union of one man with one woman is to contradict Hebrew and Christian
Scripture, Jewish law, Christian theology, and Christian understandings of
natural law. As anyone who has read the Hebrew Scriptures can tell you,
the patriarchs were polygynists.[5]

The plain facts of scriptural history—if not of Jewish practice—have
posed multipartner relations as a perennial question to Christian marital
theology. At important moments of church history, the question has been
both theoretical and actual. It has been both solicited and eclipsed by the
ghosts of the patriarchs. While most Christians have chased off the ghosts,
have denied polygamy or concubinage, they have typically done so for ascetic or evangelical reasons, not because having multiple partners was always contrary to divine will or to the nature of marriage. For communities
that suffered recurring doubts about the legitimacy of any sex in marriage,
the prospect of multiple sexual partners was not so much impossible as in-
tolerably self-indulgent.[6]

The wispy ghosts of the patriarchs appear in famous theological texts. I
give here the merest sample, beginning with Augustine's *De bono coniugali*
(On the marital good). This booklet entered decisively into the rationale
both of Western church law on marriage and its theological elaborations—
at the expense of some complexities. Augustine's purpose in the booklet is
more complicated than the title indicates. At first reading, and so for too
many readers, he apparently aims to establish that marriage is not intrinsically sinful. Christians can enter into marriage for the sake of procreating
children and in order to enjoy the special bond between husband and wife.
Christians should give their bodies to one another as if they did not own
them, to open the way for children and to fight off the temptation of lust.[7]
At the same time, Augustine repeats that celibacy is the preferred state. He
argues at length that Christians live under very different conditions from
those of the Old Testament patriarchs.[8] The patriarchs were obliged to
marry and to beget numerous children in order to build God's Chosen
People and hasten the coming of the Messiah. There is no need for numerous children in the Christian church. Indeed, it would not be a bad thing,
according to Augustine, if every Christian were to be celibate. Universal
abstinence would bring the completion of the City of God.[9]

Augustine applies the distinction between Israelite and Christian marriages at a number of points. He remarks, in regard to the patriarchs, that

polygyny "is not against the nature of marriage," but he refuses to permit it for Christian marriages, which are evidently held to a higher standard than mere nature.[10] The contrast is drawn so severely that Augustine is compelled to say more in defense of the Israelites—who are, after all, claimed by Christians too as moral exemplars. *On the Marital Good* ends by defending the patriarchs' marriages against the Christian endorsement of celibacy over marriage.[11] How could the Scriptures present holy figures who are married—who, indeed, are polygynous? Augustine replies by pleading historical changes (such as ancient underpopulation) and by urging that Christians cannot guess what virtues of self-restraint were exercised by the patriarchs. Times were different then, and Christians really do not know how chaste their polygynous predecessors were.[12]

Augustine was hardly the first to make this sort of argument. Similar reasoning can be found in Tertullian.[13] In Augustine's time, it had been taken up and elaborated by Jerome.[14] Then again, Augustine did not encounter polygyny or concubinage merely as matters of Israelite antiquity or theological dispute. On the evidence of his *Confessions,* Augustine's sainted mother, Monica, had at least tolerated his own choice of a concubine in place of a premature (that is, socially unprofitable) marriage. Concubinage was no impediment to prominent marriage later on: Monica is represented as the main proponent of Augustine's arranged marriage to a girl from a wealthy family.[15] Though she was two years under the minimum age of twelve, Augustine found his intended attractive enough to be willing to wait, though not without taking another woman for the interim (6.15.25). With an eye to the impending marriage, Monica separated Augustine from his longtime companion, a woman with whom he had fathered a son and for whom he felt a deep and sexually exclusive love (4.2.2, 6.15.25). Monica would not have been alone among mainstream Christians of the fourth century in tolerating or manipulating various sorts of unblessed unions or social improvisations.[16]

Look beyond the biographical resonances to a profusion of erotic relationships in and around early churches. Note then the logic of Augustine's distinction between patriarchs and Christians. He distinguishes natural arrangements under the urgency of procreation from evangelical arrangements under the eschatological ideal of spiritual companionship. On this logic, a marriage theology that stresses nature and unlimited fertility is a theology for the patriarchs, not for Christians. Many contemporary "Christian marriage theologies" would be, for Augustine, precisely non-Christian in their emphases. Within his account, procreation is justified for Christians only as a dispensable and early stage in a marriage that ought to tend toward unerotic companionship.

Whatever his failings before conversion, or his regrets after, Augustine's texts and arguments on polygyny and concubinage were cited as authoritative in hundreds of medieval Christian texts. Still the ghosts of the patriarchs had to be exorcised anew with every shift in the grounds for Christian reasoning about marriage. In his so-called *Against the Gentiles,* Thomas Aquinas discusses marriage at the boundary between philosophy and theology, between natural demonstration and the reasoning that cites divine revelation. His arguments point toward Christian conclusions, of course, but they are drawn mainly from what modern readers would call biological, historical, or ethical premises. In the chapter on whether marriage should be between one man and one woman, Thomas begins with two biological principles: all animals want access to copulation without competition, and all animals want to be certain that offspring are their own.[17] Thomas admits that the second principle would allow men to have multiple wives. So he provides additional arguments to forestall polygyny. He argues, first, and biologically, that in any species that requires fathers to care for offspring, males will only have one female partner.[18] He follows with reinforcing ethical arguments. If women cannot have more than one husband (on the principle of certainty of offspring), then friendship requires that men not have more than one wife. So too does domestic concord.[19] Thomas buttresses these biological and ethical arguments with that most significant citation in Christian marriage theology, though not in Jewish marriage law: "They two became one flesh" (Gen. 2 : 24). He concludes by setting aside the corresponding errors on the sharing of wives in Plato and the supposed sect of Nicholas, one of the first seven deacons.[20]

The troubling patriarchs are carefully omitted from the paragraph. Their ghosts linger. The difference between arguments against polyandry and polygyny is not only a biological asymmetry, it is a historical fact. Thomas must adjust any claim from natural law, since history is the great teacher when it comes to specific inferences about it. One sign of the adjustment comes in the sentence that concludes Thomas's supplementary arguments against polygyny: "It is therefore not fitting (*conveniens*) for one man to have many wives." *Convenientia* is a technical term in Thomas, associated with arguments from appropriateness or aesthetic congruence that cannot rise to the level of demonstration. Their relative weakness can be grasped by contrasting this summary sentence with one that has come before: "And thus, since certainty of offspring is the principal good which is sought from marriage, no human law or custom permits that one woman be the wife of many men." The conclusion against polyandry is a strong inference from natural law, while arguments against polygyny are only reasoning by *convenientia*. Thomas has warned his readers at the very beginning

of *Against the Gentiles* to be careful about deploying arguments of appropriateness in theology before nonbelievers, who might well ridicule their
weakness.[21] A reader should exercise that same caution here—and so recognize that the argument against polygyny is not drawn as surely from natural law as the argument against polyandry.

Thomas spells out the difference quite explicitly elsewhere. In his first
major work, for example, Thomas says that the prohibition against many
wives belongs to the natural law not as a primary or fundamental teaching,
but only as the kind of inference that can change with historical circumstances. The need for high rates of reproduction among the Israelites justified polygyny and concubinage for them.[22] In other places, Thomas invokes
a more powerful principle: God can override ordinary notions of adultery
or fornication. If God tells a man to take a woman, the woman is licit to
him—this in response to the testimony of the prophet Hosea.[23] The case
of Hosea is striking, because the woman God commanded him to marry
had many previous male partners, thus undoing the allegedly natural desire
for certainty of offspring. Inferences about the nature of marriage are not
only historically mutable, they are subject to God's direct veto or contrary
inspiration.

For Thomas, polygyny and concubinage are not actual practices within
the Christian community. If they appear in his present, they do so only at
the margins of Christendom, in heretical groups or among the Muslims.[24]
Still Thomas is confronted inside his Christian present with the historical
fact of the patriarchs. The historical fact requires him to characterize natural arguments against polygyny as historically contingent. Thomas is constrained to make the adjustment because he cannot dismiss the patriarchs
as an example of an immoral society that mistakes the dictates of natural
law—the reasoning he uses to deal with Caesar's report that ancient Ger-
mans tolerated theft.[25]

In the Continental reformation, new understandings of remarriage and
new critiques of celibacy opened a number of old issues, including concubinage or multiple simultaneous marriages. They opened them both theo-
retically and practically. For Luther, who generally rejected polygyny, the
issue became particularly acute in the case of Philip of Hesse. Philip explained to the reformers that he could not have sex with his first wife for
reasons of aversion and yet could not give up sex entirely. He resorted to
prostitutes, but then repented of the practice. Philip finally entered into an
apparently monogamous relationship with one woman, not his wife. He
wanted now to marry this concubine, but without divorcing his first wife
for fear of scandal. Dreading scandal to the reform movement, Luther and
Melanchthon authorized him to have a secret marriage. Luther cited Isra-

elite cases to argue that bigamy was superior to concubinage.[26] Here the
patriarchs are being used to settle an exceptional case within a Christian
community. You may want to regard the exception as Luther's throwing
whatever scriptural rag he could find over an embarrassing incident. The
remarkable thing is that he could conceive the second, bigamous marriage
as valid without dissolving the first. To admit the validity of bigamous Christian marriage in even a single case opens the possibility of multiple simultaneous marriages—which is to say, of polyamory.

Calvin was equally engaged with questions of polygyny, though not with
such counsel to prominent Calvinists. For Calvin, as for Thomas, the controlling biblical texts lie on either side of the Israelite patriarchs, either in
Genesis 2 : 24 or in the New Testament. Calvin applies to Israelite polygyny the sort of explanation Matthew's Jesus applies to Israelite divorce: it
was God's concession to hardness of heart. Permission given to the patriarchs was entirely superseded by the law of Christ or, rather, of Paul.[27]
These arguments were not hypothetical. They were required both by
Calvin's binding Christians with much Old Testament law and by challenges
from more radical reformers. When Calvin's associate Theodore Beza devoted a whole treatise to polygamy, he had before him the claims and practices of Anabaptists.[28]

Polygamy has been an exegetical crux for Christian theology. It has also
been continuously imagined as a necessary boundary on the other side of
which stood heretical Christians or nefarious non-Christians—including,
in recent centuries, the "pagans" or "heathens" of missionary lands.[29] There
was a tradition, cited by Augustine and Thomas, that one of the original
Christian deacons was a polygynist. The practice is an original deviation in
Christian erotic arrangements that is repeated through the centuries. So
polygamy—or polyamory, or mere swapping—figures in innumerable
descriptions of heretical groups. In orthodox imagination, heretics are typically inclined to polyamory and orgies—and to seduction, masturbation,
sodomy, pederasty, and bestiality. Sexual license is a distinguishing feature
of heretics, because sexual restraint is, of course, the distinguishing feature
of the orthodox.

Some heretical or marginal groups may have invoked the example of the
Israelite patriarchs. American religious groups certainly did, the first Mormons chief among them.[30] Indeed, American law still records polygamy as
a place where there can be no freedom of religion—not even by appeal to
biblical precedent. Still there is a more important theological point: Even
if it were admitted, the precedent of the Israelite patriarchs would be very
limited. On traditional Christian understandings, the patriarchs could
authorize nothing more than polygyny for reproductive ends. While this

is enough to undo dogmatic claims on behalf of natural law or of a single Judeo-Christian tradition, it is not enough to authorize reconceiving erotic relationships, for however many partners, as equal and affectional arrangements.

The ghosts of the patriarchs are ghosts of patriarchy. You can see this in large asymmetries and in legislative details. For example, the Mishnah sets the number of wives according to a man's wealth, up to a limit of five.[31] Rich men could not have more than five wives because they would then compete with the king, who was allowed eighteen. The restriction cannot be understood simply as a requirement for adequate support. It is sumptuary legislation, a restriction on any ostentatious display that might detract from royal power. The number of wives is a sign of status and a luxury. The primary basis of the multipartner relation does not seem to be an ideal of expansive affection.

The patriarchs are not an ample precedent for polyamory, but they may point to one, precisely because they have sometimes been used to distract attention from it. If some marginal or dissenting groups invoked the patriarchs, many justified their behavior by appeal to Christian notions of love or agapic community, often in connection with Eucharistic practice or direct inspiration by the Holy Spirit. Think how often charges of debauchery are linked by patristic authors to disordered Eucharists or agapic suppers.[32] Think of the claims of Spirit-led marriages in sixteenth-century Anabaptist groups.[33] The most unsettling calls for Christian polyamory are not appeals to the Israelite patriarchs. They are exhortations to indiscriminate life in the Spirit of Christian love. The Old Law proves less disconcerting to monogamous marriage than the New.

The most urgent challenge for Christian marital theology has been to prevent the universality of the agapic feast from reaching erotic relationships — how to prevent agapic community from enactment as erotic community. Christianity is latent polyamory. The cycling return of the patriarchs — the need for their repeated disavowal as historical precedent — distracts from more anxious issues underneath mainstream views of Christian marriage and so underneath current quarrels over the blessing of same-sex unions. When same-sex unions are imagined as suspiciously unbounded erotic relationships, they call up theological scripts developed to rebut the challenge of polygamy and (more urgently) to delimit unbounded Christian love, agape itself.

The old fear of agapic excess shoots through debates over church blessings for same-sex unions, which are fantasized as intrinsically polyamorous. As pictured by Christian orthodoxies, unrestricted queer desire disrupts the tidy fiction that sex has been managed — has been captured and categorized—by admitting marriage into the Christian church on a kind of perpetual probation. To bless open relationships that will not agree to abide by the fiction would undo the fiction for everyone. Queer relationships, so far as they are presumed to be "open," do destroy Christian marriage in this sense, that they destroy cherished fictions about what it has accomplished. The chief theological accomplishment of Christian marriage is supposed to be that it settles the ancient enmity between eros and agape by granting a restricted title for eros within the universal field of agape.[34] "You can exercise eros so long as you do so with the minimum number of *other* (!) people—namely, one." To increase that minimum number at all throws the truce into doubt. Traditional Christian marriage theology relies at its core on an ascetic imperative, not a model of procreation or social order. To moderate the imperative is to undermine it. Hence early churches emphasized the rule about one wife over the span of a lifetime.[35] Of course, Christian churches long ago mitigated that principle—by permitting remarriage after the death of a spouse or after annulment or after no-fault divorce or . . . The bad conscience of the churches over these incoherent accommodations is projected onto debates over blessing same-sex unions. As so often in Christian history, queer desire must bear the burdens of desire simply.

Intellectual hygiene, if nothing else, requires greater candor. Christian theologians would think more clearly if they would admit that they have a polyamory problem not just with the patriarchs, but with the Eucharistic table and the Spirit that has been poured out into their hearts (Rom. 5 : 5). Jesus practiced the sharing of meals with disgraced or ritually impure individuals. The special meal that Jesus is remembered as instituting, the meal that became the Christian Eucharist, is table-sharing pushed to the limit. The feasting table without edges is linked in many Christian liturgies with unsettling claims about the food for the feast. "Take it . . . this is my body." "This is my blood, the blood of the covenant, poured out for many."[36] The indiscriminate feast is the joining of many, body to body, regardless of sex, with the one-and-many body of Jesus, from whose sex Christology has been a long and terrified flight. Joining bodies promiscuously is the great Christian Mystery. So any Christian advocacy of monogamous marriage will necessarily have its anxieties—not to say, its burden of proof. Efforts at restricting the feast of Christian love will always be interrupted by the memorial and anticipation of another feast in the Eucharist, the meal of the new paradise, the Wedding Feast of the apocalyptic Lamb. As an anticipation of the end of time, the Eucharist threatens to remind Christians of time's beginning and so of the original arrangements for human relationships.

POLYAMOROUS FUTURES

Behind the polygyny of the patriarchs lies the story of the Garden of Eden, so often invoked by Christian writers against them. According to many traditional interpretations, Adam and Eve fell from Paradise because of a sexual transgression. Eve's consorting with the serpent does look to be a sort of adultery, even if she did tell Adam about it immediately. One result of the sin was that the two humans recognized their nakedness, whatever exactly they had done and whoever exactly was to blame. Behind patriarchal families lies an original story that links disobedience to a third party as well as to shame, deceit, and desire. The backdrop of patriarchal polygamy is a failed sexual prohibition curiously if tacitly linked to monogamy.

Adam and Eve are the only humans in the Garden. They are the only humans around—or so it seems until we get to Genesis 4:14, where Cain fears violence from a larger human population. To speak of Adam or Eve as monogamous is then oddly inappropriate. They could not be anything but monogamous unless they were to engage in bestiality, which is another way to describe Eve's lapse. Their solitude led to various speculations in Jewish tradition. There is the rabbinic suggestion, for example, that Adam had to have two faces and two sexes before Eve was taken out of his side. Otherwise there would have been no source for her femininity. Something more radical than this possibility is explored in contemporary fiction, where Edenic innocence is taken to mean honest sexual relations with as many other humans, of any gender, as one wants to include. In the canonical version of the Garden, Eve happened to be the only other one available. Polyamory was impossible as a matter of fact. In principle, so the fictions seem to suggest, there could have been more.

Sexually radical speculative fiction often imagines other stories than the tale of the Fall. It presents future worlds or alternate ones in which human sex has never been marked by sin. Omnisexual and multipartner relations are typical, if not normative. Sometimes the reversal of the Genesis account is quite explicit. Starhawk's *The Fifth Sacred Thing* imagines San Francisco as a new Garden built in resistance to the totalitarian regime of the corporate-evangelical Stewards. The Garden is rich in religious rituals held together by neopagan tolerance. Its erotic relationships are equally eclectic. One of the male protagonists, Bird, tries to explain it to an outsider, Littlejohn, a young man with whom he has been sleeping in the Stewards' prisons near Los Angeles. "When I say my family, I mean all my lovers and all their lovers and kids and ex-lovers and everyone—and half of them are faggots, at least half the time. We consider it a word to be proud of."[37] Littlejohn still worries that he will be viewed jealously if he returns with

Bird to San Francisco. Bird denies it: "I'm not saying nobody ever gets jealous. But we work it out" (87). Later, when Bird returns (alone) to San Francisco, his first sexual encounter is heterosexual and coupled (124). After all, his love for a particular woman helped guide him through perils back to the city—in the best tradition of romance. A bit later, however, Bird takes part in a properly erotic ritual that includes one other man and three women (including his main love). Bird feels no jealousy when the chance presents itself, only a moment's uncertainty whether he is actually being invited to join. He does. "The dance went on until each had been healed and renewed. The skylight in the ritual room was beginning to glow blue with dawn light when they pulled blankets from the corner, curled up in a pile, and fell asleep" (146). Love in the (new) Garden.

Starhawk's stories include Christian elements, but they are not preeminent. More interesting Edenic visions come from writers who (sometimes) claim a Christian identity—who have been queer activists in religious settings. For example, a more deliberately scriptural retelling of erotic life without the Fall is Toby Johnson's *Secret Matter*. Its denouement is the revelation that it really has been the story of Eden without the Fall, of a parallel universe in which the human choice to eat the forbidden fruit was countered by a choice not to taste it. The inhabitants of that garden cannot lie because they show their emotions, including sexual arousal, quite literally on their skins. They also have a reproductive physiology in which females conceive whenever they achieve orgasm in heterosexual intercourse. So "heterosexual intercourse became a sacred act for them—engaged in a ritual context—and homosexual sex became the basis for relationship and for recreational sex."[38] The homoerotic relations or recreations are apparently expected to admit multiple partners and to avoid jealousy, as the (fallen human) protagonist concludes when he tries to understand the behavior of his (unfallen "Visitor") boyfriend. "He was again aware of how strange it was to be with somebody who lived in openness and innocence" (126). Edenic innocence is erotic "openness" in the slang sense: it makes for open relationships.

Sally Miller Gearhart's *Wanderground* is more mixed as imagination and as theology.[39] Its Eden is a community of lesbian separatists who are trying to heal the earth after it has been poisoned by patriarchy. "Love men? The idea did not fit. It was uncomfortable and backwards in her mind" (2). There are still men on the planet, but most of them are trapped in decaying, totalitarian cities; neither their machines nor their penises function properly outside them. A few other men, "gentles" or "unmanly men" who "touched no women at all" because they recognize that male touch is inherently violent, live both in the cities and outside (2, 172). Inside they have male lovers; outside, they seem grateful for impotence (148, 168). The "essential fundamental knowledge" of gender is that "women and men cannot yet, maybe not ever, love one another without violence; they are no longer of the same species" (152). The separated women of the Wander-ground go forward in remaking Eden: they have already learned to fly and to talk with animals. They are also suspicious of exclusive, dyadic relations. They recognize that "first bonds are very taut," but after them they en-courage more fluid erotic couples, though they still describe the partners in them as "lovers" (92, 29). The intense grief felt by a woman at the ap-proaching death of her former lover elicits this gloss: "[Grief] used to be quite common among us. Some of us still occasionally felt it, but it's counted a product of possessiveness" (245). The antidote to possessiveness, to the tight couple, is administered by the telepathic and ritual uniting of the whole community.

Gearhart's novel also divides Christianity into female and male versions, peaceful and violent. There were once "vigilante Christian groups who pa-trolled the parks with clubs looking for queers" (111). "People, particu-larly religious fanatics, were outraged against the women" (200). Yet "Les-bian Priest" appears in a flashback of headlines illustrating the women's progress (185). Christian terms have also carried over into the Wander-ground's language, though their original meaning has been forgotten: "This was the grace-making, the creation of extra attention and love, either to-ward one woman or toward a number of them. Zephyr did not understand what *grace* meant: it was now an archaic word" (157). The women's central council turns out to be "Long Dozen" (160), members of an apostolic col-lege. And so on. If Toby Johnson's Eden is a parallel world, Gearhart's is a separate, half-world in which the liberating elements of Christianity have been taken up by a religion of the creation, of earth herself.

These two utopian visions rewrite biblical materials so that Paradise be-comes polyamorous. Notice in them a feature in much fiction that prides itself on imagining queer relationships beyond or after Christianity. How much persists through the "after"—say, in the very preoccupations brought to sex? Gayle Rubin asked long ago why contemporary debate privileges specific questions in evaluating sexual relations.[40] We can certainly ask that about our preoccupation with number: restricting to the couple and des-perately wanting to get beyond the couple. The ghosts of Christian theol-ogy that produce the preoccupation don't advocate nonfamilial universal love or yearn for an agapic feast. These ghosts whisper pliant accommoda-tion to reproductive and property schemes. Sex-radical fiction finds itself haunted by Christian theology at its worst, by the ideology of Christendom. The surest sign is the way that polyamory is both thought and practiced in relation to the couple.[41]

Given the historical development of Christian cultures, the couple appears to many after Christendom as the obvious unit of erotic thinking and so the standard against which polyamory has to be justified. It would not be so obvious in Christian theology if one took seriously the latent universality of agape or remembered that the revolutionary call of the Gospel is never primarily to couples or families. Since the eschatological assembly of the church supersedes the biological family, eschatological rethinking of human relations need not begin with the couple. The long effort to contain sex within monogamous marriages was an effort, not a certainty. Yet the efforts of Christendom's history live on after Christendom. The imagination of polyamory in cultures "after" Christendom is spooked by the couple. The couple still constrains both imagination and life.

The best way to chase off the couple might seem some absolute version of radical agape or radical eros (at their convergence), one that would reject my definition of polyamory as "relatively stable" relationships of some defined number in favor of perfect, transient universality. Why draw any boundaries around eros? The boundaries are drawn, not so much by my definition, or even by the finitude of bodies in their circumstances of place and time, as by the imagination of the space of the erotic encounter. Defenses of the broadest queer love also suppose the boundary of some community—as do the most generous conceptions of the agapic feast. Kathy Rudy argues that gay sexual-social life, in at least some of its varieties, may follow a model that is "fundamentally communal" rather than bound within committed, monogamous relationships.[42] The operative word is "communal," which is not the same as "universal." For example, Rudy's analogies between radical agape and anonymous sex in bathhouses emphasize that no names are needed because of the strong sense of shared community. "Sex in these communities is completely relational because it functions as a way of inscribing memories into an identity larger than the individual."[43] Quite so, but the identity is marked off in turn against other identities and other communities. Again, when Eric Rofes argues against imposing heterosexual models of family on queer lives, he falls back not only on the notion of the "gay friendship network," but on the creation of "meaningful bonds of intimacy and affection within the broader gay tribe."[44] A tribe is precisely not universal.

Free love is bounded more than ever by a strong sense of the community's distinctive space, not to speak of its norms for sexual attraction, both implicit and explicit. After a while, dogmatically promiscuous gay men tend toward a select group of sexual partners, in fact or in cherished imagination. Actual promiscuity is circumscribed by an ideal Mr. Right, My Type, the Perfect Circuit Boy/Twink/Bear, which only rarely gets expanded so far as an ideal set of Buddies, a Troop. You could empty the shelves of gay pornographic novels by removing every book that dreams erotic perfection in one elusive partner. The couple persists into multipartner arrangements as their origin, center, or fantasized end. It is the origin, because multipartner relations often appear as a second stage after the "failure" of a monogamous relationship. It is the center, because an erotic couple (or formerly erotic couple) often remains at the core of any more complex picture of erotic networks. It is the end, because the sweet song of Romance still plays through many open trysts.

Kathy Labriola proposes a typology of "open relationships."[45] She distinguishes three main models: primary/secondary relationships, multiple primary partners, and multiple nonprimary relationships. Each model has variations or subtypes. The primary/secondary model comprises couples who bring in outsiders for sexual activity or who agree that each partner may seek outside sexual relationships, usually subject to certain conditions and vetoes. The model of multiple primary partners includes both sexually exclusive group marriages and nonexclusive arrangements that grant much more autonomy to individual partners. Labriola's multiple nonprimary relationships resemble what many people think of as single life: intermittent if continuing contacts with two or more regular lovers in which there are few commitments and no preemptive claims.

I have been using *polyamory* restrictively to name relatively stable arrangements of more than two partners in which there are negotiated covenants about sexual or emotional exclusivity. I distinguish open relationships from polyamorous relationships partly to pursue possibilities for Christian blessing on multiple partners and partly to notice how quickly the ghost of the couple returns whenever we begin to think about group marriages. The couple appears not only as the origin of polyamorous relationships, but as their recurring temptation and unit of power. We can miss both the theological issues and the power regimes when we combine the transience of "open relations" in the same category with what I want to set off as polyamory.

Let me illustrate the concerns and the difference in terminology with a story about what Labriola would call the primary/secondary model. Two people try hard to be a sexually exclusive couple. After growing dissatisfactions and a few adulteries, deftly or clumsily concealed, the couple decides that it must either separate or else contrive another arrangement. For some heterosexual couples, the new arrangement may be "swapping" with another couple.[46] For others, as for many same-sex couples, the new arrangement means bringing in a third.[47] Sometimes a couple decides to bring in a third for a single night or repeat visits—to have "three-ways" with mutually agreeable outsiders. They may continue in this arrangement over years or else turn toward an officially open relationship in which the partners have sex sometimes together, sometimes separately, with a shifting range of others. In my definition, polyamory begins when a temporary or transient third is invited into more permanent status. That is the difference in terminology. Here is the point it allows me to make: In these relatively stable arrangements, the newly arrived member is often subordinated to the original and abiding couple, so that the primacy of the couple as quasi-metaphysical unit remains intact even within polyamory.

Consider a published account by Jim Marks.[48] Jim and Nick had been together as a couple for ten years, cohabiting and pooling financial resources. During that time, Jim began at least two serious relations with other men, each of which disrupted the coupled arrangement with Nick (144). Then Jim met Brian and fell in love a third time. He decided that he would introduce Brian to Nick and try combining the loves rather than letting his life "be divided into two camps" (138). Once Brian was introduced, the three men began a shared affective and sexual relationship, spending every few nights together and traveling even to family gatherings as an unexplained trio (140, 145–46). After three and a half years, Brian moved in with Jim and Nick (148). Did this mean that the original dyad was dissolved in favor of a new triad? Not exactly. Sometimes in the narrative Brian appears as the child of Jim and Nick, a rambunctious adolescent or "'our baby'" (144). He is helped to find jobs, to get through tough times, and even to date other men. "He gives us someone to worry about and to help out" (148). Jim cooks and Nick does the laundry, but Brian's chore is to keep the two of them "entertained" (148). Symbolically, the three are joined in a "marriage" of equals when they get cross-referenced tattoos in San Francisco (149). Yet the relationship as described is that of an older and financially secure couple adopting a young man of different economic and social class. This may be polyamory, but it is polyamory in the shadow of the couple.

Relationships in which a third is added to a strong original couple might in fact be understood more exactly as forms of concubinage. For Christendom, concubinage has been contrasted with legal or full marriage and has sometimes been justified in view of procreation. If *concubinage* means more generally a secondary relation entered into for sexual or emotional satisfactions not found in the primary couple, then many multipartner relations among men could be reclassified as concubinage. They would appear as

variations on older models in which well-established gay men take on a
"protégé"—or in which prosperous husbands support mistresses over
many years. Such relations might raise other questions about the importance of socially enforced gradients of power in multipartner relations. Too
often heterosexual polyamory has meant polygyny, in which an older,
wealthier, more powerful male controls the sexual or emotional exchanges
within an erotic network of women. A two-plus-one arrangement among
men can be the same sort of male-prerogative adapted to the more strait-
ened circumstances of middle-class gay life. Relative economic privilege is
one prerequisite for experimenting with erotic arrangements beyond the
couple or within the household.[49]

It could be argued that two-plus-one arrangements among men do mark
an important stage. So far as they are acknowledged, at least within gay
circles, they differ from aristocratic or bohemian domestic arrangements
that were purely private. Quite so, but they do not differ from many forms
of recognized concubinage, say in the patriarchs' Israel or Augustine's
Rome. Again, someone might claim that having a three-partner relationship among men undoes many expectations about male gender. To which I
would answer: Wealthy, powerful men, precisely as men, have had rather
visible arrangements with one or more men in the past. Think of foppish
courtiers, of acolytes and seminarians, of artistic protégés. If such arrangements sometimes provoked complaints of degeneracy or effeminacy, at
other times they were tolerated to vindicate an absolute right of male domination. Male privilege, sufficiently exalted, can keep male harems too,
even while retaining its compatibility with official heterosexuality.

I don't want to generalize about all two-plus-one relationships, much
less to judge them. I certainly don't want to judge the relationship Marks
describes. I am reflecting on his text, not on his life. My point is that
polyamory just by itself does not make for revolutionary equality. It may
not even be revolutionary. Polyamory, especially when it is built from a
couple out, may carry forward the power relations in and around the
couple. Negotiating power relations can be pleasurable, as inhabiting them
can be consoling or sustaining. Unacknowledged power relations can be
damaging, especially when carried by something so infused with power-
through-sex as the couple.

Polyamory beyond the couple's shadow requires more egalitarian arrangements from the beginning. Examples might be found in the early liberationist communes. Consider the account by John Knoebel of New York's
"95th Street Collective," "the first gay male living collective in the country."[50] Knoebel was twenty-two and only a few months "out" when he
joined the collective in July 1970 (301). The collective itself was then

barely a month old, and it would last only six (301, 303). On strict com-
munitarian principles, the members of the collective were supposed to have
erotic relations with every other member of the group: "We knew we
should in theory, but theory was not supported by our feelings" (306). In
practice, most of the members had little sex; when they did, it was with men
outside the collective and on the assumption of transience (303, 306).
Within the group, much effort was spent on consciousness-raising and other
exercises to overcome barriers to perfectly shared eros. The collective fell
into crisis when a new member, Lane, started an exclusive sexual relationship with another member, Robert (310–11). The relationship not only di-
verted energy from the drill of sexual retraining, it raised scandalous walls
of privacy: the two wanted one of the bedrooms for their separate use. After much group criticism of the relationship, Robert was given an imperative and left. Lane, who had joined later, broke with Robert to stay on. Still
the damage was done. The collective unraveled.

What is the moral of the cautionary tale? Some might find in it a vindi-
cation of monogamy and its privacies—or at least of the capriciousness of
erotic taste and its resistance to political dictates. According to Knoebel,
the lesson is not that the principle of erotic community was wrong: "I do
not consider the failure of the collective to work out its internal contradictions an indication that the group process is a failure, or that I don't have to
struggle anymore to change myself" (315). There were circumstances
enough to scuttle the social experiment, including the youth of the participants, their newness to public gay life, and the brevity of their time together. Absent external compulsions and lifelong training in ideals of
romantic monogamy, how many heterosexual marriages between newly
sexual twenty-somethings would survive six months? But this hypothetical
question reveals a more fundamental problem: In assessing radical socio-
sexual rearrangements, what could it mean to carry out a convincing
experiment?

So long as the underlying religious or social imaginary remains un-
changed, any failure can be attributed to its tenacious grip. Having been
trained in coupled heterosexuality, most contemporary Americans are of
course likely to do badly (or, rather, worse) at anything else. As Knoebel
writes, "Surely we saw that the homosexual experiences of each of us had
consisted of . . . relationships that always ended because people were victims of their romantic illusions, clung to untenable role-playing, were ir-
responsible to one another, or simply failed to understand that relationships
must be worked at and not assumed. All of this could be traced largely to
our oppression as gay men" (307). The failure of polyamorous queer com-

munities may not vindicate monogamous heterosexuality so much as disclose its reach over those who try to escape it.

Many Christians will want to retreat from the uncertainty of such testimonies and countertestimonies to some basic moral or liturgical principles. It is one thing for people to join threesomes or collectives, they might conclude, but it is something else entirely for theologians to justify them or churches to bless them. It becomes the more interesting, then, to remember not just the longer history of Christianity's entanglement with polyamory, but the more recent advocacy for polyamory by Christians or Christian groups. To my knowledge, the only denomination with an organized polyamory caucus or subgroup is the Unitarian Universalist Association (UUA). The group holds meetings, both national and regional, and maintains a website.[51] This is one of dozens of public polyamory sites on the web. They combine education or mutual reinforcement with a sort of switchboard or dating service. The single UU organization can remind us that a number of Christians, including ordained clergy, practiced or advocated polyamory in the 1960s and 1970s as part of liberating experiments. Gay men were hardly the only groups attempting to live in absolute community or to renegotiate received gender roles and erotic expectations. In the 1970s, a number of books appeared advocating polyamory or open relationships on Christian grounds.[52] The communities may have dissolved and the public renegotiations collapsed under the leaden weight of America's conservatism, but a number of people carried forward or retrieved the notion of Christianity as a warrant for alternate relationships.[53]

The notion of a Christian warrant for polyamorous relationships can perhaps explain some of the liturgical experiments of recent years. When I taught a course on same-sex unions at a national theological school, our most heated discussions concerned a draft ceremony for blessing a leather household of several men, one of whom was to be addressed as "boy." The heat was fueled not by disagreements over polyamory, but by concerns over violence and domination. When the members of the seminar were asked to agree on criteria for a Christian blessing on relationship, number of partners did not figure as a criterion. Most members of the seminar were studying for ordination in one or another Christian denomination. I would consider our conversations fantastical (in the way classroom talk often is) were it not for actual liturgical improvisations in the face of multipartner relations. Metropolitan Community Church (MCC) and UUA congregations do receive requests to bless multipartner relations. Sometimes they respond favorably. Again, the rite of hand-fasting has sparked new interest among Christians not only because it permits term relationships, but because it remains indefinite about the number of those who can be bound together.

What then are the theological objections to blessing multipartner relations? Some traditional objections have already appeared in the sample of classic responses to patriarchal polygyny, but they were often combined in confusing or contradictory ways. There are also objections not invoked by the texts mentioned; they deserve restatement and reconsideration. Here I can only consider four principal objections, ancient and modern. Those objections are from procreation, adultery, asceticism, and intimacy.

The objection against multipartner unions from *procreation* is the most obvious and perhaps the most absolute: Multipartner relations violate the principles of well-ordered procreation. The objection is related to a grander principle that any moral use of the genitals must remain open to procreation. The grander principle, literally interpreted, rules out not only same-sex activities that involve the genitals, but masturbation, oral sex, and artificial or (to my mind) "natural" means of contraception.[54] If the principle stands unmodified in its most literal sense, then no same-sex erotic relations ought to be blessed in churches. Of course, the principle does not stand unmodified in any Christian denomination. Churches make exceptions of all sorts, from the marriage of sterile couples or the teaching of "natural family planning" to approval for masturbation and oral sex. I might also add, at the risk of being captious, that an argument from procreation does not by itself rule out multipartner relations in which many men are copulating with many women. To prohibit those relations, some other principle must be invoked. Thomas Aquinas appealed to certainty of offspring to rule out polyandry, but he had no stronger argument against polygyny than the alleged example of nature and a plea from equity. It is hard to contrive a procreative argument that rules out polygyny so long as the sole husband can take good care of the children of his multiple wives. The limit would be set here, as for a monogamous marriage with many children, by material, psychological, and spiritual limits.

The next theological objection against multipartner relations holds that they somehow *violate the biblical prohibition against adultery,* known to Christians as the sixth commandment. The objection is nonsense historically, given polygynous marriages in Israel. The Israelites obviously thought having multiple wives was not an act of adultery. The objection also raises other embarrassing questions about the commandment. Is the gist of the adultery prohibition more than property rights, lineage, and deceit? What if procreation is not an issue and there is no deceit? Or what if we conceive children not as a means for transmitting name and property, not as extensions of the self, but as gifts of God who come into our care entirely apart from dynastic ambitions or ego-gratification?

The reading of the sixth commandment is further complicated for Christians by a saying attributed to Jesus in the canonical Gospels. In Matthew, and as part of a string of contrasts between prevailing religious practice and the divine standard, Jesus says, "You have heard that it was said, 'Do not commit adultery.' But I say to you that every man looking at a woman so as to desire her has already committed adultery with her in his heart" (5:27–28). The dominical saying, taken literally, reinterprets the commandment as applying to all (unmarried? heterosexual?) erotic desire. It combines with systematic pressures to bring every species of sexual sin under the meaning of this commandment. The commandment then becomes the site for constructing whole treatises against sensuous self-indulgence, from soft towels to bestiality. The enormous expansion can only cause trouble. It ignores the plain sense of the Hebrew text to project a sexual morality constructed on other bases. The sixth commandment is taken to prohibit sexual immorality without giving any guidance about how to define it. One might do better to interpret Jesus' saying in other ways— say, as a challenge not to restrict sexual morality to external acts.

Read expansively, the commandment against adultery rehearses Christianity's *ascetic complaint against all sexual activity*. It objects further against blessing polyamory by condemning it as undisciplined pleasure. The ascetic argument, like the expanded commandment on adultery, is an elastic clause that can cover any number of acts. It is a screen onto which mutating valuations, personal or collective, get projected. On a scale from no sex to profligacy, different Christian commentators draw the line of licit sex at very different points. Some object to polyamory as too much pleasure. Other Christians object to remarriage after the death of a spouse. Others still reject marriage altogether. The objection against multipartner relations is merely a cipher for the contentious and cycling history of Christian sexual prohibition. Emphasizing sexual prohibition diverts attention from more important ascetic practices. I have no doubt that Christian living requires discipline of the senses, but I wonder whether sexual denial is now the most urgent discipline. Resisting advertising or restricting hours spent before television screens or computer monitors might be a more significant and arduous ascetic practice than restricting the number of one's sexual partners. So too the urgent Christian discipline for sex might be to engage in it generously and attentively rather than greedily and abstractly, with one's partner or partners rather than with today's selection from an Internet gallery of images.

A final objection against polyamorous relations, often presented as the-ological, is an argument from the *psychology of intimacy:* human beings can only be truly intimate with one person at one time. The claim is usually enunciated so broadly that it applies equally or more emphatically to the single and "promiscuous" than to the polyamorous. Most arguments against "casual" sex now reduce to the claim that engaging in it violates, exhausts, or damages a limited and fragile capacity. Often the claim is not supported by any evidence, theological or secular. It can sound like either a confession or an expression of envy. At other times, the evidence is tendentious or faulty. The capacity for intimacy with multiple partners is probably another human characteristic liable to considerable variation—and one that has hardly been given public scope for exploration. Anecdotal evidence from male-male relations suggests as wide a range of abilities and experiences with intimacy involving multiple partners as with a single one. Some people do it well; others, badly.

While reviewing four objections against recognizing multipartner re-lations in church, I have kept one topic deliberately to the side: child-rearing. Until recently, it has not much figured in public discussions of same-sex relationships, which were presumed to be intrinsically infer-tile. Advances in reproductive technology have challenged the presump-tion. They have also brought into public view older forms of queer child-rearing, whether the children came to the same-sex relationship from a prior marriage or by adoption. The presence of children has suddenly sup-plied opponents of queer multipartner relations with one of the staple ar-guments against straight polyamory: It cannot be good for the children. This argument clearly disregards the evidence of the Hebrew Bible—or else it supposes that God authorized reproductive arrangements that were not good for children born into them. The scriptural evidence is not enough, of course, to address a range of questions about raising children in contemporary arrangements with multiple partners. The questions are worth pursuing further, especially because they are the only respect in which I will consider the issues of childbearing and child-rearing.

CHILDREN BEYOND PROCREATION

One of the oldest arguments against gay unions has been that male-male couples are ludicrously nonprocreative.[55] Various replies have been made, from noticing that churches have allowed nonprocreative marriage in other instances to expanding the notion of procreation into spiritual and creative realms.[56] Now the old argument from the infertility of gay couples sounds curiously outdated, because gay couples are having children "of their own."

The facts of queer families have changed the terms of arguments for all families, not least by showing how complicated family facts have always been.

Children were never as tightly tied to marriage as the marriage movement sometimes professes to believe. If Christian marriage was often justified for the sake of having children, it could hardly be forgotten that marriage was never a prerequisite for conceiving or delivering them. Procreation may have justified marriage, but marriage was never a requirement for procreation. It is equally clear that people now labeled as queer have long been engaged in birthing and raising children. The obvious example is provided by lesbians and gays in heterosexual relations who became mothers and fathers. Often enough, after a death or a divorce, these "natural" parents kept on with the care of their children as they entered into same-sex erotic relations with one or another degree of explicitness. This is only the obvious example. The history of Christendom is full of children entrusted to spinster aunts or bachelor uncles, not to mention children given as "oblates" to same-sex religious communities or abandoned at the doors of religiously sponsored orphanages. Christian communities have tolerated or approved many arrangements by which the unmarried and the queer raised children.

Contemporary arrangements for same-sex adoption or *in vitro* fertilization must be understood against a complicated history. Same-sex individuals or couples may press against the boundaries of reproductive technology or "black-market" services. The results they obtain often push the boundaries of religious law as well. Still, the issues of queer parenting are not some brave new world for which there are no antecedents whatever. Christian social history records many same-sex couples or communities who raised children, as Christian legend and hagiography remember many miraculous births in defiance of ordinary reproductive biology. It is only when Christian morality gets confused with a particular scheme of "nature" that theologians forget how often Christian families have played with and against biology. Queer unions only remind Christians how tenuous the link between marriage and reproduction has always been.

In the opposite direction, gay fathers and lesbian mothers pose sharp questions for queer relationships. The most distinctive public images for same-sex coupling don't make much room for children, as the most heavily marketed queer scripts have not included parenting. Much will have to be rethought and reinvented. There are dangers to be avoided. Acknowledging that queer adults have and raise children can become quickly enough an occasion for once again regulating queer relationships. One sign of this is the way in which children have been used by church officials as grounds for extending tacit recognition to their parents. For example, some church officials have conceded that social benefits might be extended to same-sex couples for the sake of their children—but only according to approved definitions of what the children need. In the same way, state permission for adoption by same-sex couples imposes on them a standard of stability and suitable home life much higher than that required of heterosexual couples that marry to have children. Adoption is regulated for all couples in a way that a first marriage hardly ever is. The "best interest of the child" is a conduit through which queer couples are brought under state control and churchly schemes of sexual regulation.

There are reasons for concern here, but interesting possibilities as well. Queer parenting can treat child-rearing as a good in its own right, distinct both from dynastic transfer and the dictates of eros. It separates child-rearing from dynastic transfer because children are often given to queer parents against the ordinary notions of social continuity. For example, states typically permit same-sex couples only to adopt "unwanted" or "difficult" children—children of the "wrong" age, race, family background, or medical condition. Queer adoptions are bridges across social locations. Children are also raised by queer parents apart from or in opposition to the alignments of eros. Frequent divorce in other-sex marriages has already weakened any connection between erotic relation and co-parenting. Mother and father may barely be on speaking terms, much less sleeping with each other. Mother has her new partner or partners, female or male, and father his. Queer couples or groups weaken the connection between eros and child-rearing even more. I know of one arrangement in which two women and two men are raising two boys. The two women are erotic partners, as are the two men. The boys were born from one of the women by donation from one of the men. They live mostly with their mothers but are raised by all four. So far as a friend can tell, the only special problems for child-rearing have come from external social disapproval and legal invisibility. In this case and others like it, erotic bonds do not underwrite or specify parental roles or legal relationships.

Queer parenting encourages candor about the great variety of relationships in which children have been raised and raised well. Some would object immediately that the issue is precisely whether children can be raised well except by one father and one mother held together in a permanent, sexually exclusive relationship. I make only two replies. The first is that the huge range of familial patterns across time and place requires that the objection produce proof. It cannot be considered self-evident that the ideal pattern for children's flourishing is one father and one mother in a nuclear household. When the claim does appear as self-evident, that says more about the prejudices prevailing in certain cultural circles than about the evidence of human history.[57] The second reply is that an ideal need not exclude alternate arrangements. Even if one father/one mother were the Christian ideal (which it is not), it would not be the only permissible arrangement among Christians for child-rearing. To argue otherwise is to suggest that Christian churches have erred repeatedly and often in permitting other arrangements—not to say, in building orphanages. If one father and one mother proves to be the best (which I continue to doubt), multiple fathers and mothers may be a close second.

Queer parenting cannot preclude queer polyamory. It may indeed reinforce it in unexpected ways.

POLYAMOROUS CHARACTERS

Buzzing controversies over the meaning of adultery or the desirability of complex parenting can turn attention away from a basic question raised by polyamory. The question is announced and concealed in the very phrase "same-sex relationship." What are the terms or poles of the relationship? Are they two bodies with the "same" genital configuration? Two scripts for erotic satisfaction? Two homoerotic "identities" or characters? Or two "persons," with all the metaphysics that oscillating term contains? To the extent that debates over blessing same-sex unions take these questions as trivial or easily settled, they encourage the debaters to misunderstand erotic life.

Here I reprise one "activist" question about blessing unions. Will the blessing of unions become a new principle of fixity in erotic roles? Must it regulate gender or sex under a new regime of "acceptance"? There is good reason to fear that incorporating same-sex relationships within an ancient system for regulating erotic life might do so. The poverty of official Christian imagination when it comes to sex hardly encourages people to sign up for Christian erotic supervision. It is as if someone in a silent film were beckoning the viewer to enter: "Leave your world of vivid color and ravishing sound to join us in mute black-and-white." So with many liberal and accepting invitations to queer Christians: "Welcome! Translate your erotic life into pidgin—just as we were forced to do!"

My gamble all along has been that incorporating queer sex explicitly into Christian discourses might disrupt them enough to vivify them. The disruption is most significant not in specific acts or arrangements, but in whole bodies, characters, and persons. "Same-sex relationship" is not the name for an exception that needs to be incorporated into the rules of Christian sex. It is a challenge to those rules. Just here the old issue of polyamory displays its force. Familiar discussions of polyamory fetishize the number of bodies in genital contact: not more than two, for reasons of reproduction, inheritance, asceticism, or scarce intimacy. Counting genitals is a rather reductive view of erotic life. It forgets that many erotic activities do not directly involve the genitals. It overlooks the complex relations between erotic roles or selves and genitals or bodies. *All* erotic relationships, except perhaps the briefest and dullest, are polyamorous. They bring together multiple erotic roles, sexual identities, and real or fictive persons. Freud famously wrote, "I am accustoming myself to the idea of regarding every sexual act as a process in which four persons are involved."[58] To which the obvious rejoinder is: Only four?

The couple can haunt polyamory, but polyamory has already possessed any couple. Here is a quick census from a single case—or, rather, the challenges for a census of even a single case. Imagine two men in the heat of passion. Begin counting with the particular characters that they inhabit, where "character" is used microscopically for the conjunction of gestures, words, looks, costumes, attitudes, and sentiments around sexual "preferences." Sharply drawn characters appear most prominently in the fully scripted encounters associated with S&M or other fetishes, but they appear as well, if less clearly (and often less imaginatively), in all erotic encounters. "Tonight I want to be on the bottom" is not just a plea for a position. It is the overture for the appearance on stage of a character. Each present character recalls by contrast the many not then present. How to count the whole repertory of erotic characters that each man carries? Or the images that each has of the characters of other? Or the figures that populate the partners' fantasies? Or the remembered friends, lovers, enemies who may suddenly appear in mind? I have taken a very easy case: two men in a single moment. If we expand the moment into a decade, we have so many more persons to count. Each man changes through time and holds those changes in memory or anticipation. The two men together may move through generations of shared scripts, with revisions, improvisations, and revolutions. If they try to stick with a single script, it too must change—say, by becoming more freighted with meanings or more stale.

The case of two men across time is still simpler than the case of a man and a woman. Their performance of gendered roles raises the number of characters even further. The polyamory implicit in a gay couple is much easier to map than the polyamory of the standard heterosexual model. Still, comparison is not the important point. Any serious count of characters involved in a continuing erotic relationship, straight or queer, quickly runs into dozens. Why then fetishize the number of bodies in it? Indeed, why not apply Jesus' saying on adultery here too and look not to the number of genitals in physical contact, but to the motions of desire in the beating hearts? If looking at another woman with lust is already adultery, then two persons engaged in intercourse while performing various characters and thinking of other people must already be polyamory.

Traditional theologies have counted bodies because bodies are easier to count and regulate than thoughts. The same logic (or illogic) is applied to same-sex copulations or unions. Yet same-sex relations show the logic's reductive fallacy. Once Christian theology recognizes that two men can legitimately refuse to do what (heterosexual) men are supposed to do, it must soon wonder whether all erotic personae are partly or largely constructions. Constructions are transient: they change in the course of a lifetime and in the succession of generations — not to say, across simultaneous cultures and subcultures. Christian theology will think sex better when it thinks transient performances of bodies and pleasures.

The same might be said of queer dating patterns. The specification of sexual tastes in handkerchief codes or online profiles can look like the exuberance of invention or the convenience of quick communication. A hundred profiles or three dozen handkerchief colors: so many experiments in fashioning erotic personae and practices and inventing shorthand for hooking up with the required partner. They can also be understood, less optimistically, as nostalgia for fixity or a compulsion to deal in brands. Having stepped out of so many roles, the queer man may find himself wanting some fixed script to inhabit. So he describes himself — markets himself — according to a limited list of options. Is that the only way into the future? A menu of choices is a system of regulation.

A sex-menu can succumb to body-counting as easily as Christian theologians do — and often for the same reason: it makes things simpler. That kind of simplification should be resisted as much in online ads or activist exhortation as in Vatican documents. If there is reason to be suspicious of emphasizing the number of bodies in critiques of polyamory, the same suspicion holds in demands for polyamory. "Two people is restrictive (or boring or antirevolutionary)." But it is never just two people: each sexual act involves a crowd. Sometimes the crowd is present in multiple bodies. Sometimes it is present in two bodies — or one. I will continue to talk of couples as a handy abbreviation, but I do not think that the number of bodies determines the number of participants in an erotic bond.

Some discussions of Christian marriage make it seem that a couple's main relation to time is through reproduction. Conceiving and rearing children is the way into the future, with its promises and dangers. Yet change is built into an erotic relationship and the persons who constitute it. A tight cluster of limited personae can, for a time, reduce the appearance of change while it limits the options for erotic expression. The erotic life of a long-term relationship will then be represented as simple continuity, a series of exact repetitions or inversions. The representation will not last long. The dynamics of erotic relation produce change and require it. No grid of roles can prevent this—even with the assistance of the police. It may succeed in attenuating eros between partners to such an extent that love dies. Then eros will appear as the great destroyer of relationships, as the monarchical agent of dissolution. Personae exiled or exhausted, the range of mutually agreed-upon acts run through too many times, the expansiveness of improvisation refused or botched, change becomes divorce.

CHAPTER SEVEN

Ending in Time

The American divorce rate is the prime exhibit for the marriage movement.[1] It is offered as the chief index for the decline of marriage, the fate of children, and the decadence or selfishness of sexual relations. While it is true that the American divorce rate increased from 1 in 10 to 1 in 2 between 1900 and 1990, the rate of marriage dissolution changed much less dramatically. Divorce must be considered alongside other factors in the dissolution of relationships, such as higher mortality rates. Since mortality rates declined sharply as divorce rates rose, the rate at which married unions dissolved looked about the same in 1970 as 1900.[2] By 1980, the combined dissolution rate stood about 25 percent above its century-long base level, but it has dropped back somewhat since. If you turn your eyes from alarmist statistics about divorce to the correlation with longevity, more interesting questions appear. As people live longer, more of them tend to outlive relationships. Divorce now does what earlier death used to do.[3] Does this mean that longer lives tend to encourage narcissism and fickleness or that there is a natural term for intimate relationships, even when they are linked to child-rearing? However one answers the question, the divorce rate by itself is hardly a transparent index of the state of unions.

An increase in the dissolution of relationships is not self-evidently a bad thing. Dissolutions can harm some or all of the parties involved, of course, including children and other dependents. Their consequences run from the psychological or spiritual through the social to the economic. Partners and their dependents are not only displaced, but impoverished or abandoned. The consequences of dissolution can spread widely. If nuclear families are sundered, so are networks of friends and relatives. The damage resulting from a dissolution can be both severe and widely distributed. At the same

time, damage from not dissolving a relationship can often be worse—for
the partners, their children or dependents, their friends and relatives. Is it
better for a child to be kept in a home with an abusive parent than for the
other parent to dissolve the relationship and take the child to safety? Is it
better for a partner to keep living with her or his own abuse rather than to
leave? For that matter, is it better for a partner to stay in an irremediably
empty relationship than to seek one that might give life—or to live in
peace alone?

"Research" reports on the effects of divorce pour out from teams, asso-
ciations, centers, and institutes. Many reports are funded by groups that expect very particular results. Results must fit into a predetermined political
platform or a church teaching. It is difficult to sort reliable from unreliable
reports without being both a psychologist and sociologist who commands a
lot of spare time. Then, again, criteria for determining reliability are hardly
clear. A statistical or clinical investigation of the effects of divorce can raise
awkward questions about moral epistemology and prediction. Is it better
for people to divorce or not? As phrased, the question is both meaningless
and empirically unanswerable. It is meaningless, because an average implies
nothing for the decisions in a particular life. It is empirically unanswerable,
because there is no instrument for measuring "better." Surveys of reported
economic status or self-satisfaction after divorce are summaries of commonplaces. They tell us what people are likely *to say* about their income,
household, or sentiments. They say it to an official stranger and often
enough in highly artificial circumstances. A sample of gossip might tell
more—a literary ethnography of stereotypical locutions after a divorce or
dissolution. If lavishly funded studies are only summarizing speech, better
to have speech with as much of its richness and variety as a sample can contain. The most telling feature of the gossip is the variation-in-repetition of
deeper rhetorical figures, the tacit patterns presupposed by the common-
est complaints and yet rarely given voice in them. A study of rhetorical figures shows the styles of representation available to Americans when they
defend or lament their broken relations.

In Christendom or its successor societies, debates around divorce are
evidently not just about the well-being of those who suffer it. Divorce is the
symbolic opposite of holy relationship. It is the lax antipodes of disciplined
domesticity, the dark Bowery of the sunlit City in which sex is properly ordered for civic ends. Divorce has been the specter against which Christian
marriage idealized itself, the enemy over which it had to triumph. The
symbolic opposition has been strengthened through the claim, anciently
made and habitually modified, that indissolubility was the hallmark of
Christian marriage. For Augustine, to cite only the best-known authority,

pagans and Jews might divorce, but Christians would not.[4] The indissolubility of their marriages would be a testimony of sexual temperance or a
witness to the coming life, but it would also be an analogue to the Great
Marriage between Christ and the Church (Eph. 5 : 32). Rhetorically figured in this way, divorce is at once the opposite of marriage and the undoing of the church. If divorce comes at the end of some marriages between
Christians, it was already there as dreadful opposite in early elaborations of
"Christian marriage."

The grand ideal of divorceless Christian marriage proved unstable from
the beginning. The ideal itself ignored too many of the tensions always
present in the churches around blessing erotic relations. The surviving evidence for Christian practice of marriage in the first millennium would ex-
acerbate those tensions and add new ones. The story of Christian marriage
is not a long slide from an original and absolute monogamy to the present
ease of divorce and remarriage, de jure or de facto, in most Christian
groups. It would be fairer to imagine an unstable cluster of religious ideals
engaged with diverse, mutating social constructions and their enforcing institutions.[5] The religious ideals made compromises with the constructions
and their police, not least because the interpreters of the religious ideals
were always already participants in the constructions—not to say members of the police. Advocating the ideals required one to argue against opposite ideals and to conceal or castigate messy marriage facts within the
churches. Divorce offered a perfect target. Polemic against divorce could
reinforce the unstable ideals by simple dichotomy, but it could also serve as
exhortation to regularize relations within the churches. In Christendom or
after it, the thought of marriage implies the threat of divorce through the
doctrine of indissolubility. Christian rhetoric of marriage insists on the
threat of divorce as its great occasion for admonition and its readiest opportunity for strategic concealment of embarrassing facts.

Male-male unions are the latest version of the threat of divorce. They
condense so many of the standard polemical oppositions. Marriage was created, so the sermon goes, to be the naturally indissoluble union of man and
woman in one flesh (by overreading Gen. 2 : 24). Male-male unions are an
unnatural attempt to unite flesh that cannot be unified—and so they dissolve quickly and violently. Or construct the polemic in the opposite direction: the male homosexual is famously promiscuous and incapable of
sustaining erotic relationships much beyond furtive encounter. So male homosexuals hate stable unions. They love to destroy heterosexual marriages
by attempting to seduce family men. The opposite of this unnatural sinner
is the Christian husband, who is joined to his wife by a naturally indissoluble and abundantly procreative bond. Real men are Christians, and Chris-

tians do not divorce. I caricature the rhetorical scheme, but not by much. Soberer Christian arguments against divorce do not deploy blatant homophobic stereotypes, but so far as they energize the old rhetorical opposition between scandalous divorce and pure Christian marriage, they run alongside homophobia. They rehearse the antinomies into which gay relationships can be too easily inducted as negative case.

The polemic against churchly divorce, in its strong or weak forms, is an attempt to shore up the ideal of permanence while drawing attention away from the always messy realities of actual marriages. Gay relationships are not the last and worst opposite of eternal Christian fidelity. They are the latest in a long series of moments that threaten to expose the limits of an ideal.

CHRISTIAN DIVORCE—AND ITS SURROGATES

So many of the quarrels about blessing same-sex unions in church sound like quarrels over words. The word *marriage* seems to matter more than the relations between people to which it refers. The same is true is of *divorce*. In some Christian groups, the word must be avoided at all costs, whatever the realities of separation and remarriage. In contemporary American Catholicism, for example, the faithful "cannot divorce," except of course that they do. They dissolve their marriages at civil law and then remarry legally. The new marriages are not officially recognized by the church, and persons contracting them are considered to be in serious sin and so unfit to receive communion—at least officially. In practice, and in some parishes, divorced Catholics play active roles and receive communion regularly. If they are willing to tolerate paperwork and invasion of privacy, American Catholics can often secure an annulment from a church tribunal. An annulment declares that their sacramental marriage was never valid because of an essential defect, such as an intention to use contraception indefinitely or a psychological immaturity—or, for that matter, homosexuality. Once an annulment is granted, the persons involved can remarry within the church, which is the principal reason for getting one. Catholics cannot "divorce," but they can marry liturgically after decades of living as spouse to someone else.

It sounds like doubletalk, but then doubletalk matters. Refusing to change contested church policies is a way of maintaining the illusion of doctrinal immutability. Rejecting plain speaking preserves verbal consistency with church teaching in earlier centuries, and verbal consistency is an urgent aspiration for official theologies. To refuse divorce, even as a word, provides an identity marker for contemporary Catholics and other Christian groups. It sets them apart. The word *divorce* matters as well because it recalls for Christian ears sayings attributed in the Gospels to Jesus. The sayings are obscure and contradictory. Taken together with other passages in the New Testament, they offer an unstable footing for the handling of broken relationships in Christian communities. Still they are authoritative words, and so they provoked or required the elaboration of a churchly rejection of divorce.

In the synoptic Gospels, Jesus makes a remark on divorce that is reported in decisively different ways. In Mark, Jesus is quizzed by "some Pharisees" about whether a man is permitted to divorce. He asks them what Moses said. They reply that Moses allowed men to draw up a writ of dismissal. Jesus replies by citing Genesis 2 : 24 on man and woman becoming one flesh. He adds: "What God has brought together human beings must not divide" (Mark 10 : 9). Confused or appalled by the answer, the disciples quiz Jesus in private. He replies, "Any man who divorces his wife and marries another commits adultery against her; and if she divorces her husband and marries another, she commits adultery" (Mark 10 : 11–12). Luke agrees with Mark in the severe version of the saying, though not in supplying a context for it (Luke 16 : 18). In the "Sermon on the Mount," however, Matthew reports the saying with an exception: "Anyone divorcing his wife, except for the reason of *porneia,* makes her commit adultery, and if any man marries a divorced woman he commits adultery" (5 : 32). Later Matthew repeats the story again, with a variant of Mark's context. Asked about divorce "for any cause whatever," and confronted with the example of Moses, Jesus replies directly to the Pharisees: "Now I say to you that any man who divorces his wife not because of *porneia* and marries another, commits adultery" (19 : 9).

Jesus does not define *porneia.* In Christian interpretation, the word was often taken to mean adultery and so to allow a husband to divorce an adulterous wife or, some centuries later, a wife to divorce an adulterous husband. Yet *porneia* is not the Greek word ordinarily translated as "adultery." That word is *moicheia.* But Jesus does not say in Matthew, "except for the reason of adultery (*moicheia*)," though that is how many Christians now hear it.[6] *Porneia* is a vaguer word than *moicheia.* Related to the word for "prostitute," it implies a range of sexual liberties outside marriage — or inside commerce. The use of the *porneia* is particularly striking in Matthew's exception precisely because his Jesus had been talking about adultery just a few sentences before (5 : 27), and then goes on after mentioning *porneia* to speak of consequences of disallowed divorce in terms of adultery. Of course, if Matthew's Jesus had couched the exception explicitly in terms of adultery, things would hardly be clearer, because he had just explained that "every man looking at a woman so as to desire her has already committed adultery with her in his heart" (Matt. 5 : 28). I have considered some awk-

ward implications of the radical saying above. Other implications would
follow here—for example, the inference that a single lustful glance would
be grounds for divorce. Let *porneia* here mean adultery in a more ordinary
sense, and other puzzles arise. Why should a wife's adultery give grounds
for legitimate divorce when every other kind of divorce is illegitimate precisely because it makes the wife an adulteress? Adam can divorce Eve only
if she is guilty of adultery. If he divorces her for another reason, he makes
her an adulteress—oh, but then he can divorce her for adultery. It would
make more sense to read the passage not as permitting the divorce of an
adulterous wife, but as permitting divorce in the case of a relationship that
is already somehow *porneia,* like coupling with a prostitute. On this more
coherent reading, *porneia* would not describe an act of the wife; it would
describe the character of the whole relation.

I emphasize conduct with a wife, because Matthew's exception is
granted to a husband. The asymmetry might be explained by pointing to
the context of Jewish law into which Jesus is made to speak by the context
in Mark and Matthew. For Deuteronomy, as much later for the Mishnah,
only the husband could issue a bill of divorce.[7] Perhaps Jesus is simply taking up the hypothetical case offered by his interlocutors. But many early
Christian authors continued to distinguish sharply between husband and
wife when it came to agency in divorce. Paul's own teaching on divorce
acknowledges a distinction: "a wife must not be separated from her husband—or if she has already left him, she must remain unmarried or else
be reconciled to her husband—and a husband must not divorce his wife"
(1 Cor. 7:9–10). Unless the word *divorce* in the last clause is meant to
cover all that has gone before, it looks as if a husband is not to initiate divorce against his wife, but that he is not under obligation to "remain unmarried" if she should leave him for another. In Romans, when Paul deploys
faithful marriage as an image for obligation to the Law only during life, it is
the woman who is also bound not to have other sexual relations so long as
her husband lives (Rom. 7:2–3). For later Christian writers, especially in
the West, Matthew's exception for *porneia* was allowed only to men—or,
indeed, required of them.[8] A Christian husband had an obligation to dismiss an adulterous wife.

I dwell on the discrepancy in the reports of Jesus' sayings on divorce to
illustrate the first difficulties that arise in trying to interpret it. The difficulties are more acute because there is only this one recorded saying, which
stumped the disciples. The canonical Gospels report no long disquisition by
Jesus on the rules for making and unmaking marriages. So his brief comment, reported in different settings (or none at all), has been subjected to
endless overreading. It has occasioned sharp disagreements among Chris-

tian groups, as it has required exegetical acrobatics from the early Christian centuries on. I am not foolish enough to attempt to recap either the debates or the interpretations. I note only some of the lines along which disagreements could be measured.

One line is the *moment* at which the exception is located. At least since the Middle Ages, some Christian theologians have contrived increasingly complicated rules for finding an exception in the moment before a marriage actually began. Most people now conceive this as the Roman Catholic doctrine of grounds for annulment, but it can be thought of more generally as a notion of latent defect. Specifying the defect's latency required an increasing exactness in defining the moment at which a marriage becomes binding. At least since the Continental Reformation, other theologians have worked to identify essential failures that undo a marriage after it has taken place. The reasoning holds that marriage comprises specifiable duties and dispositions. If any one of them disappears irremediably, then the merely nominal marriage should be dissolved so that the partners may go on to real ones. On this reasoning, the decisive moment falls after the marriage—at the time when one or more of the goods disappeared, in the projected future of lack.

Another line for measuring Christian debates over divorce runs through the *character of the decisive fault,* whether latent defect or later failure in a requisite good. Some faults have been physical: genital deformity, copulatory malfunction, and sterility or physical interference with conception. Other faults have arisen from status: genealogy or blood relation, legal minority, previous marriage, criminal conduct, egregious public sin, pastoral or ritual relation, and consecration to virginity or celibacy. There have been faults of cohabitation and parental consent, of mistaken identity and physical abuse. Still other faults, and the largest group, can now be classed as psychological. They are faults of consent, intention, affection, or erotic passion. Every detailed theological analysis has combined types of fault. Each type has shifted its boundaries with time.

A third line in the theology of divorce can be drawn through the *consequences* or meaning of dissolution. The obvious distinction here is between actions that permit remarriage and those that do not. Some churches have allowed or required separation of spouses without authorizing one or both to remarry. Other churches have viewed official separation of spouses as generally implying the right to remarry. The disagreements are embedded within an ontology of divorce, which is the reverse image of the ontology of the marriage bond. At its most abstract, the ontological speculation churns endlessly around whether marriage makes something that can never be undone, but only demonstrated not to have existed. The speculation issues in more concrete and, indeed, political considerations: Which institutions have the power to decree divorce among Christians? What is the force, if any, of a civil divorce between Christians?

Another sort of ontology, and so a fourth line in theological debate, has been the relation of marriage to its *spiritual opposites*. I use the plural to suggest that various oppositions gain prominence in different churches. In Christian traditions that prefer virginity or celibacy to marriage, to separate without remarriage can be a good thing—indeed, an evident improvement. For many more churches, the claims of church membership or ministry can take precedence over a marriage, even to the point of dissolving it. In 1 Corinthians 7:12–16, Paul urges converts to Christianity to stay with their unbelieving spouses so long as they can do so peacefully. If the unbelieving spouse leaves, the new Christian is no longer bound by the marriage. The "Pauline privilege" (as it is called) allows for dissolution with remarriage when a convert's faith is endangered by the marriage. A related exception has been made in favor of church ministry. The "Petrine privilege" allows a Christian to leave a marriage for the sake of a calling to ministry— in the way that Peter left his wife to preach the Gospel.[9] There is ambiguity as to whether the partner left behind could remarry. Remarriage after such a dissolution was allowed by some communities.[10] At other times, a couple could separate so that each could pursue religious vocation, but if either partner left afterward, she or he would not be allowed to remarry.

The last line I point out runs along theological *analogies of marriage* and how they should be applied to the dissolution of actual marriages. The controlling New Testament text is Ephesians 5:21–33, which derives the mutual obligations of husbands and wives from Christ's relation to the church. At the end of the moralizing analogy, Paul quotes Genesis 2:24 on "one flesh" and then adds: "This mystery is great: but I speak of Christ and the assembly [*or* church]." His analogy has been reversed: husband and wife becoming "one flesh" signifies something of the great mystery of Christ's union with the assembly of Christians. Generations of Christian readers have wanted to reverse the analogy yet again: In the same way that Christ is permanently and irrevocably united to the church, so husbands and wives are bound to each other. How far can such analogies provide marital regulation?

The five axes suggest the dialectical range of Christian debates over divorce. They also correct or supplement historical simplifications. For example, I have already noted the temptation to tell the story of Christian divorce as a long slide from strict prohibition to utter laxity. Early Christians, suspicious of marriage, permitted only one chance with one spouse. Contemporary Christians, so the long-slide story goes, allow divorce for any transient reason whatever. Denominations that want to approve some divorces tell a shorter version of the slide: "At the Reformation—or two centuries ago—or in the last century, believers sought divorce only for the most serious causes. Now they do it on a whim." There is some truth to the stories, but also much falsehood. The evidence for how marriage was lived among Christians in the early centuries is slight and scattered. As soon as historians do have more information (say, for the early modern period), they discover many accommodations to human circumstance. They recognize the importance not only of local custom and law, but of social and demographic contexts. In thirteenth-century Europe, as in nineteenth-century America, church-sanctioned marriages were less widespread than theologians like to imagine, and they were liable to dissolution by abandonment. In divorce, as in marriage, Christians have long found ways to square their misfortunes or hard choices with Scripture and doctrine. "What God has joined, let no man separate": right, but God may not really have joined them, or God may have already performed a separation.

Recently there has been a change in what Christian churches *say* about marital dissolution. The actual theology of divorce and remarriage has shifted markedly in many denominations during the last hundred years. With divorce, as with contraception, the shift is concealed with some historical subterfuge. But it contributes as much to contemporary anxieties over marriage as any alteration in the rate of dissolution. I suspect that many defenses of marriage are provoked rather by recent words than by new facts about divorce and remarriage. After all, divorce is not just disruption. It can be a liberation. It can open new possibilities for life—and not only for queer people who were compelled to enter other-sex marriages. Remarriage is not always betrayal or adultery. It creates new social goods. The blended or "recombinant" families that most Americans know by experience or acquaintance are a highly generative form of extended family. They break down many social barriers, as they require more deliberate partnering and parenting. They can remind us that the "Christian extended families" of two hundred years ago, so fetishized in nostalgia, were constructed by any number of dissolutions and recombinations. They were peopled by abandoned "spinsters," by remarried widowers and widows, by orphans and "illegitimate" offspring—not to say by the ghosts of same-sex lovers who could never be recognized.

Whatever the history, concealed or acknowledged, and its variable relation to words, both private and official, nostalgia for settled families remains potent. The change in church speaking on divorce produces anxiety, and the anxiety, in its turn, fuels debates and elicits policies. Denominations have begun to tighten their policies on annulment or divorce. Loud Christian voices now urge reform of civil divorce law or the introduction

of new kinds of marriage, such as covenant marriage, that are more difficult to dissolve. The new advocacy of same-sex unions also bears traces of
the push to bind couples more tightly. However much some queer advocates want to secure equitable legal benefits or to combat promiscuous
stereotypes, others want to reduce untethered, impermanent relations between persons of the same sex. The wish is a desire for domestic stability
and satisfaction—that is, reduced anxiety—through fixed relations.

I worry about the rush to blame divorce, whatever the sexes of the
couple. The last thing queer people should want is to sign on to efforts at
propping up failing models of relationship. Shifts in church teaching on divorce may have been sloppy or precipitous, but they were also plausible.
They reflected important and positive changes in the expectations that
Christians brought to relationships—often after being tutored by nonbelievers. The changes may be particularly evident or advanced in same-sex
relationships. Anthony Giddens takes lesbian couples as the best example
of the emerging "pure relationship" and its more frequent dissolution.[11]
Gay relationships, precisely as relationships between men, would for Giddens be less advanced examples, though perhaps still better than heterosexual marriages. In both kinds of same-sex relationships, Giddens finds au-
guries of the future direction of coupling. I agree with him this far:
Same-sex uncouplings are a privileged occasion for reconsidering the limits on relationship in time. Since so much in them has to be invented, they
are good sites for studying the improvisation of ending.

GAY DIVORCEES

In some cultural stereotypes, gay men's relationships are supposed to nasty,
brutish, short, and theatrical. They should end quickly and badly. These
stereotypes enter gay anxieties, but they also animate gay imaginations.
Anecdotes about particularly spectacular breakups are retold both as accusation and as entertainment. A clever analyst could sort the stories by dominant motif. There are break-ups by "cowardly message": a relationship of
several years ends with an e-mail, a voice-mail, or a typed note on the pillow. Sometimes the message can be amplified or replaced by an "abrupt departure": Bob returns from a business trip to find that Chuck has left their
shared apartment, taking all his possessions and more than his share of CDs,
but leaving his incontinent cat. Abrupt departure finds its mirror-image in
the "unannounced eviction": Jorge comes home to find that Manuel has
piled his possessions on the lawn by the curb. Then there is dissolution by
"dramatic encounter." In the middle of an argument over something trivial,
David tells Nathan that he has been "seeing" someone else for two years and
that he and his other lover are taking a new apartment next week. Or, in

the tritest stereotype of them all, Roger's lover, Pierre, is out of town on a business trip, so Roger decides on a whim to return to the bar where they first met. He does not much like going out any more, but he hopes it will cheer him up to visit a sentimental location. As soon as Roger enters the bar, he sees Pierre, shirtless, grinding against a gorgeous younger man directly under the disco ball at the epicenter of the dance floor. Roger goes quietly to the bar to purchase two chocolate martinis. He carries them gingerly onto the dance floor. He pours them over the heads of Pierre and his new love. This is the "diva rising above adversity" or the "club discovery."

I invented the particular stories in the last paragraph — and I made nothing up. I have heard them, read them, or listened to them in musical setting. The gay duo, Ron Romanovsky and Paul Phillips, combine motifs in a number of breakup songs, including the camp favorite, "Tango Indigesto."[12] An unfortunate is summoned by his lover to a Mexican restaurant. The lover arrives very late only to tell him that he is being dumped for not being "macho enough." The jilted unfortunate finally musters enough courage to leave the table mid-enchilada, noting that his lover has guacamole splattered down his shirt. On his way out, he discovers surprising hope for a better life. The diva rises, indeed.

Gay relish for melodramas of dissolution can be read as the application of camp to the sad facts of loss. It marks the survival of one of the oldest stereotypes of same-sex romance, the obligation to end tragically. Consider, for example, Gerald Glaskin's story (published under the pseudonym Neville Jackson) of male-male love in Australia during the early 1960s.[13] The narrator, Ray Wharton, falls in love with a Dutchman, Cor Van Gelder. Cor turns out to be married to Mia (with child on the way) and to be maintained by a rich boyfriend. Ray and Cor are able to overcome these challenges, but not the ghosts of lovers past or the doldrums of domesticity. When they move in together, Ray becomes obsessed with his work and increasingly neglectful. He suffers through a serious bout with hepatitis in the course of which he loses his business. Ray is finally offered a second chance at a career: a job in Hong Kong. He knows at once that he cannot possibly take Cor with him. Seized by the fear of (another) abandonment, Cor falls further into alcoholism and then into violence. In the climactic sequence of the book, Cor chases Ray through the streets, repeatedly assaulting him. While convalescing, Ray is told by a disapproving psychiatrist that he must be the one to be abandoned. He must let Cor leave him. After violent disintegration, the only therapy is a dissolution that reverses trauma. There must be dissolution, of course. The thing is to do it therapeutically. Musing at last on the drift in male-male relationships, Ray acknowledges that some endure: "There are some couples you know who have been together for ten, fifteen, twenty, twenty-five years. It's been a bit of a strain at times, now and again, but whose life isn't? But these are the lucky ones. Or else they've got strong enough character to carry them through and keep them together. For, yes, if it takes anything, then it takes a good deal of character to be a decent homosexual" (231). Luck or character may preserve a few relationships. Less luck or weaker character means that you try to break up well, because break up you must.

Glaskin's novel can stand in for hundreds of others from the beginning and middle of the last century in which the main fate of gay unions is to end. Then remember that in the last part of the century, the motif of violent separation was applied to gay couples, savagely, grotesquely, by AIDS. The grief of lovers lost to the epidemic has been told compellingly, in memoir and fiction. The deaths became often enough the occasion for the scandalous exposure of relationships or of their shameful denial. Long-term but mostly invisible couples were suddenly exposed to hostile scrutiny — only to be denied as "real" in comparison with the briefest, most unserious heterosexual marriages. The courage of partners who stayed through these denials and the humiliating tricks of the virus are familiar enough. They may seem tediously familiar to those who did not live them. So too are the stories of lovers who refused to stay, who bolted out of fear or selfishness or self-loathing. Tony Kushner's *Angels in America: Millennium Approaches* turns on just this kind of abandonment. Relationships dissolved by the pressures of AIDS are more numerous than gay mythology might want to admit. They must be balanced against the number of relationships begun under the heel of the epidemic, with grim (un)certainty about the future.

The old slanders about gay instability and the new myths (or antimyths) of AIDS still border any discussion of gay dissolutions. They surround as well the new genre of advice to gay men about breaking up. A book of counsel for gay men in troubled relationships is a sign of the times in too many senses. The genre is another form of mainstreaming—you know you have arrived in America when they write self-help books for you. The genre also shows that some gay men conceive their relationships as equivalent to heterosexual marriages, if only therapeutically. Yet the genre's most poignant implication is that gay men have some control over how their relationships end. They are no longer at the mercy of a fated instability. They do not die so rapidly. Their relationships last long enough and have enough substance to merit careful thought about whether or how they should end.

Deliberate control is the refrain of Neil Kaminsky's *When It's Time to Leave Your Lover.*[14] The back-cover copy describes it as "a book specifically for gay men who need help in leaving their partners!" It offers help through a model of relationship management in no way specific to gay men. The main tenets of the model are universal. They begin with a doctrine of appropriate autonomy: A successful dissolution will require that the partners communicate their (deliberately calculated) decisions and police their (sharply drawn) boundaries. Then come tenets of sequenced grieving and sober self-knowledge. Running throughout is the exhortation of recourse to "a competent mental health professional" (6).

For Kaminsky, the mature dissolution of a relationship begins with a review of "red flags" that "signify serious problems" (30). If the review indicates that "it is not going to work," then you must have the courage to "reinvent your life" (69 and chapter title). You can begin by reminding yourself that the decision is necessarily unilateral (83–84). Once you take it, you should plan one or more meetings in which you communicate your resolution to your ex-partner and plan briefly for the immediate future. Kaminsky provides exemplary scripts (88–102). After the meeting(s), you must count on a turbulent and trying period of undenied grief. Get through the period by reconnecting with your friends, reminding yourself of activities you enjoy, combating anxiety, and resisting the urge to get back together with your ex. You are not to date anyone seriously for about six months and should be careful about sexual adventures, unless you are sure that you can have them without romance (231). Regard your time alone as a "mental health vacation" (204–5). Consider what dispositions or expectations led you into your former relationship. "Address" them so that you will not repeat them (220). Only then will you be ready to go forward into a new relationship—eyes open, checklist of red flags in hand.

Kaminsky cautions against falling for popular romantic myths, but he shows himself an ardent advocate for love. Having a lover gives solace, companionship, "ego boosting," vivid shared history, and a general increase in pleasure (197–98). "Being in love will profoundly enhance your life" (13). Kaminsky rejects some clauses of the romantic creed, but endorses many more. He is suspicious of love at first sight, but insists on a romantic entitlement: "Being with a lover should never be a 'settle for' experience. The man you are with should be the man of your dreams" (68).[15] Being in love is "a feeling universally acknowledged and ubiquitously mystical" (1). Part of its "mystical" character is providing a space in which "the real you" can be known (48). The "real you" is the ultimate arbiter of what is right "for you."[16] More important, the "real" or deep "you" addressed by Kaminsky's book is the principal agent for bringing about a proper dissolution. "Remind yourself that you don't need his approval to leave him. *Your decision to leave him makes it so. Period*" (97). "The real you" is not absolute, of course. Self-interpretation is subject to the therapist's challenge and approval. The therapist possesses a certain measure or standard for helping to find "the *right* Mr. Right" (211). Still the authentic self is autonomous enough in Kaminsky's account to be the chief agent of its destiny in relationships. "The power to direct your life for happiness or for unhappiness is all in your hands at this very moment in time. What are you going to do with that power?" (77).

The question can be read in many rhetorical registers. It could be likened to the advertiser's pitch or the preacher's altar call or the manager's careful warning. A more suggestive context would be the conviction—or mythic assurance—that gay relationships operate outside the ordinary frame of domestic life and so have to be made or unmade by the men in them. Because queer loves have no institutional place, there is (so the myth goes) no institutional or ritual power over them. Gay men pronounce their own wedding blessings and grant their own decrees of divorce. As soon as the myth is told in that way, it reveals itself as part of the dazzling tale of Romance. How many heterosexual epics are filled with secret vows and more secret disavowals? No one may know of this love, and no one of its dissolution. The separateness of romantic love is the autonomy of the selves in it.

When romance was distributed or relinquished by the leisured classes, it was handed out to many, not just to gay men. On some accounts, it was passed out widely enough to become the general type of the contemporary erotic relationship in such countries as America. For Anthony Giddens, the recent and current meaning of the term *relationship* carries with it the notion of the self empowered to control its romantic bonds. The pure form of relationship is now "entered into for its own sake, for what can be derived by each person from a sustained association with another; and . . . continued only in so far as it is thought by both parties to deliver enough satisfaction for each individual to stay within it."[17] I think that Giddens is right about the recent shift in the term's meaning. Many who worry about the increase of divorce would add that the contemporary notion of relationship is one of the main causes of rising failure in marriage. They would argue that people now consult only their transient satisfaction rather than family duty or the common good.

Simple narratives of change are suspect, whether the change is praised or blamed. Such a narrative cannot make clear, for example, whether a new idea of relationship causes more dissolutions or is caused along with them by deeper forces—assuming that there are adequate notions about the causality of ideas. Once you begin searching for the relation of general ideas to divorces, you ought to remind yourself that certain old ideas also put marriages at risk. Christianity has long allowed marriages to be dissolved for a variety of religious reasons, including conversion and vocation.

The self that responds to the call of God is empowered to leave a marriage that hinders the call. Since the Reformation, Christian groups have worked out successive justifications for dissolving marriages in view of less dramatic spiritual calls. A person's vocation to live as a baptized Christian might give grounds for leaving a spiritually damaging relationship, even with another Christian. It is not just the outlaw existence of gay men or the prevailing notions of "pure relationship" that grant power to undo relations judged seriously harmful. Christian theology offers the same power—and the same urgency to use it.

Here a lesson from Kaminsky and the other manualists of gay divorce does become useful. Cultural commonplaces about the worthlessness and instability of male-male relationships afflict gay men too. They are widely circulated in gay subcultures as joke and complaint. The lessons can prescribe quick dissolution, but they can also prescribe useless persistence in a damaging relationship. Either prescription denies the value of relationship. A counterprescription, derived as much from the Christian sense of vocation as from prevailing psychological models, would be that any morally justified relationship may have to be dissolved at some point on moral grounds. If gay relationships are entered into for deep human purposes, there may come a moment when they must be left to fulfill those purposes.

The conclusion may sound like psychobabble. I suggest that it follows out the logic both of gay liberation and of Christian conversion. If erotic relationships are morally weighty, as they are for both liberationists and evangelists, then their beginnings and ends are subject to moral scrutiny. Scrutiny may produce opposed moral conclusions about them. A gay activist may argue that the purgation of the heterosexist poisons always requires erotic relations to be ended quickly or constructed as nonexclusive and changing. A Christian theologian may argue that dissolutions should be done slowly and carefully, because the temptations to self-deception in the service of selfishness are so potent. Or a subtler activist argues that revolution requires persistence in the face of slanders against queer love, while the more radical theologian regards mere persistence in relationship as devotion to the World rather than the Kingdom of God. The principle remains: If moral reasoning can judge the beginning of a relationship, it can dictate its end. The principle is violated by making the end of relationships subject merely to chance, whether the chance is the appearance of a new body in the bathhouse or the death of a spouse in a car accident. "Till death do us part" deserves admiration when it is the declaration of hope that love will be interrupted only by death. Respecting death alone as the solvent of committed love is either a naive view of divine providence or a denigration of relationships in favor of chance. Committing oneself to a lifelong mar-

riage no matter what is no different, morally speaking, than choosing a
partner by rolling the dice.

Much more could be said, but the main point will be obvious enough: If
the decision to enter into a marriage is subject to serious deliberation, then
so is the decision to leave one. The decision to dissolve a relationship is
more complicated. Changes produced by the relationship must be taken
into account—including, of course, children or other dependents. Lives
connected over time cannot be separated without loss, and so the loss must
figure into discernment. Of course, a dissolution is not a simple ending. It
produces changes and consequences of its own that debates over divorce
tend too often to treat as items for calculation: Are they positive or negative, local or diffuse, psychological or material? For an inquiry into the
blessing of unions, there is a more pertinent question: What might be accomplished by blessing the undoing?

RITES OF DISSOLUTION

In Christian communities, the beginning or public recognition of an erotic
relationship is celebrated with public rites. So too should its end be a ritual.
Celebrations of marriage call down grace and community support; celebrations of divorce should do the same. They must be celebrations, however
odd as that might sound. Every day on the liturgical calendar is at least a *fe-
ria,* a feast day. Every Christian rite is a celebration of the world's redemption. Celebration may include repentance and grief, as in rites for reconciliation or burial. Still the overriding note of any celebration will be saving
hope. The task of a Christian blessing on dissolution is to encourage hope.

There is every reason to perform the rites in public, however private the
disappointment or anger. The blessing at the beginning of a union is partly
the promise by the church community to support and nurture a relationship. The failure of the relationship (so far as dissolution is a failure) must
then be a communal failure. Especially if there are children or other dependents, the community must reassert its willingness to share in caring for
all those involved. When the strongest powers are invoked at the optimistic beginning, they should be invoked more ardently at what is sure to
be a sad ending—no matter how prudently deliberated and well chosen.
The dissolution of a relationship cannot be left as a private shame any more
than a death can be. It has to be enacted by a church as an occasion for hope.

More Christian groups perform same-sex unions than offer rites for
their dissolution. For example, the Metropolitan Community Churches
(MCC) have procedures for dissolving a holy union, but do not generally
perform a rite to mark the fact. Some Christian denominations or individ-

ual ministers have published or circulated rituals for divorce, but these typ-ically do not take account of same-sex unions. Let me rehearse two that do.

An explicitly Christian rite of dissolution has been published by James Lancaster.[18] Lancaster's text is dominated by the image of the journey through the wilderness with trust in God. It begins with God's calling out Abram (soon to be Abraham) from his ancestral home. The congregation figures as ministering angels accompanying the separating couple into a new homeland. Lancaster's suggested scriptural readings teach forgiveness, providence, compassion, and reconciliation. The separating partners are given little to do, which might count as a mercy. Each is asked to forgive the other, to continue cherishing shared goods, and to go forth having learned whatever must be learned. The response is "I do." The only ritual action for the two is to pull apart "loosely tied" ribbons. The congregation is reminded of its witness to the original union ceremony, and it is asked to commit itself to upholding the two partners after the separation. At the end, the minister pronounces that the former partners are "free to live your lives in the fullness of God's gifts and in the mercy of life in Christ" (41). This text shows Lutheran sensibilities both in its emphasis on the Word and on its willingness to leave many of the circumstances or consequences of marriage outside the church, in the hands of the state.

A feminist liturgy by Diann Neu contains no explicitly Christian refer-ences, but perhaps more ritual insight.[19] The ceremony opens with the marriage certificate or other record of the relationship on a central table, along with one rose for each child under the care of the dissolving couple. After an announcement of the dates on which the union began and ended, the two partners speak briefly some of their reasons for declaring the rela-tionship closed. Metaphors of journey and inner calling are strongly sug-gested in the sample formulas. When there are children, the partners reaf-firm their parental covenant and receive from the children reaffirmations of love. The partners ask forgiveness from each other. More formulas are suggested. The faults mentioned in them range from "taking a path that is different from yours" to inappropriate anger and incomprehension (250). Each of the two tears the marriage certificate or other record while pledg-ing respect within "a new relationship" (251). Rings are returned to the presider, who passes them on to the other partner. The presider pro-nounces the union dissolved and then leads the community not only in af-firming its support, but in blessing the two who have separated. The bless-ing is conferred by laying on of hands. Each member of the congregation then greets each of the ex-partners. The words of dismissal are an exhor-tation to reconciliation and new life.

The two rites contain some clichés in what they propose as words for the couple. Still the many "journeys" and "paths" recall that the blessing of a relationship was a communal rite on behalf of eros in time. The dissolution of a relationship is an end neither to time nor to eros. (It may not even mark the end of eros between the partners.) Rites of dissolution should console the wounded and pledge the community's care again to all those who might need it. The rite must also reaffirm the possibility of blessing eros in time. It should reaffirm blessing, I suggest, not only as an abstract possibility, but as a possibility for the individuals standing before the congregation, according to their present characters or characters yet to come. Same-sex relations carry particularly explicit investments in the mediation of eros through character. Because heterosexuality is presumed to be natural and universal, its desires are presumed to inhere in the human. Homoerotic desire by contrast has typically come through a character—through what has been conceived as an identity of sin or perversion, a peculiar history or physiology. Even on more benign accounts, it is almost always a character in the minority. It must then be aware of itself as a character. The dissolution of an erotic relation between two such characters brings them once again into prominence and perhaps into doubt. Failure in queer love looks to confirm, if not the worst condemnations and the most malignant stereotypes, at least a certain doubt about the coherence or practicability of homoerotic "identities." All the more reason to have rites of dissolution in which the fate of queer eros in (heteronormative) time is not foreclosed.

A variant on the rite of dissolution would be a rite ending or recommitting a "term" relationship. In a term union, the partners, whether two or more, agree to be bound together for a specified period of months or years. At the end of that time, the union dissolves automatically, as it were. When the partners choose to continue with it, they have to recommit themselves for another period and (typically) in another ceremony. I have heard people explain that setting a term increases seriousness about the relationship. Nothing can be let go, because nothing is guaranteed. The end of the term can also be described as a fixed point for evaluation, like a regular "performance review" on the job. It provides a recognized occasion for breaking things off if they are not going well. I hear the arguments and the testimonies, but I am not entirely convinced. Many queer relationships are under continual review—no matter what the vows said. At a time when any straight marriage can break up in any season, unsanctioned queer relationships are not likely to be lulled into a sense of permanence. Why fix a term for review when review is ongoing? Why wait for the end of the term if things are in fact going badly? And would having an expiration date really make it any easier to say that you want out if your partner does (partners do) not?

Every erotic relationship has a term, and not just because of life's hazards. Every relationship is subject to a moral term: Once the relationship becomes morally damaging, it should be finished. Fixing the term in years or months is just another effort at managing the transit of eros through time. Erotic love waxes and wanes. People "fall out" of love and then, unpredictably, fall back into it. Eros disappears only to reappear in subtler form, with the agency of a reinvented character.

Whether the term of an erotic relationship is artificially calculated or discovered with surprise and regret, it is important to mark it ritually. The rite is a reminder that coming to a term is not coming to the end of time. Among other things, dissolution of a relationship is returning to the community of one's friends and to the eros in them.

FRIENDS AND EXES

Some American gay men report a taboo against sex with good friends. "There is," Andrew Holleran writes, "a strange and powerful taboo that prevents us from mixing friendship and sex, in the vast majority of cases."[20] The taboo on sex with friends sometimes means that one has to choose between having a friend and having a lover. Yet it can also mean that lovers become friends. An unhappy sexual connection can begin a strong friendship. Either kind of friend can, with time, be described as a sibling. Michael Rowe begins an essay by declaring, "I have made brothers out of my two oldest friends. I'm not sure where the line between friendship and brotherhood is drawn and crossed, but it has to do with trust and time."[21] One of these friends was a first lover from prep school who, after a painful rejection, came back into Rowe's life as a gay comrade. The other friend, also from childhood, is a straight man. Michael Clark writes of a mentor in "leathersex" as a "big brother."[22] Arnie Kantrowitz writes, more synoptically, "First we went to bed and later we exchanged names. Casual tricks often turned into lifelong friends." But in the case of his two best friends, there was never sex. "We discussed it, but we agreed it would have seemed incestuous. We had met each other and become 'sisters' first."[23]

In a study of gay friendship, Peter Nardi summarizes the more complex frame ignored by any simple analogy to the incest taboo (which is, in itself, hardly simple). "A central narrative of gay men's lives is that of how important their friends are to them, how this 'rich network of friends' is like a family, how sex has been a dimension of their earlier friendships with some of their friends, and how, for some, their friends mean more and last longer than do their romantic relationships."[24] You do not sleep with your friends—unless they were once your lovers, tricks, or fuck buddies. Friends last longer than lovers—perhaps especially when they began as lovers. According to the stereotypes, holding on to ex-lovers is supposed to be the lesbian habit. Paul Phillips (of Romanovsky and Phillips) poses this brain-teaser as part of his queer literacy quiz: "Mary and Kay are lovers. Mary has six ex-lovers. Kay has four ex-lovers. How many best friends do Mary and Kay have?" The answer is, of course, ten.[25] The joke is told on women, but men may also feel its punch line. Many gay men experience a widening network of friends that is constituted by ex-lovers and their new lovers, friends, and children.

The network may welcome the dead, who remain real presences through later unions and dissolutions. When death raged along lines of erotic exchange, it pressed passion up against mortality. You could not know which of your lovers had brought you the virus—and to whom you had given it in turn. It hardly mattered. Networks of coupling became networks of dissolution. The losses made other networks—new "buddies," friends of friends, lovers of ex-lovers now gone.[26] Christian hagiography has long remembered the "faithful departed" as pioneers and companions, those who have gone before and yet remain behind. They remain part of the church. They share in the communion of saints. New churches and communions were constituted by AIDS. Out of dissolution, larger communion.

I suggest the analogy to expand the view of friends ranged around gay relationships. Friendship has often served as a euphemism for queer love. When erotic connection is too disconcerting, it is refigured as friendship. The person your parents cannot call your "lover" or "partner" becomes your "friend." More positively, friendship has provided many models for queer relationship, especially between women.[27] As we have seen in Alan Bray's *The Friend*, Christian rites of friendship have attracted same-sex couples over centuries. The circle of one's queer friends may offer more enduring support than the sequence of one's lovers. They can be mobilized as a troop of matchmakers or scrutinized as candidates for future partners. Meeting friends is often a more important test of a new relationship than meeting parents, as jealous friends can meddle more effectively than a distant father-in-law.

In each of these ways, the network of friends, queer or straight, constitutes an eroticized space within which sexual bonds form. The space is eroticized most basically by the stories of eros that get told in it. Friends of queers are friends to whom queers can talk candidly about their desires. When friends share words about the accomplishments and frustrations of queer desire, they mark off a sphere of discourse against heteronormative speech. The sphere is distinguished by the eros within it—by the eros that can find words safely only within it. The gossip of queer love—its sightings, meetings, ecstasies, griefs—is the home of queer character. Characters live in its words. Things may go more easily for same-sex love in future decades and other places, but so long as it remains the eros of a significant minority, it will depend on the elaboration of characters to act it in distinction from the majority. Those characters need the protected space of speech among friends.

Friends' speech is the dense set of relations on top of which stable erotic unions can be built. It stands under them so long as they endure. It receives the individual partners if the union dissolves. A dissolution does not stop time or cancel memory. It does not bring silence. The couple's history is taken back into the discourse of queer loves—as a cautionary tale, perhaps, or as a remembered gift. The antidote for dissolution is the continuing speech about queer love. Eros gives time meaning. Its yearning dilates minutes into hours, hours into days. Its ecstasies stop the clock—at least for a while. Its cycles mark beginnings and endings, unions and dissolutions. Most of all, eros spins out human time in onrushing speeches that seduce, repent, analyze, propose, praise, blame, regret, mourn. Friends share and protect erotic speech.

A Comic Exhortation

∝

Christian churches should bless same-sex unions. They should do it as a matter of justice, after reading the real signs of the times, with prayerful enthusiasm for the Gospel, and by way of securing some credible future for their marriage theology. Some churches will bless unions sooner, some later, some never — in ordinary time. Churches will split over the blessings as they have over a hundred other issues, large and small. Church history will then rumble on. Blessing same-sex unions will not by itself either reform or destroy the churches.

The stewards of American queer politics should take an interest in how Christian churches proceed. Rapid legal change by itself cannot deliver queer utopia — or even accomplish "mainstreaming." Entering more fully and candidly into American society will require engaging the churches not only as agents of social recognition, but as reservoirs of potent accusation against same-sex desire. For that matter, queer stewards might look beyond the churches as electoral, legislative, or judicial levers and recognize them as places where many queer people still live. Of course, winning over some or many churches will not eradicate violent hatred against queer people. It will only shrink it.

Queer Christians who want a blessing should seek one out. They should petition their churches as stubbornly as some Gospel characters petitioned Jesus, but they should never confuse a particular church with Jesus. If their petitions are refused long enough, and if receiving a blessing remains important enough, they should consider it a vocation to join other Christian communities where they will be welcomed, supported, and blessed. Most of all, queer Christians should use the occasion of a blessing to examine themselves, to scrutinize and revise the characters through which they perform erotic relationship.

Christian lives are not confined to churches. Queer lives are not subordinated to movements. The most interesting effects of my rhetorical mediations are to be looked for in the characters through which queer Christians might go on to conduct erotic lives. The book ends not by announcing its arrival in a promised land of pure speech, but by disclosing itself as a series of modest proposals for replotting the comedy of manners. Its exhortation has been comic. It has played an *opera buffa:* the avuncular parson's winking approval, the bar-stool soliloquy of a hustler with a heart of gold, your favorite drag queen's smile, your prayer partner's uncondemning and amused gaze.

Can comic opera possibly be enough? No other genre will do, either for queer romance or Christian marriage. Camp is the condition of queer critique—and of Christian liturgy. Every serious theology laughs at itself.

In the end, will queers get married in a real church with a real minister? Just like everyone else—unless they are very careful.

Notes

INTRODUCTION

1. Her devoted readers will recognize these words as the opening of Jane Austen's *Pride and Prejudice.*

2. The ceremony I describe occurred on June 29, 2002. There was a substantially similar ceremony a year later, as there had been the year before.

3. California State Assembly, AB 26, Chapter 588 of the Statues of 1999, codified as Cal. Fam. Code §297 (1999). This makes up Division 2.5, which is grafted onto the code right before the divisions on marriage.

4. The official founding date of the Sisters is Easter Sunday, 1979. See the essays by Sr. Dana Van Iquity and Sr. Missionary P. DeLight in Leyland, *Out in the Castro,* 213–18, at 216; and 201–9, at 205, respectively. The Sisters have participated in other activities on behalf of same-sex unions, such as a ceremony on April 1, 2001, in celebration of the first legal same-sex unions in the Netherlands (218). They have also figured in comic imagination as marriage officiants. In 1994, Gerard Donelan drew a cartoon showing a Sister towering in the background, unamused, as two grooms quarrel. One says to the other: "*You're* the one who insisted on a religious ceremony!"

5. *Christian* and *Christianity* are never neutral descriptions. Especially for believers, the terms remain claims or provocations. When I use *Christian* or *Christianity* in the following pages, I make claims based partly on a historical judgment about what has distinguished Christian communities and partly on a theological conviction about what might justify them. In saying even that much, I reach a point where Christian and non-Christian discourses diverge to the point of incomprehension. Christians and non-Christians may agree to describe certain discourses as Christian because they have more or less evident relations to Christian texts, authors, institutions, or cultural configurations. For the Christian believer, this will seem a relatively superficial description, but an intelligible one. When it comes to churches, but more especially to lives, the thoughtful Christian must immediately confront questions about the offer and acceptance of divine grace.

6. Attentive readers will have noticed that I move back and forth between *marriage* and *union.* I do so deliberately, because I regard *marriage* as an incorrigibly equivocal term. If some

original of marriage was laid down in creation, it is as inaccessible to us as the Kantian Thing-in-Itself. So I let the term *marriage* float through these opening pages. In chapter 2, I propose that *union* should be for Christians the genus of which marriage is an unhappily compromised species. For me, *union* is not the name for a marriage substitute. It points rather to the higher and better possibility out of which marriage has fallen.

7. I imagine the mutual interrogation more sharply—and perhaps more broadly—than Michael Vasey, who sees a question and a danger. See his *Strangers and Friends* (237): "The question faces the churches: What is it about their understanding of Jesus Christ that leads them to a poorer grasp of some fundamental Christian insights than the gay movement? The danger faces gay people: they may fail to hear in their experience of love and their intuitions of beauty the mysterious call of God."

8. On most pages of this book, I will be criticizing or at least questioning common terms that figure in the debates over blessing same-sex unions, especially when these terms are applied as identity markers to individuals. I have considered various typographical devices for highlighting the suspect terms. The simplest is the use of quotation marks. It can also be the most distracting. Because so many terms will be under suspicion by the end of the book, each page risks becoming a thicket of quoted terms. So I adopt the convention of enclosing problematic terms in quotation marks only at their first few appearances. The reader is asked to remember.

9. I use *character* for its older and newer meanings. According to the newer meanings, it refers both to moral personality and to a figure in a novel or a script. It also names an eccentric—a "character"—that is, someone queer. The older meanings of the term refer to the combination of moral features and dispositions, to an abiding comportment, that Theophrastus was understood to have parsed into so many quasi-natural traits (in his *Characters* [*Charactēres*]). In Christian theologies, *character* has meant, among other things, an indelible imprint of membership in the community that confers ritual agency. (See the discussion of sacramental character below, chapter 5.) Gay or lesbian "identity" ranges across all these meanings, from allotted performance through recurring quasi-species to ministerial office. I hope to make my meanings clearer in the course of the book—along with my reasons for finding the term "identity" now mostly misleading. It is at once too external, like an identity card, and too internal, like self-consciousness.

10. Persky, *Autobiography of a Tattoo,* 18–19.

11. I say here aphoristically what a general account of church-state relations or the religious-secular distinction would have to develop much more subtly. See, for a good example, Jakobsen and Pellegrini, *Love the Sin,* especially 19–44. In later chapters, I argue for the limited autonomy of religious rite and teaching so long as religious membership is voluntary. Thus I disagree with the hypothetical suggestion that citizens who enter a religious marriage under particular rules should remain bound by them when they contemplate divorce or dissolution. See Carter, "'Defending' Marriage," 225. I also and obviously disagree with Carter about the "solemn religious origins" of (a univocally conceived) marriage.

12. A selection of news photographs will show how religious symbols were deployed in the civil space—and contained by it. See, for example, Amy Rennert, *We Do,* especially 36–37, 39, and 44–45.

13. You can watch me falling under the spell of the picture in *Telling Truths in Church,* 34–58. Some of the ideas in that lecture escaped the spell and are carried forward in the next few paragraphs here.

14. My colleague Ted Smith said something very like this in an early conversation—and so redirected the course of my thinking.

15. I used to describe these as *scripts,* using that term not in some pseudo-precise psychological or sociological sense, but as a loose theatrical metaphor. I have come to think that *script* causes confusion—and not only for readers of psychology and sociology. What I am trying to describe is not just a set of words and actions, but a response to an anxious craving for instruction about how to carry oneself, how to comport oneself as a particular sort of self. If you find this use of *etiquette* misleading, please substitute *script.*

16. Among recent examples, see in particular Ellison, *Same-Sex Marriage?* 56–77 and (in a different way) 88–94. See also Crysdale, "Christian Marriage and Homosexual Monogamy"; Williams, "Toward a Theology for Lesbian and Gay Marriage."

17. There is a growing sense among queer Christian theologians that they have fallen into a trap of mistaken questions. See, for example, Ellison, *Same-Sex Marriage?* 1–2, but also Stuart, *Gay and Lesbian Theologies,* 3–4, 11, and throughout. There is much less agreement on how to reframe the questions. For example, Ellison seeks a "progressive Christian ethic" that engages law, relies on a stable sense of justice, and wants to notice history only at a clean distance. My own proposal is the reverse of the three points. I am especially concerned to abolish a sanitary separation of past and present. Our historical narratives are inevitably about the present, into which the past keeps erupting as the repressed.

18. Kierkegaard, *Philosophical Fragments:* "In all human probability the centuries-old echo, like the echo in some of our churches, would not only have riddled faith with chatter but would have eliminated it in chatter" (71). Elsewhere I have argued that the chatter of repetition can be a cunning device for insuring churchly silence around unsettling topics; see Jordan, *The Silence of Sodom,* 54–59.

19. Theophrastus *Characters* 3.

20. See Sedgwick, *Epistemology of the Closet,* 23, on "the precious, devalued arts of gossip" as providing human taxonomy for survival.

21. Doing this, I resemble the character Elias Canetti, in *Earwitness,* labels the "earwitness": "The earwitness makes no effort to look, but he hears all the better. He comes, halts, huddles unnoticed in a corner, peers into a book or a display, hears whatever is to be heard, and moves away untouched and absent. . . . He is already somewhere else, he is already listening again" (43). A related character, though a less detached one, is performed through an auditory memoir disguised as subcultural history in James McCourt's *Queer Street.*

22. Bernardino of Siena, *De horrendo peccato contra naturam,* 3:267–84.

23. Gagnon, *The Bible and Homosexual Practice,* 37 and then throughout. The book gives no evidence that Gagnon has engaged these fundamental theoretical questions. His views on "homosexuality" seem to have been formed instead from dubious "scientific studies" promoted by religious politicians, from notorious "psychological" claims about gay men as "sissies," and from the propaganda of "ex-gay" ministries (see, respectively and as examples, 396, n. 83; 408, n. 113; 423, n. 139). The heavy reliance on Joseph Satinover is indicative (see especially 471–73). Gagnon's book shows the hypocrisy of the "conservative" accusation that "liberal" biblical exegesis has been driven by an imported political agenda. There could be no more politically driven exegesis than Gagnon's own.

24. James Alison provides a vivid application of this passage in *On Being Liked,* 101–2.

25. I summarize these views in *Ethics of Sex,* 76–106.

26. For recent examples, see the essays in Stone, *Queer Commentary and the Hebrew Bible,* and the comprehensive reading in Jennings, *The Man Jesus Loved.*

27. See Bawer, *Stealing Jesus.*

28. Warner, *The Trouble with Normal,* 81–147. Cited by page number in parentheses in the rest of this section.

29. For the authorized account, see Perry, *The Lord Is My Shepherd and He Knows I'm Gay*, 133–38.

30. The churches continued to be engaged by queer marriage issues after the 1960s— and even more so. For a good survey, see Baptiste Coulmont, "Églises chrétiennes et homo- sexualités aux États-Unis, éléments de compréhension."

31. Keeping religion out of sight also requires hiding queer social groups or locations in which religion remains prominent. Denigrating religion in queer politics renders invisible the lives of many queers who don't inhabit Enlightened urban enclaves. To cite a single coun- terexample: MCC congregations have served in many southern cities as centers for activism. See Howard, "Protest and Protestantism," especially 216–19.

32. I here step around a very important question: Why in America are so many citizens' rights routed through "families" of a certain model? If I were writing about civil recognition of same-sex unions, I would also argue (with Martha Fineman) that many of the benefits now given through marriage and its families ought rather to be given to citizens as dependents and caretakers. But I am not writing about civil recognition.

33. The double-ring ceremony for Neva Joy Heckman and Judith Ann Belew was per- formed in their Los Angeles home on June 12, 1970.

34. Perry, *Lord Is My Shepherd*, 206–8.

35. For example, "The Wedding" was a union of 2,600 couples performed as a demon- stration at the 1993 March on Washington for Lesbian, Gay and Bi Equal Rights and Libera- tion. The text of the ceremony is reproduced in Cherry and Sherwood, *Equal Rites*, 106–9.

36. The weddings of Anne and Elaine Vautour and Joe Varnell and Kevin Bourassa were performed on January 14, 2001, at the MCC church in Toronto by its pastor, Brent Hawkes. Beyond the numerous press and website accounts, see Varnell and Bourassa, *Just Married*.

37. I recall the cover of *Gay Sunshine* no. 8 (August 1971), as reproduced in Leyland, *Gay Roots, Twenty Years of "Gay Sunshine,"* 204.

38. The qualification "in America" should be heard with full force here and throughout. American discourses are distinguished both by the character of the dominant Protestantism and by the ambivalence of its domination. For an introduction to contemporary discourses in European state churches and other Christian groups, see Merin, *Equality of Same-Sex Couples*, especially 64–65 and 76–77 (Denmark), 84–85 (Norway), 99 n. 160 (Sweden), 118–19 n. 44 (Netherlands), and 156 and n. 135 (Italy).

39. I do not use the acronym LGBT (Lesbian Gay Bisexual Transgender). It implies that the most general description is gotten by summing four particular identities. I use *queer* as a term that leaves the number and fixity of identities unspecified just in order to emphasize that they have in common some deviation from majority norms for sex, gender, and bodily pleasures.

40. This comment is not superfluous. Many Christian critics of same-sex unions pride themselves either on not having any contact with same-sex couples or on encountering them only through the antiseptic barrier of a revulsion buffered by "pastoral" concern.

41. Laura Kipnis writes that "What the hell now?" is the "prohibited question" at the end of the love film. See her *Against Love* (100), with reference to the closing shot of *The Graduate*. I am more interested in how to get through the "contradictions" that "often [erupt] hysteri- cally at the level of form" when the question is raised (Kipnis, 96–97n).

CHAPTER ONE

1. *Queer as Folk* [U.S. version] 2000.

2. Predictably, the opening of the original British version requires neither the strobe light

nor the sound effect to make the point that something important is happening. The tension of the encounter is maintained only by the rhythm of glances and the possibility that the older man will simply keep on walking to his jeep—rather than pivoting to stare a final time before approaching. *Queer as Folk* [U.K. version] 1999.

3. Sandra Bernhard, "You Make Me Feel (Mighty Real)," from *Excuses for Bad Behavior, Part 1;* Sylvester, "You Make Me Feel (Mighty Real)," from *Step II.*

4. Sylvester was active in the Castro at this time, but there are also other clues. Bernhard has "MacArthur Park" playing on the dance floor. The reference is probably to the version on Donna Summer's double album, *Live and More,* which redid the coda of a longer piece by Jimmy Webb.

5. I am not sure that it is helpful to distinguish gay codes of etiquette from lesbian ones as between boys' adventures stories and girls' romances. The readerly identifications and the gender performances of queer boys are more complicated—as I assume they are for queer girls. Compare Rose, "Lesbian and Gay Love Scripts." For much more nuanced representations of queer genders, see the criss-crossing essays in Miles and Rofes, *Opposite Sex.*

6. Although I am often intrigued by Denis de Rougemont's *Love in the Western World,* I can endorse neither his story about the origin of Romance in Eastern heresy (Catharism) nor his reading (against Nietzsche) of the larger cultural opposition between eros and agape. The popular American version of true love that I rehearse is decidedly more ambiguous about marriage than the death-wishing and adulterous love Rougemont finds epitomized in the myth of Tristan. See Rougemont, *Love in the Western World.*

7. And not only American etiquettes, of course. The highly romantic notion of the "true (homoerotic) friend" espoused from the 1930s on by the group associated with Der Kreis began from and continued to play on Christian motifs, even as it wished to rehabilitate the language of a divine Eros. See the many translated selections in Kennedy, *The Ideal Gay Man.*

8. Compare the notion, found in not a few gay novels, that the first sexual intercourse, no matter how painful or abusive, creates a bond that can never be equaled. For examples, see Jackson, *No End to the Way,* 80 (the narrator: "You know that something like that only happens the first time—Cor with this fellow, you with Uncle Kev"); and Merrick, *The Lord Won't Mind,* 24–25 (the original copulation) and 232 (Peter's confession: "It's never been the same with anybody else").

9. Compare Field, *Over the Rainbow,* on the circulation of romantic fictions in the "pink economy" in order to make a false and politically incapacitating haven (29–33). For the hype in and about gay-targeted advertising, see Chasin, *Selling Out,* 29–56 and 101–43; Walters, *All the Rage,* 235–72.

10. Laura Kipnis reminds her readers of the many (heterosexual?) "anti-love stories" in circulation: they show "the anxiety, perversity, boredom, sadism, and frustration that riddle couples life" (*Against Love,* 98). The gay films that might fall into this category actually seem to me more like what Kipnis calls "'serial love' films," which "purport to remain confident about love as an enterprise—if you can find a better object the next time around" (99n). Of course, gay filmmaking tends still to choose either the relentlessly tragic or the clammily hopeful.

11. Mau, *Life Style,* 41–43.

12. Fans will see that I simplify. For a fuller and nicely historicized description, see Thomas, "The House the Kids Built."

13. Madonna, "Material Girl," by Peter Brown and Robert Rans, from *Like a Virgin;* issued later as a single with an extended dance mix (1985). Numerous other dance mixes were released.

14. See, for example, Drukman, "Why I Want My MTV," 86–88.

15. "Vogue," by Madonna and Shep Pettibone, was released as a single by Sire in the spring of 1990 and then included on Madonna's retrospective album, *Immaculate Conception*. *Paris Is Burning*, directed by Jennie Livingston, was also released in 1990. The drag "houses" it documents go back several decades before, but do not figure much in (white) histories of gay New York.

16. Barthes, *A Lover's Discourse*, 9.

17. Surveys of gay characters both argue and illustrate the tedious similarity of their fates. I draw here on Slide, *Lost Gay Novels*.

18. See Rennard's fable from Waldo Frank's *The Dark Mother* (1920), as quoted in Slide, *Lost Gay Novels*, 88.

19. See Slide, *Lost Gay Novels*, 47 (wedding bands), 79 ("playing man and wife"), 95 ("happier household"), 109 (Rex and Jack as settled couple promoting the same).

20. Susan Stryker has analyzed both the confusions of blurbs and their design conventions in *Queer Pulp*. A number of Stryker's covers are for books mentioned by Slide in *Lost Gay Novels*.

21. From the cover of Percy Fenster, *Hot Pants Homo* (1964), reproduced in Stryker, *Queer Pulp*, 43, with further discussion on p. 45.

22. From the cover of Victor Jay's *So Sweet, So Soft, So Queer* (1965), reproduced in Stryker, *Queer Pulp*, 39.

23. From the cover of André Tellier's *Twilight Men* (1957), reproduced in Stryker, *Queer Pulp*, 101. For the novel itself, see Slide, *Lost Gay Novels*, 165–69.

24. Rougemont, *Love in the Western World*, 15: "Happy love has no history. Romance only comes into existence where love is fatal, frowned upon and doomed by life itself." Compare Kipnis, *Against Love*: "Nor until relatively recently was marriage the expected venue for Eros or romantic love, nor was the presumptive object of romantic love your own husband or wife (more likely someone else's), nor did anyone expect it to endure a lifetime: when practiced, it tended to be practiced episodically and largely outside the domicile" (26).

25. On the change in mass-market fiction, see Stryker, *Queer Pulp*, 97–98, 107–18.

26. Stills from *Pink Narcissus* and a number of other projects were published in James Bidgood, *Bidgood*, with a text by Bruce Benderson.

27. Review of *Pink Narcissus*, in *Variety*, May 25, 1971; Murray, *Images in the Dark*, 428; and Benderson in Bidgood, *Bidgood*, 62.

28. Review of *Pink Narcissus*, in *Variety*, May 25, 1971. The film was also reviewed by Vincent Canby for the *New York Times*, who judged it "sad and very vulnerable and as serious as it is sappy" (May 24, 1971, 44).

29. *A Night at Halsted's*, directed by Fred Halsted (1981). Halsted's best-known film was released nine years earlier under the title *LA Plays Itself*. For an argument about his role in distributing the aesthetic of leathersex, see Moore, *Beyond Shame*, 58–69.

30. For Barthes, *déclaration* veers away from avowal into the "endlessly glossed form of the amorous relation," into the "generalized suasion" that characterizes the speech of love. See *Lover's Discourse*, 73–74.

31. Altman, *Homosexual Oppression*, 131. Altman repeats the slogan on p. 145.

32. Altman, *Homosexual Oppression*, 130.

33. Let me repeat that I use the word *gay* to refer to modern male homosexuals and the discourses about them. Many of my sources use *gay* to refer both to men and women, as they use *homosexual* to refer to same-sex activities or dispositions in any place or time. I reproduce their language when quoting, but I revert to my own usage when commenting.

34. "Mattachine Society Missions and Purposes" (adopted July 20, 1951), reproduced in Harry Hay, *Radically Gay,* 131.

35. R. H. Crowther [Julian Underwood], "Homosexual Culture," *ONE Institute Quarterly of Homophile Studies* 3 (1960): 176−82, quoted in Legg et al., *Homophile Studies in Theory and Practice,* 120; see 117−22 generally on debates about culture, and 128−45 on the survey.

36. "Working Paper for the Revolutionary People's Constitutional Convention," reprinted in Jay and Young, *Out of the Closets,* 346−52, at 350−51.

37. Originally published as "Statement" in *Chicago Gay Pride,* June 1971; reprinted in Jay and Young, *Out of the Closets,* 252−59, at 259.

38. I quote from the later edition, edited by Bruce Rogers and published as *Gay Talk: A (Sometimes Outrageous) Dictionary of Gay Slang,* 124.

39. Hanson, "The Fairy Princess Exposed," 266.

40. "Checking the Transmission (1976)," reprinted in Gay, *The View from the Closet,* 30−32. The essay is an appreciation of Hamilton's *Christopher and Gay.*

41. Altman, *Homosexual Oppression,* 28−49 (on "gayworld"), 39 ("counterculture"), and 49 ("pseudo-community"). Altman takes "gayworld" from Hoffman, *The Gay World.*

42. Ibid., 37−38, 46. The acknowledged subtext here is Susan Sontag's "Notes on Camp" (1966), which defines it as a sensibility, but not as a culture or subculture. See Sontag, *Susan Sontag Reader,* 105−19.

43. See, for example, a column from 1976 in Gay, *View from the Closet,* 14.

44. Bronski, *Culture Clash.* Consider, for example, p. 190: "At the end of the 19th century, a distinct homosexual identity emerged in Western culture, and *along with* that identity, a distinct culture and sensibility. This sensibility was a *product* of homosexuality and the ways society had treated it. *This gay sensibility and culture* evolved over time during the past 100 years" (emphasis added).

45. Young, "No Longer the Court Jesters," 23. On the essay's earlier version, see p. 493.

46. Murray, *American Gay,* 195−98.

47. Compare the opening exhortation in Grahn, *Another Mother Tongue,* xiv.

48. Herdt and Boxer, "Introduction: Culture, History, and Life Course of Gay Men," 3.

49. I paraphrase what I take to be one of the repeated charges in Harris, *The Rise and Fall of Gay Culture.* Harris wisely avoids defining "culture," but he lists some of its elements as "rituals . . . obsessions . . . methods of communication . . . commodities . . . political institutions . . . and styles of bodily adornment" (3).

50. D'Emilio, *Sexual Politics, Sexual Communities.* The book is based on D'Emilio's 1981 dissertation at Columbia.

51. D'Emilio, *Sexual Politics, Sexual Communities,* 39; cf. 5, 31, 33, 37, and passim.

52. Katz, *Gay/Lesbian Almanac . . .* , 15.

53. Chauncey, *Gay New York,* 1.

54. Weeks, "Discourse, Desire and Sexual Deviance," 18. The essay was published originally in Plummer, *The Making of the Modern Homosexual.*

55. Boswell, *Christianity, Social Tolerance, and Homosexuality,* 243.

56. Chauncey, *Gay New York,* 133.

57. Norton, *Myth of the Modern Homosexual,* 239−41, attacking David F. Greenberg's *The Construction of Homosexuality.*

58. This remains true despite efforts to make a distinction, as in Richard Trumbach, "Sodomitical Subcultures, Sodomitical Roles, and the Gender Revolution of the Eighteenth Century."

59. Bronski, *Culture Clash,* 9.

60. For example, *Revolve: The Complete New Testament* does contain the canonical text in the "New Century Version," but it also assigns quizzes (e.g., "Are You Dating a Godly Guy?") and "Love Notes from God." The publication is designed to resemble a magazine like *Seventeen,* including pictures of rapturously smiling models with wind-machine-blown hair.

61. Norton, *My Dear Boy.*

62. Ibid., 24–25.

63. Ibid., 33–36; quotation at 33. On what view of historiography—not to mention historical causality—can a "prejudice" "sweep across" a continent in a given century?

64. Thus Matthiessen in a letter to Davenport half a year later, as reported in Hyde, *Rat and the Devil,* 15–18; quotations at 17–18. The Matthiessen/Cheney correspondence is cited in what follows by the page numbers in Hyde.

65. Matthiessen quotes Whitman, "So Long!" lines 25–27.

66. The brackets mark Hyde's insertion of an explanatory paraphrase.

67. The controlling passage is Ephesians 5 : 22–33. I will consider the force and limits of this analogy below in chapter 7.

68. Matthiessen had applied the same notion to his own flirtation with a church workman; see Matthiessen to Cheney, April 18, 1925, 123–25, at 124.

69. See the reminiscence by Joseph H. Summers in Sweezy and Huberman, *F. O. Matthiessen (1902–1950): A Collective Portrait,* 141–44, at 142: "Matty stated his position as a Christian in the simplest terms. He believed that love was the greatest value man could know, and he believed its power and absolute value could not be accounted for by any naturalistic or rationalistic explanation." For other mentions of Matthiessen's religious belief and practice in the letters, see Hyde, *Rat and the Devil,* 86–88 (on God and love), 90 (visit to chapel), 91 (idolatry in notion of God), 214 ("early church"), 257 (Cheney's Bible brought to Matthiessen in hospital), 282 (Easter communion), and 341 ("service").

70. Compare Matthiessen to Cheney, February 9, 1925, where Matthiessen commends Cheney for beginning each day with a prayer (93).

71. Though Cheney may not have known it, the depiction of the relationship between Jesus and the "beloved disciple" in John had long been appropriated by Christian same-sex couples as supreme precedent. See Bray, *The Friend,* especially 116–22.

72. Russell, *Jeb and Dash,* 1 (on pseudonym), 4 (on the family relation).

73. For references to Whitman or quotations of him, see Russell, *Jeb and Dash,* 55, 65, 92. As telling examples of the terms, consider the following: "a glorious companion and freedom" (22); "a friend, a lovable, handsome fellow, a realization of the friend I have dreamed of" (31); "my dear Dashie, my beloved companion" (166); "my dear comrade Dashie" (168); "joined forever with a loving friend and companion" (188); "sweet friend" as euphemism for boyfriend (198); "my charming companion" (210); "my best friend Dash" (226).

74. Ibid., 43 (in 1924), 80 (in 1925), 159 (in 1929), 236 (in 1938), 276 (in 1945). An imaginary lover is the best romantic object—and, indeed, the only romantic object.

75. Ibid., 40. Since Russell has combined "Alexander's" five siblings into one (4), it is not clear which brother this might be—or whether it is in fact a brother. For other passages on the potency of "forever" or "always" as expressed in popular music, see 151 and 203.

76. Ibid., 42.

77. Ibid., 100.

78. Compare Kristeva, *Tales of Love:* "Eros is thus homosexual, and homosexuality must be understood, beyond love for *paides,* boys, as an appetite for homologation, for identification of the sexes, under the aegis of an erected ideal. Of the Phallus" (62).

79. Genet, *Our Lady of the Flowers,* 97. Page numbers of this translation are cited parenthetically in the rest of this paragraph.

80. Baker, *Fantabulosa: A Dictionary of Polari and Gay Slang,* 33, 61, 149, 211.

81. Marge Piercy, *Woman on the Edge of Time,* 66.

82. Ibid., 56 ("rigid"), 66 ("sweet friends"), and so on.

83. Ibid., 56.

CHAPTER TWO

1. *Metrosexuality,* DVD, 2001.

2. From act 1 of *The Importance of Being Earnest,* in Wilde, *The Importance of Being Earnest and Related Writings,* 39–40.

3. See, among many examples, Cromey, *In God's Image,* 44–45.

4. Cory, *The Homosexual in America,* xvi. Subsequently cited in the text by page numbers in parentheses.

5. In what follows, I describe the voice of the narrator in Cory's book. I do not try to describe Cory/Sagarin himself. For an effort at psycho-biography, see Duberman, *Left Out,* 59–94.

6. The contrast "gay"/"straight" is no anachronism. Cory explains the distinction himself at some length; see *Homosexual in America,* 109–10.

7. Kleinberg, "Modern Arrangements." Cited parenthetically by page number in the rest of this section.

8. One explicit invocation of Freud juxtaposes him with Catholicism: "Michael's fears are partly Catholic, partly Freudian, and mostly his own" (125).

9. Compare the movement for "second virginity" or the stipulations of Roman Catholic premarital counseling.

10. John D'Emilio makes a related point: "Rather than identify the Stonewall Riots of June 1969 as the *birth* of gay liberation at the *end* of the 1960s, perhaps we would do better to see them for what they were: as symbolic of a shift that had been in the making for a number of years" (*The World Turned,* 30; original emphasis; see also 49, 67, 147–53, 218–21). He proposes that we understand Stonewall "not as an event of great historic significance but as a kind of queer shorthand for a larger historic phenomenon: 'the sixties'" (*The World Turned,* 227). I add only that the "the sixties" is also a mythic symbol. All of this is opposed to the conclusions David Carter wants to draw in *Stonewall.* Consider just this double claim: "Certainly [Stonewall] was an event of a rare kind in history, one where without any planning of any kind all the necessary elements came together in just the right way to start a revolutionary change in human consciousness that is profoundly for the better. Rather than being an inevitable event that could have happened almost anywhere, the riots could have occurred only at the Stonewall Inn" (*Stonewall,* 259).

11. Compare Mitulski, "Lavender Lunch."

12. The critiques were not invented in the 1960s. Their genealogies run back at least into feminist and other reformist discourses of the nineteenth century. (I note below some obvious echoes of Engels.) For the reemergence of these critiques more generally, see Ingraham, *White Weddings,* 9–10, 17. Compare the difficult balance of historical "shifts" and actual plurality in Eskridge, *The Case for Same-Sex Marriage,* especially 44–50; Stiers, *From This Day Forward,* 12–24.

13. The discipline can take benign forms, such as efforts to identify points of agreement under conflict. For example, Marvin Ellison writes that "internal LBGT conflict [about marriage] is not about the status of homosexuality, the desirability of increasing support for

alternative families, or even the value of committed intimate partnerships" (*Same-Sex Marriage?* 101). The statement is not accurate, I think, for either the past or the present—unless "internal" refers to a very specific group of public advocates.

14. Saunders, "Reformer's Choice." If the editorial note can be taken at face value, the author (male or female) was unknown to the editors. Cited parenthetically by page number in the rest of this section.

15. All of these comments come from the generous selection of replies to Saunders printed in the October 1953 issue of *ONE* (11–22). I cite these parenthetically by page number here and in what follows.

16. Handwritten notes on these conversations are preserved in the papers of Don Lucas, GLBT Historical Society (San Francisco), box 1, folder 5, which is labeled "Matt[achine] Foundation Discussion Groups, 1952–1953." If the date "Thurs., Mar. 5" is correct, these notes followed an earlier set prepared by Marilyn Rieger in February 1953, which is mentioned in the adjacent correspondence.

17. The text was originally published under the headline "Refugees from Amerika: A Gay Manifesto" in the *San Francisco Free Press,* but it entered into wider circulation with the shortened title "Gay Manifesto." The version printed under that short title in Jay and Young, *Out of the Closets,* 330–42, differs at many points from the original in the *Free Press.* I follow the original version.

18. Earlier, Wittman was visible as president of the Swarthmore Political Action Club. He passed from organizing integration actions in Chester, Pennsylvania, to the National Committee of the SDS and its Economic and Action Research Project. In 1967, Wittman moved to San Francisco, where he continued antiwar activity. See Sale, *SDS,* 104–5.

19. See Wittman's brief items in the newsletter of San Francisco's Committee for Homosexual Freedom, April 22 and 29, 1969.

20. On the protest action, see Donn Teal, *Gay Militants,* 29–32.

21. It was republished in 1970 in New York by (among others) the "Red Butterfly" collective, which added its own commentary. See Teal, *Gay Militants,* 86, 95. Teal himself wrote in 1971 that the "Manifesto" "has become, in effect, the bible of gay liberation" (95). Allen Young describes his first reading of it in Greenwich Village almost as emphatically: "A very important piece for me personally. . . . I was very moved by it." See Young's remarks in "Reminiscences of Pre-Stonewall Greenwich Village," 333. The "Manifesto" is listed among pamphlets available from Berkeley's Committee of Concern for Homosexuals in its newsletter, *Agape and Action,* no. 1 (June 5, 1970), no. 2 (June 23, 1970). It was dropped from the list ten months later in order to make more room for women's material; see *Agape and Action,* no. 7 (February 1971): 3.

22. Wittman, "Refugees from Amerika," 3–4. The quotations following are from p. 4.

23. Wittman, "Refugees from Amerika," 3–4. The quotations following are from the subsection headed "Alternatives to Marriage," 4.

24. Wittman's tentativeness about the future is emphasized in other tracts. Compare the somewhat later piece by McCubbin, *The Gay Question:* "Marxism is a potent tool in the struggle for a better world but it is not a crystal ball. Yet Marxists are concerned with the questions of love and sexuality. We are confident that with the end of exploitation and oppression will come the possibility of much fuller, richer, and more profound human relationships."

25. The gay liberationist critique was inspired by and then outdistanced by lesbian feminist critiques. For a quick introduction to the history and a restatement of the argument that monogamy is patriarchy, see Stelboum, "Patriarchal Monogamy," especially 42–44.

26. See, for example, Engels, *Origin of the Family,* 105–15 on monogamy, masculine privilege, and capitalism.

27. Red Butterfly, untitled article in *Come Out.*

28. Thorp, "I.D., Leadership and Violence," 356, 357. This text was read in August 1970 at the National Gay Liberation Front Student Conference.

29. Third World Gay Revolution, "What We Want, What We Believe," 365. This text was originally published in March 1971 (see Jay and Young, *Out of the Closets,* lxvii).

30. "It Can Happen Here!" 19.

31. See, for example, Diaman, "On Sex Roles and Equality" (1970), 262; Third World Gay Revolution (Chicago) and Gay Liberation Front (Chicago), "Gay Revolution and Sex Roles" (1971), 253, 258.

32. The series was inaugurated with *Fag Rag*'s first issue (June 1971). The newspaper was the project of Boston's members of the Gay Liberation Front, Shively prominent among them. His essays are accompanied by explicit illustrations, but they are more striking for their alternation of elegantly sardonic distance and revolutionary fervor. For other accounts of Shively's biography and views, as well as his importance to *Fag Rag,* see Shand-Tucci, *The Crimson Letter,* 260–62; and Moore, *Beyond Shame,* 6–10.

33. The reference to Whitman is not only a cliché. As "Charley," Shively wrote on Whitman and, in a pamphlet of San Francisco poetry, after Whitman. See his *Nuestra Señora de los Dolores.*

34. Charles Shively, "Group Sex," 8, pt. 4 of "Cocksucking as an Act of Revolution."

35. Shively, "Group Sex," 8.

36. Ibid., 9.

37. Shively, "Indiscriminate Promiscuity As an Act of Revolution," 3.

38. Ibid., 4. Subsequently cited parenthetically by page number in the text.

39. I follow the account in Clendinen and Nagourney, *Out for Good,* 312–16. Their account draws from contemporary news stories and interviews with Shively.

40. A narrative of the 1964 gathering and its genesis was produced by Don Kuhn of the Glide Urban Center as *The Church and the Homosexual: A Report on a Consultation.* I cite from the typescript in the papers of Phyllis Lyon and Del Martin, #93-13, GLBT Historical Society (San Francisco), box 17, folder 14. An abbreviated version appears as "The Church and the Homosexual" in Gearhart and Johnson, *Loving Women/Loving Men,* 3–20. For a somewhat later account of the founding of CRH, see Martin and Lyon, *Lesbian/Woman,* 239–42.

41. John Preston makes this joking aside: "It was a time when 'alternative lifestyles' were the fad as well as alternative forms of ministry." See Preston, "A Eulogy for George," 84.

42. Despite promises to the contrary, the police harassed those attending the fund-raising event in many ways (e.g., by photographing anyone entering and repeatedly demanding access to the hall). When two lawyers with CRH asked to see a warrant, they were arrested—along with the woman collecting tickets from those courageous enough to attend. It would be just another enraging story except for what happened next: seven straight-identified clergyman called a press conference at Glide Memorial Church to protest police intimidation. For a summary account, see D'Emilio, *Sexual Politics,* 192–95; Loughery, *Other Side of Silence,* 285–87; and Boyd, *Wide Open Town,* 233–35, but beware her conclusion that the event shifted the council's concern "from theology to police harassment and abuse" (235). Board minutes for that spring and summer are obviously preoccupied with the event and its sequel, but over a longer period the CRH continued to be much concerned with theology—as I show below.

43. Kuhn, *Church and the Homosexual,* 11. The whole summary of Lucas's survey occupies pp. 9–20 of the typescript.

44. The outline is in the Lyon-Martin Papers, GLBT Historical Society, box 17, folder 14.

45. Kuhn, *Church and the Homosexual,* 39–62.

46. The discussion was conducted by "Billie Talmij." The three other members were Cleo Glenn, Phyllis Lyon, and Del Martin. A typescript exists of the questions prepared for the discussion, entitled "Gab 'n' Java: August 28, 1964," Lyon-Martin Papers, GLBT Historical Society, box 17, folder 14 (4 pp.).

47. Wood, *Christ and the Homosexual.* Wood describes homosexual "marriages," including those between active churchgoers; see, for example, the story of David and Paul (38–40). In general terms, Wood asserts "the validity of a union between two men or two women who are truly in love and who really want to spend the rest of their lives together," though only when it comes as close as possible to "the established conventions of society" (198–99). He also advocates blessing such unions: "If a gay couple came to me and requested a religious marriage ceremony, I would not automatically turn them away. . . . [If they met substantially the same requirements for heterosexual couples,] I would then be inclined, God willing, to give such a blessing in my capacity as an ordained minister of the Gospel" (200).

48. "Gab 'n' Java," 3.

49. Council on Religion and the Homosexual, minutes of the general meeting of July 7, 1964, in the Lyon-Martin Papers, GLBT Historical Society, box 17, folder 17.

50. "Goals and Purposes of 'The Council on Religion and the Homosexual,'" single sheet, Lyon-Martin Papers, GLBT Historical Society, box 17, folder 15. Correspondence related to the document in the same folder is dated from February 1965.

51. Council on Religion and the Homosexual, *A Brief of Injustices.* In what follows, the four pages of this broadsheet are cited parenthetically in the text.

52. Episcopal Diocese of California, Joint Committee on Homosexuality, Minutes of the meeting of February 9, 1966, in Lyon-Martin Papers, GLBT Historical Society, box 18, folder 11, p. 1.

53. Ibid., 2. The mention of a "situational ethic" recalls that a debate over situation and context in distinction to regulation and principle was already raging in Christian circles, especially with regard sexual matters. The debate was fueled later in the year by Joseph Fletcher's *Situation Ethics.*

54. Gale Thorne, "A Sexual Bill of Rights," 38.

55. The history figures in chapter 6, which considers the genealogy of same-sex union ceremonies.

56. In July 1970, the *San Francisco Chronicle* was already running a two-part series under the headline "The Boom in 'Gay' Marriages." The first part features a picture of Troy Perry, with the caption "He's wed 36 same-sex couples already." See Grieg, "Boom," 1.

57. Individual members of the CRH or its allied groups would later endorse gay unions or marriages quite explicitly. For example, Robert Warren Cromey was one of the straight-identified clergymen who joined in organizing the early work of the CRH, including the New Year's Day dance and its aftermath. An Episcopal priest, he spent the ensuing years first as a private counselor and then as Rector of Trinity Episcopal Church, San Francisco. From 1982 on, Cromey provoked controversy by advocating the development of union ceremonies and then blessing same-sex couples in the church at a Eucharist. He writes of the ceremony as a "marriage." See Cromey, *In God's Image,* 16–18, 41–45, 66.

58. See Gearhart and Johnson, *Loving Women/Loving Men,* 3−20 (Kuhn); 23−58 (Treese); 61−88 (Gearhart and Johnson on the narrative history).

59. "Homosexual Identity," 6.

60. Dean, "Gay Marriage." Subsequent citations are by page number in the text.

61. Troy Perry writes in the same period: "We [presumably the MCC] insist that the couple has a close ongoing relationship for at least six months. We counsel them about special problems, promiscuity, and how to cooperate in establishing a fulfilling and meaningful relationship" (*The Lord Is My Shepherd,* 208).

62. Consider these examples from the first-person accounts in Yost, *When Love Lasts Forever:* anniversary of moving into first shared apartment, 45−56, at 48, and 139−46, at 142; anniversary of being "together," with no beginning specified, 119−29, at 129; anniversary as first date (first kiss and first copulation), 149−58, at 151.

63. The "engagement" can be confused with other events. In another account from Yost, the parents of a gay man start sending anniversary cards at the end of "the first year." The anniversary date seems to be the day their son "came out" by announcing his involvement with another man. The men did not celebrate a commitment ceremony then or at any later time. See Yost, *When Love Lasts Forever,* 17−28, at 23, 27.

64. Michael Foley, no friend of gay unions, complains that the function of (heterosexual) betrothal rites must be clarified quite carefully if they are not to "collapse into the wedding" ("Betrothals," 61).

65. Beatrice, quoted in Mackey, O'Brien, and Mackey, *Gay and Lesbian Couples,* 61.

66. Yip, *Gay Male Christian Couples,* 2 (date); 5 (sample); 141−42 (date, sample, criteria). Subsequent citations are by page number in the text.

67. Other studies, while not quite so dramatic, confirm that only a low percentage of long-term couples have had a ceremony. See, for example, Berger, "Men Together": "Only 12.6% of couples in this study reported having had such a ceremony." Of those who had not yet had a ceremony, "over a third (36.5%) said they would choose one if given the opportunity" (39). The next question should have been: What opportunity are you waiting for that you don't already have?

68. Yip here condenses material already published as "Gay Christian Ceremonies and Blessing Ceremonies." Compare Marcus, *Together Forever:* most of the couples interviewed "expressed little interest in or negative feelings toward the idea of a public ceremony" (146). It might be, of course, that the antipathy expressed toward unions condenses a more general—and more upsetting—antipathy toward Christian churches, even by those who are actively involved in them. Many gay men who stay on "in church" do so just barely, struggling from week to week to control anger and despair.

69. As should become clear, I am thinking of betrothal not as a legal requirement, but as a moment in a full liturgical cycle. I am definitely not proposing betrothal as a second-class marriage for same-sex couples. Betrothal remains for me a period of preparation before a rite of blessing on the union, whether that blessing is conceived as marriage or in more promising terms.

70. The queries were drafted by the Lesbian, Gay, and Bisexual Concerns Committee of Putney Friends Meeting, September 1992; see Hill, *Marriage,* 27−28.

CHAPTER THREE

1. "Normal Heights" and untitled photo spread, *XY* no. 38 (December 2002), 44−55 and 59−66, respectively. The photographs are by James Patrick Dawson.

2. Condé Nast Bridal Infobank American Weddings Study 2002 as reported in Condé Nast Bridal Group, *Future Impact of Demographic Trends on the Bridal Industry,* page entitled "Today's Average Wedding Costs Over $22,000."

3. Jennifer Bayot, "For Richer or Poorer." Bayot's source for these figures is apparently the Condé Nast Bridal Infobank. Earlier statistics, also chiefly from Condé Nast, are reviewed in Ingraham, *White Weddings,* 27−30. The Condé Nast figures, of whatever vintage, are admittedly skewed toward affluent, white couples. See Ingraham, *White Weddings,* 89.

4. Condé Nast, *Future Impact,* page entitled "Over a 16-Month Time Period, They Decide How to Spend $120 Billion."

5. Parenthetical citations in the text refer to the pages of this issue until otherwise noted.

6. Whenever there is a gender prohibition, there's an occasion for camp. So, of course, two "boys" in a playful mood shake up some Cosmos, put on two veils, and spend an evening with *Modern Bride.* The veils are the key, though. They show the gender-specificity of the magazine's address. Could the two boys put on their gym gear or their business suits and read *MB* with quite as much pleasure?

7. Compare the main headline for the ad by WeddingChannel.com, "How do you know it's the right dress? The same way you know he's the right guy" (82−83). See again the advertisement for kitchenware and small appliances on 221: "Like the perfect husband—clever *and* attractive."

8. The whiteness of both female and male bodies is remarkable. For a more comprehensive analysis, see Ingraham, *White Weddings,* 93−95.

9. There is, I readily admit, a more complicated story to be told here about how "bridal culture" can open space for adolescent women. See, for example, Driscoll, *Girls,* 175−91.

10. The phrase appears in Condé Nast, *Future Impact,* page entitled "Average Engagement."

11. Ingraham, *White Weddings,* 139−46.

12. Freeman, *Wedding Complex,* 2.

13. Beginning with *Queer Eye for the Straight Guy,* episode 3, originally aired July 29, 2003, on the Bravo Network.

14. One of two advertisements that show multiple male bodies is meant to look like a slightly faded wedding snapshot (230−31).

15. See 2, 51, 114, 616, 626, 628, 629, 632, 636, 639, and so on. A photograph on 27 is ambiguous. It appears in an ad for rings and so may represent a proposal at a bistro. But it might also be a moment of romantic infatuation that the astute bride will want to see preserved in precious metal.

16. See respectively 29, 39, and the unnumbered foldout after 48.

17. See respectively 36−37, 79, 619, 92, 95, 105, and the inside of the front cover together with 1.

18. The same model appears in a second spread for the same company on 366−73. In the second series, he sports many of the same shirts and usually stares off into (his own?) space, but does once look at the camera (368).

19. Ingraham, *White Weddings,* 80−81.

20. *Gay Weddings* aired on the Bravo Network beginning on September 2, 2002, in eight episodes of 30 minutes each. I cite this series in the text parenthetically by episode number.

21. For this reason, the remarks following should be read as pertaining to the named characters of the fictional series and not to the actual persons who acted in it. Their feelings and actions around the series were presumably more complex. The same must be said of the ceremonies pictured. With fuller access, it would certainly have been possible to analyze the

ritual processes according to one or another model. (See, for example, McQueeney, "The New Religious Rite.") But the Bravo series is of course not trying to document the rites. It stages them to "entertain," that is, to attract and hold the attention of viewers.

22. Ayers and Brown, *Essential Guide to Lesbian and Gay Weddings,* 40.

23. Ayers and Brown, *Essential Guide,* 40.

24. Ibid., 16.

25. See, for example, www.GayWeddings.com; www.PlanetOut.com, under "Families/ Commitment"; www.TwoGrooms.com. Five Star Software offers a planning program, "My Gay Wedding Companion."

26. Steve Hymon, "Gay, Lesbian Wedding Expo Honors 'We Do,'" *Los Angeles Times,* February 24, 2004, consulted on the web.

27. Ingraham, *White Weddings,* 49.

28. "Daniel Gross and Steven Goldstein," *New York Times,* September 1, 2002, late edition—final, sec. 9, p. 12.

29. Bronski, "I'll Cry Tomorrow," 44–45.

30. Ayers and Brown, *Essential Guide.* I quote from the blurbs on the back cover of the 1999 edition. Subsequent parenthetical citations in the text are to the pages of this book until otherwise noted. Some readers might think that I am picking on the *Essential Guide;* others will imagine that I chose it because it is easy to mock. In fact, I chose it because it is the most comprehensive queer wedding planner I could find. I could make roughly the same arguments from other books: for example, Martinac, *Lesbian and Gay Book of Love and Marriage,* especially 80–137—but it hasn't as many colorful details.

31. Freeman, *Wedding Complex,* 9.

32. Ingraham, *White Weddings,* 71–72.

33. Laderman, *Rest in Peace.*

34. Condé Nast, *Future Impact,* page entitled "A Snapshot of the American Wedding."

35. *Absolutely Fabulous,* "In New York," 45 minutes. The episode was originally broadcast by the BBC on December 27, 2002, as a Christmas special under the title "Gay."

CHAPTER FOUR

1. The latter is the notion of "Levirate marriage" that figures so prominently in Genesis 38:8–10, the story of Onan. Onan "spills his seed on the ground" rather than supply heirs to his deceased brother. God then kills him.

2. For an accessible summary, see Blenkinsopp, "The Family in First Temple Israel," 63–66.

3. For the slow development of the theology of Christian marriage in the West, see Reynolds, *Marriage in the Western Church;* for medieval constructions of the canon law on sexual acts in and out of marriage, see Brundage, *Law, Sex, and Christian Society in Medieval Europe;* for a classification of Christian "models" of marriage, especially from the Reformation to the present, see Witte, *From Sacrament to Contract.*

4. I return to these texts and topics in chapter 7.

5. For quotations from the Bible, I use the New Revised Standard Version for the Hebrew, and translate directly from the New Testament Greek.

6. See, for the preeminence of continence, Augustine *De bono coniugali* 6.6 and 8.8, 195, lines 23–24, and 199, lines 6–17. Compare the translation by Roy J. Deferrari in *Saint Augustine: Treatises on Marriage and Other Subjects,* 17, 21.

7. Some Christian groups have adopted more "sex-positive" views in recent decades, and theologians have called for their adoption in many more. These recent views depart from the

mass of Christian traditions as clearly as approval of same-sex desire. In other decades, the views would have been judged and punished as heresy. Tim and Beverly LaHaye, in the kind of sexual exhortation they offer in *The Act of Marriage: The Beauty of Sexual Love,* align themselves not only with the most "liberal" theologians of a previous generation, but with some notorious "heretics" in church history. The same can be said of the new wave of evangelical pillow books. While claiming to be following the letter of Scripture, they appropriate many lessons from the "sexual revolution" that they elsewhere condemn.

8. Peter Lombard *Sententiae* 4.28.4.2, in *Sententiae in IV libris distinctae,* 2:435.17–20.

9. I argue the point more fully in *Ethics of Sex,* 107–30.

10. Boswell, *Christianity, Social Tolerance, and Homosexuality* and *Same-Sex Unions in Premodern Europe;* Brooten, *Love between Women;* Bray, *The Friend.* I raise some objections against Boswell and Bray in the next chapter. Here I emphasize that their work, whatever its limitations, takes the history of Christian relationships much more seriously, as both Christian and historical, than do many of their opponents. I cannot stress enough that most "traditional" defenses of Christian marriage are thoroughly untraditional both in their historical claims and in their notions of theological method.

11. See the extraordinary meditation on an equally extraordinary essay by Rowan Williams, in Eugene F. Rogers, Jr., *Sexuality and the Christian Body,* 237–48, to which compare Williams, "The Body's Grace."

12. Here I come close to some of the central themes in Stuart, *Gay and Lesbian Theologies,* especially with regard to repetition. We differ, I think, on the causes of repetition in the past and on prospects for the future.

13. For example, Canon Jeffrey John, who was forced to withdraw from appointment as Bishop of Reading because of his honest homosexuality, was in a committed relationship for twenty-seven years. He was quoted by the BBC as saying, "My own view is that there is a sound argument from Scripture and tradition in favour of Christians accepting same-sex relationships, provided they are based on a personal covenant of lifelong faithfulness. I would not term such a relationship a 'marriage,' but I believe it could be understood as a legitimate covenanted relationship." See "Gay Priest Rejects Bishop Post," reported July 6, 2003, by the BBC News online service. Jeffrey John had laid out his views with slightly different emphasis in *"Permanent, Faithful, Stable": Christian Same-Sex Partnerships:* "Homosexual relationships should be accepted and blessed by the Church, provided that the quality and commitment of the relationship are the same as those expected of a Christian marriage. . . . The theological, ethical and sacramental status of such a partnership between two men or two women is comparable to that of a marriage whether or not the word marriage is used to described it" (1). For the circumstances of John's withdrawal, see Bates, *A Church at War,* 160–75.

14. For example, and to remain with Anglicans, see Cromey, *In God's Image:* "If, as a typical [queer] parishioner, you want to celebrate your relationship with your lover, the bishop may interfere if he hears about it. You may be shunted off to a garden or living room. You can likely get some priest to say some prayers, making you feel like a second-class citizen of the Body of Christ" (32).

15. Yip, *Gay Male Christian Couples.* In what follows, this work is often cited parenthetically by page number in the text.

16. Ibid., 109 (Calvin, celebrating Eucharist with his partner); 110 (James, public and private prayer); 110 (Nigel, on private prayer and Bible study; cf. 112, where he rejects liturgy).

17. Ibid., 109 (Calvin, with his remarks on 93; Neil); 110 (Nigel); cf. 92–93 (Robert, Paul, and Clive).

18. Religion can disappear almost entirely in interviews or first-person accounts that are trying to construct a political or legal narrative of same-sex unions. See, for example, Lahey and Alderson, *Same-Sex Marriage.*

19. Tyler, *Divine Comedy of Pavel Tchelitchew.*

20. Ford, *Water from a Bucket;* Wescott, *Continual Lessons.*

21. Kirstein, *Pavel Feodorovitch Chelitchew, 1898–1957;* Lynes, "Pavel Tchetlichev in his studio with Jonathan Tichernor" (1944), reproduced in Leddick, *Intimate Companions,* 128; Tyler, *Divine Comedy of Pavel Tchelitchew,* plate facing 283.

CHAPTER FIVE

1. A number of Christian bodies in America now bless such unions. Blessings have been approved, with various restrictions of terminology and options for local choice, by at least the Universal Fellowship of Metropolitan Community Churches, the Unitarian Universalist Association, the United Church of Christ, the Religious Society of Friends (Quakers), the Presbyterian Church (U.S.A.), and some Episcopalian dioceses. The list changes almost weekly and will doubtless be out of date by the time you read this note. The rapid change is only another sign of the contentious role that same-sex unions have been assigned to play in church politics: they are right now the pretext for the main battles of church power.

2. Frank Howell, "Sacred Ceremonies," 14–15.

3. See Reynolds, *Marriage in the Western Church,* 324, 374, who cites and generally agrees with Ritzer, *Les marriages dans les églises chrétiennes du Ier au XIe siècle,* 81–94, 104–23. Compare Stevenson, *Nuptial Blessing,* 21–32, on Eastern and Western evidence in the fourth through the sixth centuries.

4. For the general point, see Reynolds, *Marriage in the Western Church,* 393–94.

5. See Marcus, *Together Forever,* 147–48 (Pam and Lindsy at Notre Dame in Paris); 152 (Jim and Martin at the Vatican); and the fictional account of a rite culminating in communion at St. Peter's in T'ien-Wen, *Notes of a Desolate Man,* 55–57.

6. Brown, *The Evening Crowd at Kirmser's,* 88–89.

7. Miller, *Place for Us,* 20–21.

8. Montaigne, *Journal de Voyage,* 231. Boswell takes this as evidence for the use in western Europe of a Latin liturgy of *adelphopoiēsis;* see Boswell, *Same-Sex Unions in Premodern Europe,* 264–65, about which more immediately below. I see it as evidence of the appropriation for same-sex purposes of existing wedding rites.

9. Johnson, *Lavender Scare,* 42.

10. There is a pious account of George Hyde's early ministry in Pappas, "Happy Birthday, Jesus!" (1976). Pappas was a member of the original group in Atlanta. In 1957, Hyde took his group into "the full fellowship and communion of the Orthodox Catholic Church of America, with specific encouragement to continue our gay Christian work" (George A. Hyde to Raymond Broshears, February 12, 1977, p. 2; in the papers of Raymond Broshears, GLBT Historical Society [San Francisco], box 4, folder "Hyde").

11. Warren, *Front Runner,* 36, 287–88. Compare the recollections reported in Stiers, *From This Day Forward,* 14–15, of "Services of Holy Union" during the 1970s at the "Church of the Beloved Joseph" on Twentieth Street in Manhattan.

12. Michael Arditti, *Easter,* 279–91.

13. See "A Covenant of Friendship."

14. Vecsey, "Minister Sponsors Homosexual Rituals."

15. Paulson, "Virtue Enough for Miss Grrrrl," 3.

16. Until otherwise noted, parenthetical citations in this section refer to the pages of Boswell, *Same-Sex Unions.*

17. Boswell died of complications arising from AIDS on December 24, 1994, six or seven months after *Same-Sex Unions* appeared in the bookstores. He had suffered "complications" and their consequences for at least several years. I am not alone in thinking that we would have had a much stronger book if he had not been so ill—as we would have any number of other books if so many had not died.

18. Goar, *Euchologion, sive rituale Graecorum . . .*

19. This is the now famous Grottaferrata MS Γ.B.II. Boswell's interpretation of the rite in this and all other manuscripts depends on reading through a scribal line that would appear to mark off the marital ceremony of crowning from the rite of *adelphopoiēsis.* Boswell justifies ignoring the line in *Same-Sex Unions* at 296–97, n. 80.

20. The strips ran in many American newspapers for several days beginning June 8, 1994—though some regular subscribers to Garry Trudeau's series refused to print them.

21. Compare Saliers, *Worship as Theology,* on the eschatological character of liturgy and its elements.

22. I quote a greeting card designed by R. N. Schachter and published by Saints Alive! In 1996, the *National AIDS Awareness Catalog* advertised Boswell's book with the blurb, "Did you know European churches in the Middle Ages formally sanctioned same sex marriages? This fascinating study by a Yale professor provides details." The same catalog offered a "Same Sex Union Medallion" that reproduces the illustration from Boswell's cover, the detail of a seventh-century icon of the saints Serge and Bacchus.

23. Compare Boswell's labored explanation for translating the various rites into something like the English of the 1928 *Book of Common Prayer (Same-Sex Unions,* 283–84).

24. Until otherwise noted, parenthetical citations will refer to the pages of Bray, *The Friend.*

25. Many would claim that if industrialized societies have tended to lose nonreproductive systems of kinship, certain segments or subcultures (including queer ones) have both retained and cultivated them. See the dazzling reflections in Judith Butler's "Is Kinship Always Already Heterosexual?"

26. Bray recounts a variety of ways for performing the ceremony before communion. See the summary in *The Friend,* 242–43.

27. Bray's fullest explanation of these connections comes in his interpretation of the great east window at Holy Trinity, Goodramgate (*The Friend,* 246–53).

28. I remain unclear how the models of friendship Bray presents are meant to differ from the notions of friendship current in homophile or homoerotic groups around the middle of the last century. On many pages of *Der Kreis,* for example, "friendship" is the treasured relationship to one special comrade within the larger movement. See Kennedy, *Ideal Gay Man,* 33, 35, 52, 61, 81, 90, 117, 173–80, and so on. *Der Kreis* traced this friendship back to the Christian God and even to such specific holy exemplars as Jesus and John (65, 106).

29. Bailey, *Homosexuality and the Western Christian Tradition.*

30. This thought-experiment can be performed on many other kinds of historical or exegetical arguments in churches. Theologians often scatter their time on the quality of evidence without wondering whether the argument would go through with the best imaginable evidence.

31. Ayers and Brown, *Essential Guide,* 120.

32. Love, "Great Ceremony Solutions," 185.

33. Cherry and Sherwood, *Equal Rites,* xviii.

34. Becky Butler, *Ceremonies of the Heart: Celebrating Lesbian Unions,* 41.

35. A fine example of this sort of process is described in a report to the local Episcopal bishop (then William E. Swing) by the Church of the Good Shepherd in Berkeley: "'In All Our Loving, We Praise You, O God': Celebrating Relationships at Good Shepherd Church" (December 1994). The parish had been authorized by the bishop to conduct an experiment in blessing same-sex couples. They ended up rethinking the liturgical place of erotico-familial relationships in church life.

36. The ceremony of Marion Hansell and Barbara Hicks (June 4, 1998), as reported in Butler, *Ceremonies of the Heart,* 149–57.

37. *Gay Weddings,* ep. 6.

38. Garner, "A Sample Service of Holy Union based on the Tradition of Kwanzaa," 99.

39. Dusty Blue and Ali Marrero (October 21, 1984); see Butler, *Ceremonies of the Heart,* 179–89, at 184. Cited by page number in the text in the rest of the paragraph.

40. Kilby Clark and Janet Osimo (May 19, 1984); see Butler, *Ceremonies of the Heart,* 173–78, 175.

41. Terry Kime and Sally Meiser (August 8, 1987); see Butler, *Ceremonies of the Heart,* 191–98. The text is not cited, but it seems to be Rosemary Radford Ruether, *Women-Church,* 196–200, a rite developed for the covenant celebration of Phyllis Athey and Mary Jo Osterman on August 19, 1982.

42. Hill, *Marriage,* 12–22.

43. For example, Linda Quiring and Cindy Reichley (May 18, 1985); see Butler, *Ceremonies of the Heart,* 243–52, especially the vows, 248–49.

44. This liturgy was first used for celebrating Piazza's union with his own partner in 1981. Composing the rite, Piazza began with a traditional Methodist wedding and then added texts from other sources. The "Apache" blessing was taken from a wedding card the couple received. Piazza, personal correspondence, July 19, 2004.

45. This liturgy arose out of the practice of the Church of St. John the Evangelist, Bowdoin St., Boston. Though McLaughlin put it into final form and fixed the theological emphasis on friendship, some of the liturgy was originally composed by Richard Valantasis and Jennifer Phillips. McLaughlin, personal correspondence, June 10, 2004.

46. Piazza, "Cathedral of Hope Holy Union" (see "Charge to the Congregation"). Subsequently cited by section title in the text.

47. Glaser, "A Celebration of Love and Commitment," 90. In the following paragraph, I cite this text parenthetically by page number.

48. McLaughlin, "Celebration and Blessing of a Covenanted Union," 100. I cite this text parenthetically by page number until otherwise indicated.

49. Witte identifies this as *the* Anglican model of marriage in his *From Sacrament to Contract,* 130–34.

50. A little treatise could be written on controversies over candle ceremonies. Are there two candles of equal size tipped together (as here)? Or two little candles used to light a single big one, so that all three burn? Or two little candles that are blown out as soon as the big one catches flame?

51. McLaughlin, "Celebration and Blessing of a Covenanted Union," 101.

52. Butler's views have been reduced to dull caricature, so let me make clear that I am

thinking of a specific sentence: "Indeed, in my view, the normative focus for gay and lesbian practice ought to be on the subversive and parodic redeployment of power rather than on the impossible fantasy of its full-scale transcendence." See Butler, *Gender Trouble,* 158.

53. See the liturgies by Malcolm Boyd, Zalmon Sherwood, and D. B. Gregory Flaherty in Cherry and Sherwood, *Equal Rites,* 7–13; William G. Storey, *Book of Prayer,* 80–86; and Elizabeth Stuart's two short pieces in Duncan, *Courage to Love,* 278–79. Each liturgy specifies or presumes a setting other than a church.

54. Mitchell, *Liturgy and the Social Sciences,* 39–41.

55. *Common Ground,* dir. Donna Deitch, originally aired on Showtime. The union segment of the anthology, entitled "Amos and Andy," was written by Harvey Fierstein. It calls up (at least visually) characters from the two earlier segments: "A Friend of Dorothy's" by Paula Vogel, and "M. Roberts" by Terrence McNally.

56. Since my concern is with Christian blessings of same-sex unions, I have not considered what many would count the most inventive gay liturgies and theologies, those that resist Christianity specifically and monotheism generally. For an introduction to such liturgies, see Conner, *Blossom of Bone,* and Barzan, "Gay Rites Primer: Ritual as a Doorway to the Sacred," in *Sex and Spirit,* 133–36. For a representation of the place of Christianity within the range of gay spirituality, see Thompson, *Gay Soul.*

57. Mitchell, *Liturgy and the Social Sciences,* 43–46.

58. Rofes, "Dancing Bears, Performing Husbands, and the Tyranny of the Family," 156.

CHAPTER SIX

1. Hyde, *Rat and the Devil,* 113–14.

2. Ibid., 127.

3. Yip summarizes the research as of a decade ago in his "Gay Male Christian Couples and Sexual Exclusivity," especially 289–91. "The issue of sexual exclusivity," he writes, "constitutes one of the most researched areas in the studies of gay male couples." He then goes on to note some problems in the research. Yip's own proposal is to shift research from sexual acts to the consonance of acts and the couple's expectations.

4. Corporate or university policies for domestic partner benefits make interesting reading on this point. Many of them impose conditions of cohabitation, financial commitment, and longevity on same-sex couples that they don't or couldn't impose on state-recognized marriages.

5. I am summarizing the facts of scriptural history, especially as they were received in Christian tradition, and not the views on the merits of polygyny discovered or imagined in one or another scriptural author or "layer" of redacted source material.

6. A brief declaration of terminology: I use the term *polygamy* to refer equally to marriages with multiple husbands or multiple wives. *Polygyny* means, of course, one husband with multiple wives; *polyandry,* one wife with multiple husbands. *Polyamory* names unconcealed and relatively stable erotic relationships among more than two partners. I stress "unconcealed," because not a few traditional Christian marriages beloved by conservative defenders have been in fact concealed multipartner arrangements.

7. Augustine *De bono coniugali* (On the marital good) 6.6. See also the translation by Roy J. Deferrari, in Augustine, *Saint Augustine: Treatises on Marriage and Other Subjects,* 17.

8. Compare Augustine *Confessiones* 3.7.13, where Augustine defends the patriarchs from charges of wickedness by explaining that God permits some arrangements at one time or place, but not in others. Compare the translation of the *Confessions* by Henry Chadwick, 44.

9. Augustine *De bono coniugali* 10.10. See also Augustine, *Saint Augustine,* trans. Deferrari, 23.

10. Augustine *De bono coniugali* 17.20. See also Augustine, *Saint Augustine,* trans. Deferrari, 34.

11. Augustine *De bono coniugali* 26.34–35, generally.

12. For a fuller discussion of Augustine's views, especially in parallel texts, see Reynolds, *Marriage in the Western Church,* 266–74.

13. Tertullian *De exhortatione castitatis* 6.

14. Jerome *Adversus Helvidium* 20; compare the translation by John N. Hrizu, *Against Helvidius on the Perpetual Virginity of Mary,* 39–42.

15. Augustine *Confessions* 6.13.23. Cited parenthetically in the rest of the text paragraph.

16. Brown, *The Body and Society,* 147, 390, 392–93.

17. Thomas Aquinas *Summa contra Gentiles* 3.124 (sec. no. 2969 in the Pera, Marc, and Caramello edition; citations in subsequent notes use only these section nos.).

18. Ibid., no. 2971.

19. Ibid., nos. 2972–73 and 2974, respectively.

20. Thomas had no direct access to Platonic texts. Here he relies on Aristotle's literal-minded reading of the marital arrangements in the *Republic.* Thomas's reference to Nicholas is grounded in Augustine *De haeresibus* 5. Augustine accuses the heresiarch of advocating not so much polygyny as male-run promiscuity: "usus indifferens feminarum."

21. Thomas Aquinas *Summa contra Gentiles* 1.9.

22. Thomas Aquinas *Scriptum in Sententiis* 4.33.1.1 corpus, responses 1 and 2, and 4.33.1.2 corpus and responses to the counterarguments.

23. Thomas Aquinas *Summa theologiae* 1–2.94.5, response 2.

24. Compare the critique of Mohammed's licentiousness in *Summa contra Gentiles* 1.6.

25. Thomas Aquinas *Summa theologiae* 1–2.94.4 corpus.

26. I follow the account in Luther's letter to John of Saxony (June 10, 1540), as reproduced and explained in Witte, *Law and Protestantism,* 225–26.

27. See the collation of texts in Witte, *Sacrament to Contract,* 99–100.

28. Namely, Ochino, *Dialogi XXX in duos libros diuisi . . .*

29. It is important to note that the Christian rejection of polygyny is being debated again in the African churches. Though these churches are often described as "conservative" and "evangelical" when it comes to sex, it might well be that they reconsider polygyny as they move farther toward an indigenous Christianity. See, for a somewhat dated introduction, Hillman, *Polygamy Reconsidered.*

30. For one attempt to put the Mormons into wider context, recall Foster, *Religion and Sexuality.*

31. Blenkinsopp, "Family in First Temple Israel," 64, and Collins, "Marriage, Divorce and Family in Second Temple Judaism," 121. There are Jewish marriage contracts in which the husband forgoes the right to take a second wife; see Collins, 115–16, 121.

32. For a particularly striking example, see Jordan, *Ethics of Sex,* 72 and n. 74.

33. See Roper, "Sexual Utopianism in the German Reformation," especially 398–402.

34. Recall the remark that eros is the "principal adversary" of Christianity in Nygren, *Agape and Eros,* 53.

35. As I suggested, this is how I read key verses in the New Testament letters that require a church elder or deacon to be "husband of one wife" (1 Tim. 3 : 2, 3 : 12; Titus 1 : 6). The reference is not, I think, to polygyny, but to notions of sexual restraint more widely diffused in Hellenistic culture. I come back to them in the next chapter.

36. I follow the words of the institution as in Mark 14:23–24. Compare the different version in 1 Corinthians 11:23–25.

37. Starhawk, *Fifth Sacred Thing*, 87. Subsequently cited by page number in the text.

38. Johnson, *Secret Matter*, 171 (subsequently cited in the text). The text is confusing here. It first says that their females "ovulate as part of orgasm," which presumably would occur in masturbation or sexual relations with a partner of either sex. It then adds that they conceive in heterosexual intercourse (?) when the man and the woman both "reach climax."

39. Gearhart, *Wanderground*. The pages of this edition are cited parenthetically in the following discussion.

40. Gayle Rubin, "Thinking Sex," 3–44, at 11–15.

41. There is considerable disagreement about how many male-male couples accept nonexclusive sexual relations. The disagreement has many causes, including competing political programs, but I suspect that one significant cause is misrepresentation by gay men themselves. In different circumstances, friends will give contradictory answers about whether their nonmonogamy is negotiated or not. See Kaminsky, *When It's Time to Leave Your Lover*, 247.

42. Rudy, "'Where Two or More Are Gathered,'" 202–3.

43. Ibid., 205.

44. Rofes, "Dancing Bears," 161.

45. Labriola, "Models of Open Relationships." A much more whimsical typology is provided in West, *Lesbian Polyfidelity*, 27–34. Much less imaginative lists can be found in advice books for gay men. See, for example, Sullivan, *Boyfriend 101*, 243.

46. See the stories in Francoeur, Cornog, and Perper, *Sex, Love, and Marriage in the Twenty-First Century*, especially the founding narrative by Bob Rimmer at 146–48, with its cross-references to his fictions about foursomes, but also the story by Masefield, 177–79.

47. Most of the heterosexual stories in Francoeur, Cornog, and Perper, *Sex, Love, and Marriage*, are actually triads. See 80–81 (the Johnsons), 95 (Triumph), 103–4 (Rosenblum), 120–21 (Robins), 161–64 (Nearing).

48. Marks, "We Three"; parenthetical citations in the remainder of this paragraph are to the pages of this essay.

49. See Fischer and Hout, "'The Family in Trouble.'"

50. Knoebel, "Somewhere in the Right Direction," 303. Parenthetical citations in this and the next paragraph are to the pages of this essay.

51. See the website maintained by Unitarian Universalists for Polyamory Awareness, www.uupa.org; last consulted on January 11, 2004.

52. Among the best known are Mazur, *The New Intimacy*; Ramey, *Intimate Friendships*; and Roy and Roy, *Honest Sex*.

53. See the following pieces in Francoeur, Cornog, and Perper, *Sex, Love, and Marriage*: Maude's Friend, "A Southern Rural Pastor," 7–10; Alicia Smith, "The Story of a Single Pastor," especially 15–16, on the views of Bill, a former seminary professor; Henry Bullmann, "This Is My Song, This Is My Sacred Journey," especially 24–29; Eleanor and John Sharp, "New Marital Patterns Work—If Lived with Principles and Patience," especially 79 (the 1968 or 1969 retreat at Kirkridge), and 82 (the 1962–64 sex survey through Yale Divinity School).

54. I include "natural" means of contraception for both substantive and traditional reasons. Substantively, I cannot see how the intention to have sexual relations only during infertile periods differs significantly from other contraceptive intentions or violates any less the alleged procreative teleology of genital acts. Traditionally, I note that Augustine, among many others, includes such allegedly "natural" practices among unnatural and antimarital acts.

55. Cf. Jordan, *Invention of Sodomy,* 35.

56. I think particularly of André Guindon on gay fecundity in *The Sexual Creators,* 159–204.

57. One of the curiosities of contemporary American debates over family is that the religious right has become the last home of a dogmatic Freudianism, that is, a certain literal espousal of the oedipal triangle.

58. Freud, *Origins of Psycho-Analysis,* 289. The context makes the quotation even more pertinent. Freud has just written: "The more the work of the past year recedes into perspective, the better pleased I am with it. Now for bisexuality! I am sure you are right about it."

CHAPTER SEVEN

1. The "official" marriage movement website points to the high divorce rate as principal motive for the movement's existence: "*We come together because the divorce revolution has failed*" (original emphasis); see Coalition for Marriage, Family, and Couples Education; Institute for American Values; and Religion, Culture, and Family Project (University of Chicago Divinity School), "The Marriage Movement: A Statement of Principles" (2000), www.marriagemovement.org/MMStatement.html, last consulted on June 8, 2004. I cite this website only because it offers an accessible summary of the *stated* goals of a much larger and more diffuse network.

2. Cherlin, *Marriage, Divorce, and Remarriage,* 25.

3. Compare Kipnis, *Against Love,* 65.

4. For example, Augustine *De bono conjugali* 7. See the careful reconstruction of Augustine's views on the marriage bond in Reynolds, *Marriage in the Western Church,* 280–311.

5. I think of Ernst Troeltsch's sobering conclusion: "One of the most serious and important truths which emerge as a result of this inquiry is this: every idea is still faced by brutal facts, and all upward movement is checked and hindered by interior and exterior difficulties. Nowhere does there exist an absolute Christian ethic, which only awaits discovery; all that we can do is to learn to control the world-situation in its successive phase just as the earlier Christian ethic did in its own way." See Troeltsch, *Social Teaching of the Christian Churches,* 2:1013.

6. The contemporary Bible translations are more varied. The New Revised Standard Version (NRSV) offers "unchastity." The New Jerusalem Bible (NJB) proposes "illicit marriage" and adds the note "within the prohibited degrees of kinship." The note means that an incestuous marriage would be an invalid marriage — that is, not a real marriage at all. Matthew's Jesus would not so much be making an exception for some divorce as registering a condition for the nonexistence of a marriage. The Catholic NJB cannot allow Jesus to permit the dissolution of a valid marriage for any reason. This is Bible "translation" as denominational catechesis.

7. See Blenkinsopp, "Family in First Temple Judaism," 65–66; Collins, "Marriage, Divorce, and Family in Second Temple Judaism," 115–19. There is (controversial) documentary evidence for the right of women to divorce (Collins, 119–21).

8. Reynolds, *Marriage in the Western Church,* 174–75, 179–87.

9. Christians inferred that Peter was married from the mention of his mother-in-law at Matthew 8:14. They inferred that Peter left his wife and family behind from his claim to have left everything to follow Jesus (Matt. 19:27). Compare Jesus' exhortation to leave parents and children behind in Matthew 10:37.

10. Reynolds, *Marriage in the Western Church,* 233–34.

11. Giddens, *Transformation of Intimacy,* 134–40.

12. Romanovsky and Phillips, "Tango Indigesto." The song is preceded by "Journal En-

try," in which the narrator stops by his ex-lover's apartment before leaving town—only to meet the new boyfriend. It is followed by "Closing Chapter," in which two men sing antiphonally about making it through their split.

13. Jackson [Glaskin], *No End to the Way.* Cited parenthetically later in this paragraph.

14. Kaminsky, *When It's Time to Leave Your Lover.* Subsequently cited by page number in the text. I choose Kaminsky's book because it is typical. Other books of the subgenre could be used to make the same points from different features. For example, Dann Hazel writes his guide to gay divorce as a cross between a diagnostic test and a workbook. He gives his readers agency by inviting participation—that is, by presenting test results and then inculcating new skills. See Hazel, *Moving On,* 23−25, 65−67, 94−99, and so on.

15. Kaminsky sometimes puts the phrase "man of your dreams" in quotation marks (e.g., 37). At other times, as here, the phrase appears without any cautionary punctuation (e.g., 30).

16. Consider the following locutions: "You may not agree with some of what I say, and it makes no sense to do that which does not feel right for you" (6). "You have made this decision because the relationship can no longer work for *you*" (87). "A principal change that succeeds often does so in great part *because it was at the right moment, meaning it was the right time for you*" (203).

17. Giddens, *Transformation of Intimacy,* 58.

18. Lancaster, "Ceremony of Dissolution," 39−42. Cited by page number in the rest of this paragraph.

19. Neu, *Women's Rites,* 248−52. Cited by page number in the rest of this paragraph.

20. Holleran, "Friends," 32−33. Compare Bonin-Rodriguez, "A Cloak and Dildo Story," 224.

21. Rowe, "Looking for Brothers," 177.

22. Clark, "Radical Reflections on Radical Sex," 41.

23. Kantrowitz, "Family Album," 286.

24. Nardi, *Gay Men's Friendships,* 3.

25. Romanovsky and Phillips, "Functional Illiteracy," on *Let's Flaunt It!* It is not only a stereotype or a joke. See Becker, *Unbroken Ties.*

26. Among the many written testimonies to these friendships, there stands out for me Andrew Sullivan's essay "If Love Were All," in his *Love Undetectable,* 175−252.

27. For salient and rather different examples, see Hunt, *Fierce Tenderness,* and Stuart, *Just Good Friends.*

Works Cited

Absolutely Fabulous: "In New York." Directed by Jon Plowman. 45 minutes. Oxygen network, February 8, 2003. Originally broadcast by the BBC December 27, 2002 under the episode title "Gay."

Alison, James. *On Being Liked.* London: Darton, Longman, and Todd, 2003.

Altman, Dennis. *Homosexual Oppression and Liberation.* Rev. ed. New York: New York University Press, 1993. This edition reprints the 1973 paperback version published by Penguin with an introduction by Jeffrey Weeks and an afterword by Altman.

Arditti, Michael. *Easter.* London: Arcadia, 2000.

Augustine. *Confessiones.* Ed. M. Skutella. Revised by L. Verheijen. Corpus Christianorum Series Latina, vol. 27. Turnhout: Brepols, 1981.

———. *Confessions.* Trans. Henry Chadwick. Oxford: Oxford University Press, 1992.

———. *De bono coniugali.* Ed. Josephus Zycha. Corpus Scriptorum Ecclesiasticorum Latinorum, vol. 41. Vienna: F. Tempsky, 1900.

———. *De haeresibus.* Ed. R. vander Plaetse and C. Beukers, 261–385. Corpus Christianorum Series Latina, vol. 46. Turnhout: Brepols, 1969.

———. *Saint Augustine: Treatises on Marriage and Other Subjects.* Trans. Roy J. Deferrari. Fathers of the Church: A New Translation. New York: Fathers of the Church, 1955.

Ayers, Tess, and Paul Brown. *The Essential Guide to Lesbian and Gay Weddings.* Los Angeles and New York: Alyson Books, 1999.

Bailey, Derrick Sherwin. *Homosexuality and the Western Christian Tradition.* 1955. Reprint, Hamden, CT: Archon Books, 1975.

Baker, Paul. *Fantabulosa: A Dictionary of Polari and Gay Slang.* London and New York: Continuum, 2002.

Barthes, Roland. *A Lover's Discourse: Fragments.* Trans. Richard Howard. New York: Hill and Wang/Farrar, Straus, and Giroux, 1978.

Barzan, Robert, ed. *Sex and Spirit: Exploring Gay Men's Spirituality.* San Francisco: White Crane Newsletter, 1995.

Bates, Stephen. *A Church at War: Anglicans and Homosexuality.* London: I. B. Tauris, 2004.

Bawer, Bruce. *Stealing Jesus: How Fundamentalism Betrays Christianity.* New York: Three Rivers Press, 1997.

Bayot, Jennifer. "For Richer or Poorer, to Our Credit Limit." *New York Times,* July 13, 2003.

Becker, Carol S. *Unbroken Ties: Lesbian Ex-Lovers.* Boston: Alyson, 1988.

Benjamin, Walter. "The Work of Art in the Age of Mechanical Reproduction." In *Illuminations,* ed. Hannah Arendt, 217–51. New York: Schocken Books, 1969.

Berger, Raymond M. "Men Together: Understanding the Gay Couple." *Journal of Homosexuality* 19, no. 3 (1990): 31–49.

Bernardino of Siena. *De horrendo peccato contra naturam.* In *Opera omnia,* 3:267–84. Ed. the Fathers of the Collegium S. Bonaventurae. Quaracchi: Collegium S. Bonaventurae, 1966.

Bernhard, Sandra. "You Make Me Feel (Mighty Real)." Additional lyrics by Sandra Bernhard, Derrick Smit, and Mitchell Kaplan. From *Excuses for Bad Behavior, Part 1.* CD. Sony Music Entertainment, BK 57693, 1994.

Bidgood, James. *Bidgood.* Text by Bruce Benderson. Cologne: Taschen, 1999.

Black, Allida M., ed. *Modern American Queer History.* Philadelphia, PA: Temple University Press, 2001.

Blenkinsopp, Joseph. "The Family in First Temple Israel." In *Families in Ancient Israel,* ed. Leo G. Perdue, Joseph Blenkinsopp, John J. Collins, and Carol Meyers, 48–103. Louisville, KY: Westminster John Knox, 1997.

Bonin-Rodriguez, Paul. "A Cloak and Dildo Story." In Preston and Lowenthal, *Friends and Lovers,* 217–24.

Boswell, John. *Christianity, Social Tolerance, and Homosexuality.* Chicago: University of Chicago Press, 1980.

————. *Same-Sex Unions in Premodern Europe.* New York: Villard Books, 1994.

Boyd, Nan Alamilla. *Wide Open Town: A History of Queer San Francisco to 1965.* Berkeley and Los Angeles: University of California Press, 2003.

Bray, Alan. *The Friend.* Chicago: University of Chicago Press, 2003.

Bronski, Michael. *Culture Clash: The Making of Gay Sensibility.* Boston: South End Press, 1984.

————. "I'll Cry Tomorrow." In Preston and Lowenthal, *Friends and Lovers,* 39–47.

Brooten, Bernadette J. *Love between Women: Early Christian Responses to Female Homoeroticism.* Chicago: University of Chicago Press, 1996.

Brown, Peter. *The Body and Society: Men, Women, and Sexual Renunciation in Early Christianity.* New York: Columbia University Press, 1988.

Brown, Ricardo J. *The Evening Crowd at Kirmser's: A Gay Life in the 1940s.* Ed. William Reichard. Minneapolis: University of Minnesota Press, 2001.

Brundage, James A. *Law, Sex, and Christian Society in Medieval Europe.* Chicago: University of Chicago Press, 1987.

Burston, Paul, and Colin Richardson, eds. *A Queer Romance: Lesbians, Gay Men, and Popular Culture.* London and New York: Routledge, 1995.

Butler, Becky, ed. *Ceremonies of the Heart: Celebrating Lesbian Unions.* 2nd ed. Seattle, WA: Seal Press, 1997.

Butler, Judith. *Gender Trouble: Feminism and the Subversion of Identity.* Tenth anniversary edition. New York: Routledge, 1999.

————. "Is Kinship Always Already Heterosexual?" *Differences* 13 (2002): 14–44.

California State Assembly, AB 26, Chapter 588 of the Statues of 1999, codified in California Family Code, Division 2.5.

Canby, Vincent. Review of *Pink Narcissus. New York Times,* May 24, 1971.

Canetti, Elias. *Earwitness: Fifty Characters.* Trans. Joachim Neugroschel. New York: Seabury, 1979.

Carter, David. *Stonewall: The Riots That Sparked the Gay Revolution.* New York: St. Martin's Press, 2004.

Carter, Stephen L. "'Defending' Marriage: A Modest Proposal." *Howard Law Journal* 41 (1988): 215–28.

Chasin, Alexandra. *Selling Out: The Gay and Lesbian Movement Goes to Market.* New York: Palgrave, 2000.

Chauncey, George. *Gay New York: Gender, Urban Culture, and the Making of the Gay Male World, 1890–1940.* New York: Basic Books/Harper Collins, 1994.

Cherlin, Andrew J. *Marriage, Divorce, and Remarriage.* Rev. and enlarged ed. Cambridge, MA: Harvard University Press, 1992.

Cherry, Kittredge, and Zalmon Sherwood, eds. *Equal Rites: Lesbian and Gay Worship, Ceremonies, and Celebrations.* Louisville, KY: Westminster John Knox, 1995.

Clark, J. Michael. "Radical Reflections on Radical Sex: A Spiritual Journey through Leathersex." In Barzan, *Sex and Spirit,* 37–43.

Clendinen, Dudley, and Adam Nagourney. *Out for Good: The Struggle to Build a Gay Rights Movement in America.* New York: Simon and Schuster, 1999.

Coalition for Marriage, Family, and Couples Education; Institute for American Values; and Religion, Culture, and Family Project (University of Chicago Divinity School). "The Marriage Movement: A Statement of Principles" (2000). Online at www.marriagemovement.org/MMStatement.html, last consulted on June 8, 2004.

Collins, John J. "Marriage, Divorce and Family in Second Temple Judaism." In *Families in Ancient Israel,* ed. Leo G. Perdue, Joseph Blenkinsopp, John J. Collins, and Carol Meyers, 104–62. Louisville, KY: Westminster John Knox, 1997.

Committee of Concern for Homosexuals [Berkeley]. *Agape and Action: News Notes for a Revolution of Concern and Service,* no. 1 (June 5, 1970)–no. 7 (February 1971).

Common Ground. Directed by Donna Deitch. VHS (105 min.). Paramount Studio, 2000.

Condé Nast Bridal Group. *Future Impact of Demographic Trends on the Bridal Industry.* New York: Condé Nast Bridal Group, 2003. Summarizes data from the Condé Nast Bridal Infobank American Wedding Study 2002 and other studies.

Conner, Randy. *Blossom of Bone: Reclaiming the Connections between Homoeroticism and the Sacred.* New York: HarperCollins, 1993.

Cory, Donald Webster [Edward Sagarin]. *The Homosexual in America: A Subjective Approach.* New York: Greenberg, 1951.

Coulmont, Baptiste. "Églises chrétiennes et homosexualités aux États-Unis, éléments de compréhension." *Revue française d'Études Américaines* no. 95 (2003): 77–90

Council on Religion and the Homosexual [San Francisco]. *A Brief of Injustices: An Indictment of Our Society in Its Treatment of the Homosexual.* San Francisco: Council on Religion and the Homosexual, June 1965.

"A Covenant of Friendship." *San Francisco Chronicle,* March 22, 1971.

Creekmur, Corey K., and Alexander Doty. *Out in Culture: Gay, Lesbian, and Queer Essays on Popular Culture.* London: Cassell, 1995.

Cromey, Robert Warren. *In God's Image: Christian Witness to the Need for Gay/Lesbian Equality in the Eyes of the Church.* San Francisco: Alamo Square Press, 1991.

Crysdale, Cynthia S. "Christian Marriage and Homosexual Monogamy." In Hefling, *Our Selves, Our Souls and Bodies,* 89–104.

"Daniel Gross and Steven Goldstein," *New York Times,* September 1, 2002, section 9.

Dean, Douglas. "Gay Marriage." *Cross Currents* 1, no. 1 (fall 1972): 6, 15. Published by the Metropolitan Community Church of San Francisco.

D'Emilio, John. *Sexual Politics, Sexual Communities: The Making of a Homosexual Minority in the United States, 1940–1970.* Chicago: University of Chicago Press, 1983.

———. *The World Turned: Essays on Gay History, Politics, and Culture.* Durham, NC: Duke University Press, 2002.

Denneny, Michael, Charles Ortleb, and Thomas Steele, eds. *The Christopher Street Reader.* New York: Perigee Books/Putnam, 1984.

Diaman, N. A. "On Sex Roles and Equality." In Jay and Young, *Out of the Closets,* 262–64. Orig. pub. 1970.

Driscoll, Catherine. *Girls: Feminine Adolescence in Popular Culture and Cultural Theory.* New York: Columbia University Press, 2002.

Drukman, Steven. "Why I Want My MTV." In Burston and Richardson, *A Queer Romance,* 81–95.

Duberman, Martin. *Left Out: The Politics of Exclusion, Essays, 1964–1999.* New York: Basic Books, 1999.

———, ed. *Queer Representations: Reading Lives, Reading Cultures.* New York and London: New York University Press, 1997.

Duncan, Geoffrey, ed. *Courage to Love: Liturgies for the Lesbian, Gay, Bisexual, and Transgender Community.* Cleveland, OH: Pilgrim Press, 2002.

Ellison, Marvin M. *Same-Sex Marriage? A Christian Ethical Analysis.* Cleveland, OH: Pilgrim Press, 2004.

Engels, Friedrich. *The Origin of the Family, Private Property and the State.* Ed. Michèle Barrett. London: Penguin Books, 1986.

Episcopal Church of the Good Shepherd (Berkeley). "'In All Our Loving, We Praise You, O God': Celebrating Relationships at Good Shepherd Church. A Report to the Rt. Rev. William E. Swing, Diocese of California." December 1994.

Eskridge, William N., Jr. *The Case for Same-Sex Marriage: From Sexual Liberty to Civilized Commitment.* New York: Free Press, 1996.

Faderman, Lilian. *Odd Girls and Twilight Lovers: A History of Lesbian Life in Twentieth-Century America.* New York: Columbia University Press, 1991.

Field, Nicola. *Over the Rainbow: Money, Class, and Homophobia.* London: Pluto Press, 1995.

Fischer, Claude S., and Michael Hout. "'The Family in Trouble': Since When? For Whom?" Presented at the conference entitled "Sex, Marriage, and Family and the Religions of the Book: Modern Problems, Enduring Solutions." Center for the Interdisciplinary Study of Religion, Emory University, Atlanta, GA, March 27–29, 2003.

Fletcher, Joseph. *Situation Ethics: The New Morality.* Philadelphia, PA: Westminster Press, 1966.

Foley, Michael P. "Betrothals: Their Past, Present, and Future." *Studia Liturgica* 33 (2003): 37–61.

Ford, Charles Henri. *Water from a Bucket: A Diary, 1948–1957.* Introduction by Lynne Tillman. New York: Turtle Point Press, 2001.

Foster, Lawrence. *Religion and Sexuality: The Shakers, the Mormons, and Oneida Community.* Urbana: University of Illinois Press, 1984.

Francoeur, Robert T., Martha Cornog, and Timothy Perper, eds. *Sex, Love, and Marriage in the Twenty-First Century: The Next Sexual Revolution.* San Jose: Excel, 1999.

Freeman, Elizabeth. *The Wedding Complex: Forms of Belonging in Modern American Culture.* Durham, NC: Duke University Press, 2002.

Freud, Sigmund. *The Origins of Psycho-Analysis: Letters to Wilhelm Fliess, Drafts and Notes: 1887–*

1902. Ed. Marie Bonaparte, Anna Freud, and Ernst Kris. Trans. Eric Mosbacher and James Strachey. New York: Basic Books, 1954.

Gagnon, Robert A. J. *The Bible and Homosexual Practice: Texts and Hermeneutics.* Nashville, TN: Abingdon Press, 2001.

Garner, Darlene. "A Sample Service of Holy Union based on the Tradition of Kwanzaa." In Cherry and Sherwood, *Equal Rites,* 94–100.

Gay, A. Nolder. *The View from the Closet: Essays on Gay Life and Liberation, 1973–1977.* Boston: Union Park Press, 1978.

"Gay Priest Rejects Bishop Post." BBC News online service. Published July 6, 2003, 14:22:01 GMT, on http://news.bbc.co.uk.

Gay Weddings. Evolution Productions. Eight episodes of 30 min. First broadcast on the Bravo Network beginning September 2, 2002.

Gearhart, Sally Miller. *Wanderground: Stories of the Hill Women.* 1979. Reprint, Denver: Spinsters Ink Books, 2002.

Gearhart, Sally Miller, and William R. Johnson, eds. *Loving Women/Loving Men.* San Francisco: Glide, 1974.

Genet, Jean. *Our Lady of the Flowers.* Trans. Bernard Frechtman. Introduction by Jean-Paul Sartre. New York: Grove Press, 1991.

Giddens, Anthony. *The Transformation of Intimacy: Sexuality, Love and Eroticism in Modern Societies.* Stanford, CA: Stanford University Press, 1992.

Glaser, Chris. "A Celebration of Love and Commitment." In Cherry and Sherwood, *Equal Rites,* 90–94.

Goar, Jacobus, comp. *Euchologion, sive rituale Graecorum* . . . Venice: Bartholomaeus Javarina, 1730. Reprint, Graz: Akademische Druck- u. Verlagsanstalt, 1960.

Goss, Robert E., and Amy Adams Squire Strongheart, eds. *Our Families, Our Values: Snapshots of Queer Kinship.* New York: Harrington Park Press/Haworth Press, 1997.

Grahn, Judy. *Another Mother Tongue: Gay Words, Gay Worlds.* Boston: Beacon Press, 1984.

Greenberg, David F. *The Construction of Homosexuality.* Chicago: University of Chicago Press, 1988.

Grieg, Michael. "The Boom in 'Gay' Marriages." *San Francisco Chronicle,* July 14 and 15, 1970. The page numbers for pt. 1 are 1 and 16; for pt. 2, 1 and 30.

Guindon, André. *The Sexual Creators: An Ethical Proposal for Concerned Christians.* Lanham, MD: University Press of America, 1986.

Hamilton, Wallace. *Christopher and Gay: A Partisan's View of the New York Homosexual Scene.* New York: Saturday Review Press, 1973.

Hanson, Craig Alfred. "The Fairy Princess Exposed." In Jay and Young, *Out of the Closets,* 266–69.

Harris, Daniel. *The Rise and Fall of Gay Culture.* New York: Hyperion, 1997.

Hay, Harry. *Radically Gay: Gay Liberation in the Words of Its Founder.* Ed. Will Roscoe. Boston: Beacon Press, 1996.

Hazel, Dann. *Moving On: The Gay Man's Guide for Coping When a Relationship Ends.* New York: Kensington Books, 1999.

Hefling, Charles, ed. *Our Selves, Our Souls and Bodies: Sexuality and the Household of God.* Cambridge: Cowley, 1996.

Herdt, Gilbert, ed. *Gay Culture in America: Essays from the Field.* Boston: Beacon Press, 1992.

Herdt, Gilbert, and Andrew Boxer. "Introduction: Culture, History, and Life Course of Gay Men." In Herdt, *Gay Culture in America,* 1–28.

Hill, Leslie. *Marriage: A Spiritual Leading of Lesbian, Gay, and Straight Couples.* Pendle Hill Pamphlet 308. Wallingford, PA: Pendle Hill, 1993.

Hillman, Eugene. *Polygamy Reconsidered: African Plural Marriage and the Christian Churches.* New York: Orbis Books, 1975.

Hoffman, Martin. *The Gay World.* New York: Basic Books, 1968.

Holleran, Andrew. "Friends." In Preston and Lowenthal, *Friends and Lovers,* 31–37.

"Homosexual Identity." *Agape and Action* (winter 1970): 6 (back cover).

Howard, John. "Protest and Protestantism: Early Lesbian and Gay Institution Building in Mississippi." In Black, *Modern American Queer History,* 198–223.

Howell, Frank. "Sacred Ceremonies: On Doing Your Own Things." *Cross Currents* [MCC/SF] (fall 1973): 14–15.

Hunt, Mary E. *Fierce Tenderness: A Feminist Theology of Friendship.* New York: Crossroad, 1991.

Hyde, Louis, ed. *Rat and the Devil: Journal Letters of F. O. Matthiessen and Russell Cheney.* Hamden, CT: Archon Books 1978.

Hymon, Steve. "Gay, Lesbian Wedding Expo Honors 'We Do.'" *Los Angeles Times,* February 24, 2004.

Ingraham, Chrys. *White Weddings: Romancing Heterosexuality in Popular Culture.* New York: Routledge, 1999.

"It Can Happen Here!" *Fag Rag* no. 2 (fall 1971): 19.

Jackson, Neville [Gerald M. Glaskin]. *No End to the Way.* London: Barrie and Rockliff, 1965.

Jakobsen, Janet R., and Ann Pellegrini. *Love the Sin: Sexual Regulation and the Limits of Religious Tolerance.* New York: New York University Press, 2003.

Jay, Karla, and Allen Young, eds. *Lavender Culture.* Rev. ed. 1979. Reprint, New York: New York University Press, 1994.

———. *Out of the Closets: Voices of Gay Liberation.* Twentieth anniversary edition. Foreword by John D'Emilio. London: GMP Publishers, 1992.

Jennings, Theodore W., Jr. *The Man Jesus Loved: Homoerotic Narratives from the New Testament.* Cleveland, OH: Pilgrim Press, 2003.

Jerome. *Adversus Helvidium de Mariae virginitate perpetua.* Migne *PL* 23 : 183–206.

———. *Against Helvidius on the Perpetual Virginity of Mary.* In *St. Jerome: Dogmatic and Polemical Works,* tr. John N. Hrizu, 1–43. Fathers of the Church: A New Translation. Washington, DC: Catholic University of America Press, 1965.

John, Jeffrey. *"Permanent, Faithful, Stable": Christian Same-Sex Partnerships.* Rev. ed. London: Darton, Longman, and Todd, 2000.

Johnson, David K. *The Lavender Scare: The Cold War Persecution of Gays and Lesbians in the Federal Government.* Chicago: University of Chicago Press, 2004.

Johnson, Toby. *Secret Matter.* Reprint, Austin, TX: Peregrine Ventures, 1995. Orig. pub. 1990.

Jordan, Mark D. *The Ethics of Sex.* Oxford: Blackwell, 2002.

———. *The Invention of Sodomy in Christian Theology.* Chicago: University of Chicago Press, 1997.

———. *The Silence of Sodom: Homosexuality in Modern Catholicism.* Chicago: University of Chicago Press, 2000.

———. *Telling Truths in Church: Scandal, Flesh, and Christian Speech.* Boston: Beacon Press, 2003.

Kaminsky, Neil. *When It's Time to Leave Your Lover: A Guide for Gay Men.* New York: Harrington Park Press/Haworth Press, 1999.

Kantrowitz, Arnie. "Family Album." In Preston and Lowenthal, *Friends and Lovers,* 281–300.

Katz, Jonathan Ned. *Gay/Lesbian Almanac . . .* New York: Harper & Row, 1983.

Kennedy, Hubert. *The Ideal Gay Man: The Story of Der Kreis.* New York: Harrington Park Press/Haworth Press, 1999. Also published in *Journal of Homosexuality* 38, (special issues) nos. 1–2 (1999).

Kierkegaard, Søren. *Philosophical Fragments.* Ed. and trans. Howard V. Hong and Edna H. Hong. Princeton, NJ: Princeton University Press, 1985.

Kipnis, Laura. *Against Love: A Polemic.* New York: Pantheon Books, 2003.

Kirstein, Lincoln. *Pavel Feodorovitch Chelitchew, 1898–1957.* Santa Fe: Twelvetree Press, 1994.

Kleinberg, Seymour. "Modern Arrangements: Careless Love." In Denneny, Ortleb, and Steele, *The Christopher Street Reader,* 109–29. Orig. pub. as "Restless Love: What Is the State of the Gay Couple in the Eighties?" *Christopher Street* 5, no. 1 (1980): 30–44.

Knoebel, John. "Somewhere in the Right Direction: Testimony of My Experience in a Gay Male Living Collective." In Jay and Young, *Out of the Closets,* 301–15.

Kristeva, Julia. *Tales of Love.* Trans. Leon S. Roudiez. New York: Columbia University Press, 1987.

Labriola, Kathy. "Models of Open Relationships." In Munson and Stelboum, *Lesbian Polyamory Reader,* 217–25.

Laderman, Gary. *Rest in Peace: A Cultural History of Death and the Funeral Home in Twentieth-Century America.* New York: Oxford University Press, 2003.

LaHaye, Tim, and Beverly LaHaye. *The Act of Marriage: The Beauty of Sexual Love.* Rev. ed. Grand Rapids, MI: Zondervan, 1998.

Lahey, Kathleen A., and Kevin Alderson. *Same-Sex Marriage: The Personal and the Political.* Toronto: Insomniac Press, 2004.

Lancaster, James. "Ceremony of Dissolution." In Cherry and Sherwood, *Equal Rites,* 39–42.

Leddick, David. *Intimate Companions: A Triography of George Platt Lynes, Paul Cadmus, Lincoln Kirstein, and Their Circle.* New York: St. Martin's/Stonewall Inn Editions, 2001.

Legg, W. Dorr [William Lambert], with David G. Cameron, Walter L. Williams, and Donald C. Paul, eds. *Homophile Studies in Theory and Practice.* Los Angeles: ONE Institute Press, and San Francisco: GLB Publishers, 1994.

Leyland, Winston, ed. *Gay Roots, Twenty Years of Gay Sunshine: An Anthology of Gay History, Sex, Politics and Culture.* San Francisco: Gay Sunshine Press, 1991. (Although this is not designated as "vol. 1," it was in time followed by "vol. 2.")

———, ed. *Out in the Castro: Desire, Promise, Activism.* San Francisco: Leyland, 2002.

Loughery, John. *The Other Side of Silence: Men's Lives and Gay Identities, A Twentieth-Century History.* New York: John Macrae/Owl, Henry Holt, 1999.

Love, Aileen. "Great Ceremony Solutions." *Modern Bride* (February–March 2003), 184–86.

Mackey, Richard A., Bernard A. O'Brien, and Eileen F. Mackey. *Gay and Lesbian Couples: Voices from Lasting Relationships.* Westport, CT: Praeger, 1997.

Madonna. "Material Girl." Written by Peter Brown and Robert Rans. From *Like a Virgin.* LP. Sire, 9-25157-1. November 1984.

———. "Vogue." Written by Madonna and Shep Pettibone. From *Immaculate Collection.* CD. Sire/Warner Brothers, 9-266440-2. November 1990.

Marcus, Eric. *Together Forever: Gay and Lesbian Marriage.* New York: Anchor/Doubleday, 1998.

Marks, Jim. "We Three." In Preston and Lowenthal, *Friends and Lovers,* 137–50.

Martin, Del, and Phyllis Lyon. *Lesbian/Woman.* San Francisco: Glide, 1972.

Martinac, Paula. *The Lesbian and Gay Book of Love and Marriage: Creating the Stories of Our Lives.* New York: Broadway Books, 1998.

Mau, Bruce. *Life Style*. Ed. Kyo Maclear with Bart Testa. New York: Phaidon, 2000.

Mazur, Ron. *The New Intimacy: Open-Ended Marriage and Alternative Lifestyles*. Boston: Beacon Press, 1973.

McCourt, James. *Queer Street: Excursions in the Mind of the Life—The Rise and Fall of An American Culture, 1947–1985*. New York: W. W. Norton, 2004.

McCubbin, Bob. *The Gay Question: A Marxist Appraisal*. New York: World View, 1976.

McLaughlin, Eleanor L. "Celebration and Blessing of a Covenanted Union." In Cherry and Sherwood, *Equal Rites*, 100–104.

McQueeney, Krista B. "The New Religious Rite: A Symbolic Interactionist Case Study of Lesbian Commitment Rituals." In Oswald, *Lesbian Rites*, 49–70.

Merin, Yuval. *Equality of Same-Sex Couples: The Legal Recognition of Gay Partnerships in Europe and the United States*. Chicago: University of Chicago Press, 2002.

Merrick, Gordon. *The Lord Won't Mind*. Los Angeles: Alyson, 1995. Orig. pub. 1970.

Metrosexuality. DVD. Directed by Rikki Beadle-Blair. London: Channel Four Television, 2001.

Miles, Sarah, and Eric Rofes, eds. *Opposite Sex: Gay Men on Lesbians, Lesbians on Gay Men*. New York: New York University Press, 1998.

Miller, D. A. *Place for Us: Essay on the Broadway Musical*. Cambridge, MA: Harvard University Press, 1998.

Mitchell, Nathan D. *Liturgy and the Social Sciences*. American Essays in Liturgy. Collegeville, MN: Liturgical Press, 1999.

Mitulski, James. "Lavender Lunch." Presentation at the Center for Lesbian and Gay Studies, Pacific School of Religion, September 20, 2001.

Montaigne, Michel de. *Journal de Voyage en Italie par la Suisse et l'Allemagne en 1580 et 1581*. Ed. Charles Dédéyan. Paris: Société Les Belles lettres, 1946.

Moore, Patrick. *Beyond Shame: Reclaiming the Abandoned History of Radical Gay Sexuality*. Boston: Beacon Press, 2004.

Munson, Marcia, and Judith P. Stelboum, eds. *The Lesbian Polyamory Reader: Open Relationships, Non-Monogamy, and Casual Sex*. New York: Harrington Park Press/Haworth Press, 1999. Co-published as *Journal of Lesbian Studies* 3, nos. 1–2 (1999).

Murray, Raymond, ed. *Images in the Dark: An Encyclopedia of Gay and Lesbian Film and Video*. Philadelphia, PA: TLA Publications, 1994.

Murray, Stephen O. *American Gay*. Chicago: University of Chicago Press, 1996.

Nardi, Peter M. *Gay Men's Friendships: Invincible Communities*. Chicago: University of Chicago Press, 1999.

Neu, Diann L. *Women's Rites: Feminist Liturgies for Life's Journey*. Cleveland, OH: Pilgrim Press, 2003.

A Night at Halsted's. Directed by Fred Halsted. 75 minutes. VHS. Chatsworth, CA: HIS Video/VCA Labs, 1990. Orig. production in 16 mm film, 1981.

Norton, Rictor, ed. *My Dear Boy: Gay Love Letters through the Centuries*. San Francisco: Leyland, 1998.

———. *Myth of the Modern Homosexual: Queer History and the Search for Cultural Unity*. London: Cassell, 1997.

Nygren, Anders. *Agape and Eros*. Trans. Philip S. Watson. London: SPCK, 1957.

Ochino, Bernardino. *Dialogi XXX in duos libros diuisi . . .* Basel: [Per Petrum Pernam], 1563.

Oswald, Ramona Faith, ed. *Lesbian Rites: Symbolic Acts and the Power of Community*. New York: Harrington Park Press/Haworth Press, 2003.

Pappas, Helen. "Happy Birthday, Jesus! Happy Anniversary, Beloved Church!" *SAGA Newsletter,* December 1976, 8–10. Published by the National Alliance of Christian Homosexuals, Anderson, SC.

Paris Is Burning. Directed by Jennie Livingston. VHS. 71 minutes. New York: Fox Lorber, 1997. Orig. released on film, 1990.

Paulson, Kevin Thaddeus. "Virtue Enough for Miss Grrrrl." In Yost, *When Love Lasts Forever,* 1–14.

Perry, Troy D. *The Lord Is My Shepherd and He Knows I'm Gay.* Twenty-fifth anniversary edition. Los Angeles: Universal Fellowship Press, 1994.

Persky, Stan. *Autobiography of a Tattoo.* Vancouver: New Star Books, 1997.

Peter Lombard. *Sententiae in IV libris distinctae.* 2 vols. Ed. members of the Collegium S. Bonaventurae. Spicilegium Bonaventuriarum, vols. 4–5. Grottaferrata: Collegium S. Bonaventurae ad Claras Aquas, 1971–1981.

Piazza, Michael. "Cathedral of Hope Holy Union." www.buddybuddy.com/vows-3.html.

Piercy, Marge. *Woman on the Edge of Time.* New York: Fawcett Crest/Ballantine, 1983.

Pink Narcissus. Directed by Anonymous [James Bidgood]. VHS. Strand Home Releasing, 1997. Orig. produced as 16 mm film, 1971.

Plummer, Kenneth, ed. *The Making of the Modern Homosexual.* London: Hutchinson, 1981.

Preston, John. "A Eulogy for George." In Preston and Lowenthal, *Friends and Lovers,* 83–94.

Preston, John, and Michael Lowenthal, eds. *Friends and Lovers: Gay Men Write About Families They Create.* New York: Dutton/Penguin, 1995.

Queer as Folk [U.K. version], episode 1. Directed by Charles McFougall. 30 min. First broadcast in the U.K. on February 2, 1999.

Queer as Folk [U.S. version], episodes 1–2. 90 min. First broadcast on Showtime, March 12, 2000.

Queer Eye for the Straight Guy, episode 3. First broadcast on Bravo, July 29, 2003.

Ramey, James. *Intimate Friendships.* Englewood Cliffs, NJ: Prentice-Hall, 1975.

Red Butterfly. [Untitled article.] *Come Out,* vol. 1 (January 10, 1970): 4–5.

Rennert, Amy, ed. *We Do: A Celebration of Gay and Lesbian Marriage.* San Francisco: Chronicle Books, 2004.

Review of *Pink Narcissus. Variety,* May 25, 1971.

Revolve: The Complete New Testament. Nashville, TN: Nelson Bibles, 2003.

Reynolds, Philip Lyndon. *Marriage in the Western Church: The Christianization of Marriage during the Patristic and Early Medieval Periods.* Supplements to *Vigiliae Christianae,* vol. 24. Leiden: E. J. Brill, 1994.

Ritzer, Korbinian. *Les marriages dans les églises chrétiennes du Ier au XIe siècle.* Paris: Cerf, 1970.

Rofes, Eric. "Dancing Bears, Performing Husbands, and the Tyranny of the Family." In Goss and Strongheart, *Our Families, Our Values,* 151–62.

Rogers, Bruce, comp. *Gay Talk: A (Sometimes Outrageous) Dictionary of Gay Slang.* New York: Paragon Books/G. P. Putnam's Sons, 1979.

Rogers, Eugene F., Jr. *Sexuality and the Christian Body.* Oxford: Blackwell, 1999.

Romanovsky, Ron, and Paul Phillips. "Functional Illiteracy." From *Let's Flaunt It!* CD. Fresh Fruit Records, DIDX 031187, 1995.

———. "Tango Indigesto." From *Be Political, Not Polite.* CD. Fresh Fruit Records, FF 104, 1991.

Roper, Lyndal. "Sexual Utopianism in the German Reformation." *Journal of Ecclesiastical History* 42 (1991): 394–418.

Rose, Susanna. "Lesbian and Gay Love Scripts." In Rothblum and Bond, *Preventing Heterosexism and Homophobia,* 151–73.

Rotello, Gabriel. *Sexual Ecology.* New York: Dutton Books, 1997.

Rothblum, Esther D., and Lynne A. Bond, eds. *Preventing Heterosexism and Homophobia.* Vol. 17 of *Primary Prevention of Psychopathology.* Thousand Oaks, CA: Sage, 1996.

Rougemont, Denis de. *Love in the Western World.* Trans. Montgomery Belgion. Rev. and augmented ed. Princeton, NJ: Princeton University Press, 1983.

Rowe, Michael. "Looking for Brothers: Barney, Chris, and Me." In Preston and Lowenthal, *Friends and Lovers,* 177–88.

Roy, Rustum, and Della Roy. *Honest Sex.* New York: New American Library, 1968.

Rubin, Gayle. "Thinking Sex." In *The Lesbian and Gay Studies Reader,* ed. Henry Abelove, Michèle Aina Barale, and David M. Halperin, 3–44. New York: Routledge, 1993.

Rudy, Kathy. "'Where Two or More Are Gathered': Using Gay Communities as a Model for Christian Sexual Ethics." In Goss and Strongheart, *Our Families, Our Values,* 197–216.

Ruether, Rosemary Radford. *Women-Church: Theology and Practice of Feminist Liturgical Communities.* San Francisco: Harper & Row, 1985.

Russell, Ina, ed. *Jeb and Dash: A Diary of Gay Life, 1918–1945.* Boston: Faber and Faber, 1993

Sale, Kirkpatrick. *SDS.* New York: Random House, 1973.

Saliers, Don E. *Worship as Theology: Foretaste of Divine Glory.* Nashville, TN: Abingdon, 1994.

Saunders, E. B. "Reformer's Choice: Marriage License or Just License?" *ONE* 1, no. 8 (1953): 10–12.

Sedgwick, Eve Kosofsky. *Epistemology of the Closet.* Berkeley and Los Angeles: University of California Press, 1990.

Shand-Tucci, Douglass. *The Crimson Letter: Harvard, Homosexuality, and the Shaping of American Culture.* New York: St. Martin's Press, 2003.

Shively, Charles. "Group Sex." Pt. 4 of "Cocksucking as an Act of Revolution." *Fag Rag* no. 5 (summer 1973): 8–9.

———. "Indiscriminate Promiscuity As an Act of Revolution." Special issue: Stonewall Fifth Anniversary Issue, *Fag Rag/Gay Sunshine* (summer 1974): 3–5.

———. [as "Charley Shively"]. *Nuestra Señora de los Dolores: The San Francisco Experience.* Boston: Good Gay Poets, 1975.

Signorile, Michelangelo. *Life Outside.* San Francisco: HarperCollins, 1997.

Slide, Anthony. *Lost Gay Novels: A Reference Guide to Fifty Works from the First Half of the Twentieth Century.* New York: Harrington Park/Haworth Press, 2003.

Sontag, Susan. *A Susan Sontag Reader.* New York: Farrar, Straus, Giroux, 1982.

Starhawk. *The Fifth Sacred Thing.* New York: Bantam Books, 1993.

Stelboum, Judith P. "Patriarchal Monogamy." In Munson and Stelboum, *Lesbian Polyamory Reader,* 39–46.

Stevenson, Kenneth. *Nuptial Blessing: A Study of Christian Marriages Rites.* London: Alcuin Club/SPCK, 1982.

Stiers, Gretchen A. *From This Day Forward: Commitment, Marriage, and Family in Lesbian and Gay Relationships.* New York: St. Martin's Press, 1999.

Stone, Ken, ed. *Queer Commentary and the Hebrew Bible.* Cleveland, OH: Pilgrim Press, 2001.

Storey, William G. *A Book of Prayer: For Gay and Lesbian Christians.* New York: Crossroad, 2002.

Stryker, Susan. *Queer Pulp: Perverted Passions from the Golden Age of the Paperback.* San Francisco: Chronicle Books, 2001.

Stuart, Elizabeth. *Gay and Lesbian Theologies: Repetitions with Critical Difference.* Aldershot, UK: Ashgate, 2003.

————. *Just Good Friends: Towards a Theology of Lesbian and Gay Relationships.* London: Mowbray, 1995.

Stuart, Elizabeth, and Adrian Thatcher, eds. *Christian Perspectives on Sexuality and Gender.* Leominster, UK: Gracewing/Fowler Wright; Grand Rapids: Wm. B. Eerdmans, 1996.

Sullivan, Andrew. *Love Undetectable: Notes on Friendship, Sex, and Survival.* New York: Alfred A. Knopf, 1998.

Sullivan, Jim. *Boyfriend 101: A Gay Guy's Guide to Dating, Romance, and Finding True Love.* New York: Villard, 2003.

Summer, Donna. "MacArthur Park." Written by Jimmy Webb. From *Live and More.* 2 LPs. Casablanca, NBLP 7119, 1978.

Sweezy, Paul M., and Leo Huberman, eds. *F. O. Matthiessen (1902–1950): A Collective Portrait.* New York: Henry Schuman, 1950.

Sylvester. "You Make Me Feel (Mighty Real)," words and music by J. Wirrick and Sylvester (S. James). From *Step II.* LP. Fantasy, F-9556, 1978.

Teal, Donn. *The Gay Militants.* Rev. ed. New York: St. Martin's Press, 1994. Orig. pub. 1971.

Tertullian. *De exhortatione castitatis.* In *Exhortation à la chasteté,* ed. Claudio Moreschini, trans. Jean-Claude Fredouille. Sources Chrétiennes, vol. 319. Paris: Éditions du Cerf, 1985.

Theophrastus. *Characters.* Ed. and trans. Jeffrey Rusten. In *Theophrastus: Characters, Herodas: Mimes, Cercidas and the Choliambic Poets,* ed. Jeffrey Rusten, I. C. Cunningham, and A. D. Knox. Loeb Classical Library, vol. 225. Cambridge, MA: Harvard University Press, 1993.

Third World Gay Revolution. "What We Want, What We Believe." In Jay and Young, *Out of the Closets,* 363–67.

Third World Gay Revolution and Gay Liberation Front. "Gay Revolution and Sex Roles." In Jay and Young, *Out of the Closets,* 252–59. Orig. pub. 1971.

Thomas, Anthony. "The House the Kids Built." In Creekmur and Doty, *Out in Culture,* 437–45.

Thomas Aquinas. *Opera omnia ut sunt in Indice thomistico . . .* Ed. Roberto Busa. Stuttgart—Bad Cannstatt: Frommann-Holzboog, 1980.

————. *Scriptum in Sententiis.* In *Opera omnia,* ed. Busa, 1 : 597–99.

————. *Summa contra Gentiles.* In *Liber de Veritate Catholicae Fidei contra Errores Infidelium seu Summa contra Gentiles,* ed. Ceslao Pera, Pierre Marc, and Pietro Caramello. Turin and Rome: Marietti; Paris: Lethielleux, 1961–67.

————. *Summa theologiae.* 4 vols. Ed. the Institutum Studiorum Medievalium Ottaviensis. Ottawa: Studium Generalis Ordinis Praedicatorum, 1941.

Thompson, Mark. *Gay Soul: Finding the Heart of Gay Spirit and Nature.* San Francisco: Harper San Francisco/HarperCollins, 1995.

Thorne, Gale. "A Sexual Bill of Rights: Rights of Civility for the Sexual Being." In *Essays on Religion and the Homosexual,* ed. Gale Thorne, 1 : 38. San Francisco: Council on Religion and the Homosexual, n.d.

Thorp, Charles P. "I.D., Leadership, and Violence." In Jay and Young, *Out of the Closets,* 352–63.

T'ien-Wen, Chu. *Notes of a Desolate Man.* Trans. Howard Goldblatt and Sylvia Li-chun Lin. New York: Columbia University Press, 1999.

Troeltsch, Ernst. *The Social Teaching of the Christian Churches.* 2 vols. Trans. Olive Wyon. Louisville, KY: Westminster John Knox, 1992.

Trumbach, Richard. "Sodomitical Subcultures, Sodomitical Roles, and the Gender Revolution of the Eighteenth Century: The Recent Historiography." *Eighteenth Century Life,* n.s., 9, no. 3 (1985): 1092–1121.

Tyler, Parker. *The Divine Comedy of Pavel Tchelitchew.* New York: Fleet, 1967.

Unitarian Universalists for Polyamory Awareness. www.uupa.org, last consulted on January 11, 2004.

Varnell, Joe, and Kevin Bourassa. *Just Married: Gay Marriage and the Expansion of Human Rights.* Madison: University of Wisconsin Press, 2002.

Vasey, Michael. *Strangers and Friends: A New Exploration of Homosexuality and the Bible.* London: Hodder and Stoughton, 1995.

Vecsey, George. "Minister Sponsors Homosexual Rituals." *New York Times,* November 27, 1977.

Walters, Suzanna Danuta. *All the Rage: The Story of Gay Visibility in America.* Chicago: University of Chicago Press, 2001.

Warner, Michael. *The Trouble with Normal: Sex, Politics, and the Ethics of Queer Life.* New York: Free Press, 1999.

Warren, Patricia Nell Warren. *The Front Runner.* Twentieth anniversary edition. Beverly Hills, CA: Wildcat Press, 1996.

Weeks, Jeffrey. "Discourse, Desire and Sexual Deviance: Some Problems in a History of Homosexuality." In *Against Nature: Essays on History, Sexuality, and Identity.* London: Rivers Oram Press, 1991.

Wescott, Glenway. *Continual Lessons: The Journals, 1937–1955.* Ed. Robert Phelps and Jerry Rosco. New York: Farrar, Straus and Giroux, 1990.

West, Celeste. *Lesbian Polyfidelity: A Pleasure Guide for All Women Whose Hearts Are Open to Multiple Sensualoves, or, How To Keep Nonmonogamy Safe, Sane, Honest & Laughing, You Rogue!* San Francisco: Booklegger, 1996.

Wilde, Oscar. *The Importance of Being Earnest and Related Writings.* Ed. Joseph Bristow. London: Routledge, 1992.

Williams, Robert. "Toward a Theology for Lesbian and Gay Marriage." In Stuart and Thatcher, *Christian Perspectives on Sexuality and Gender,* 279–300.

Williams, Rowan. "The Body's Grace." In Hefling, *Our Selves, Our Souls and Bodies,* 58–68.

Witte, John. *From Sacrament to Contract: Marriage, Religion and Law in the Western Tradition.* Louisville, KY: Westminster John Knox, 1997.

———. *Law and Protestantism: The Legal Teachings of the Lutheran Reformation.* Cambridge: Cambridge University Press, 2002.

Wittman, Carl. "A Gay Manifesto." In Jay and Young, *Out of the Closets,* 330–42.

———. Notices in newsletter of the Committee for Homosexual Freedom (San Francisco), April 22 and 29, 1969.

Wood, Robert W. *Christ and the Homosexual: Some Observations.* Introduction by Albert Ellis. New York: Vantage Press, 1960.

Yip, Andrew K. T. "Gay Christian Ceremonies and Blessing Ceremonies." *Theology and Sexuality* 4 (1996): 100–107.

———. "Gay Male Christian Couples and Sexual Exclusivity." *Sociology* 31, no. 2 (1997): 289–306.

———. *Gay Male Christian Couples: Life Stories.* Westport, CT: Praeger, 1997.

Yost, Merle James, ed. *When Love Lasts Forever: Male Couples Celebrate Commitment.* Cleveland, OH: Pilgrim Press, 1999.

Young, Allen. "No Longer the Court Jesters." In Jay and Young, *Lavender Culture,* 23–47.

———. "Reminiscences of Pre-Stonewall Greenwich Village." In Duberman, *Queer Representations,* 331–39.

Index